Economic and Philosophic Manuscripts of 1844 and the Manifesto of the Communist Party

©2011 Wilder Publications

Wilder Publications, Inc.
PO Box 10641
Blacksburg, VA 24063

ISBN 10: 1-61720-293-2
ISBN 13: 978-1-61720-293-3
First Edition

10 9 8 7 6 5 4 3 2 1

Economic and Philosophic Manuscripts of 1844 and the Manifesto of the Communist Party

Karl Marx and Frederick Engels

Translated by Martin Milligan

Economic and Philosophic Manuscripts of 1844

Contents

Translator's Note on Terminology. 5

Preface. 8

Wages of Labor. 12

Profit of Capital. 24

    1. Capital. 24

    2. The Profit of Capital. 25

    3. The Rule of Capital over Labor and the Motives of the Capitalist. . . . 27

    4. The Accumulation of Capitals and the Competition among the

Capitalists. 28

Rent of Land. 37

Estranged Labor. 49

Antithesis of Capital and Labor Landed Property and Capital. 60

Private Property and Labor Views of the Mercantile System and Physiocracy, Adam Smith, Ricardo and His School. 66

Private Property and Communism Various Stages of Development of Communist Views. Crude, Equalitarian Communism and Communism as Socialism Coinciding with Humaneness. 70

The Meaning of Human Requirements Where There Is Private Property and under Socialism. The Difference between Extravagant Wealth and Industrial Wealth. Division of Labor in Bourgeois Society. 82

The Power of Money in Bourgeois Society. 97

Critique of the Hegelian Dialectic and Philosophy as a Whole. 102

Outlines of a Critique of Political Economy, by *Frederick Engels*. 123

Translator's Note on Terminology

(The translator offers the following notes on certain important German terms which are frequently used in the material translated in the present volume, partly to explain the way in which they have been translated, and partly as an aid to understanding the texts.)

Aufheben (past tense: *aufhob*, p.p. *aufgehoben;* noun: *Aufhebung*).

Aufheben (literally "to raise up") has two opposed meanings in popular speech. (i) It can mean "to abolish," "to cancel," "to annul," "to do away with," etc. (ii) It can mean "to preserve." Hegel, valuing the word just because of this double, negative and positive, meaning (see *The Logic of Hegel*, tr. Wallace, 2nd ed., p. 180), uses it to describe the positive-negative action by which a higher logical category or form of nature or spirit, in superseding a lower, both "annuls" it and "incorporates its truth." Unfortunately, there is no single English word with the same double meaning, except "sublate," a technical term adopted for the purpose by some translators of Hegel; but as this is likely to be unintelligible to the general reader, it has not been used in the present volume. Instead, "supersede" has generally been used to render *aufheben*, where it seemed that the word was being used in this double, positive-negative sense, and occasionally it has been rendered as "transcend." Where, on the other hand, it seemed that *aufheben* was being used simply or predominantly in its commonplace negative sense, the negative words listed above—"abolish," "annul," etc.—have been employed.

Entäussern (p.p. *entäussert;* noun: *Entäusserung*).
The ordinary dictionary meanings of *entäussern* are "to part with," "to renounce," "to cast off," "to sell," "to alienate" (a right, or one's property). The last of these best expresses the sense in which Marx usually uses this term. For "alienate" is the only English word which combines, in much the same way as does *entäussern*, the ideas of "losing" something which nevertheless remains in existence over-against one, of something passing from one's own into another's hands, as a result of one's own act, with the idea of "selling" something: that is to say, both "alienate" and *entäussern* have, at least as one possible meaning, the idea of a sale, a transference of ownership, which is simultaneously a renunciation. At the same time, the word *entäussern* has, more strongly than "alienate," the sense of "making external to oneself," and at times, when this has seemed to be the aspect of its meaning uppermost in the author's mind, the

word "externalize" has been used to render it in English. *Verdussern*, whose occurrence is noted at one point in the text, means "to sell" and "to alienate" in the same way as *entäussern*, but without the overtone of "renunciation" or of the counter-position of the thing alienated to the one who has alienated.

Entfremden (p.p. *entfremdet*; noun: *Entfremdung*).

The ordinary dictionary meanings for *entfremden* are "to estrange," "to alienate," but in the present volume "estrange" has always been used. The reason is not only that "alienate" was needed for *entäussern* (see above), but also that *entfremden* is only equivalent to "alienate" in *one* sense of the English word— in the sense in which we speak of two people being "alienated," or of someone's affections being "alienated." *Entfremden* has not the legal-commercial undertones of "alienate," and would not be used, for instance, to describe a transfer of property. Hence, despite the fact that translators of Marx have often rendered *entfremdet* as "alienated," "estranged" seems better, especially as Marx does also use *entdussert*, which *is* the equivalent of "alienated" in its legal-commercial sense.

Wesen

There is no English word with the same range of meaning as *Wesen*.

Wesen can mean, for one thing, "essence," and some translators of Marx have treated it as if it could mean nothing else. But even when it does mean "essence," "essence" should be understood, not in the sense of something super-mundane or rarefied, but almost in the opposite sense of the "solid core" of something—its essential, as against its inessential, characteristics—its "substance" as against its accidental features—the "essential nature" or even the "very being" of something.

But secondly, *Wesen* is also the quite commonplace German word for a "being," in such phrases as "a human being" {*ein menschliches Wesen*}; or the "Supreme Being" (*das hochste Wesen*).

Thirdly, *Wesen*, as Hegel points out, "in ordinary life frequently means only a collection or aggregate: *Zeitungswesen* (the press), *Postwesen* (the post office), *Steuerwesen* (the revenue). All that these terms mean is that the things in question are not to be taken singly, in their immediacy, but as a complex, and then, perhaps, in addition, in their various bearings." Hegel adds that: "This usage of the term is not very different in its implications from our own." (See *The Logic of Hegel*, tr. Wallace, 2nd ed., p. 209, and p. 202 f.)

This last usage of the term is also not very different from Marx's, when, for instance, he seeks to make positive use of the concept of *das menschliche Wesen*. "The essence of man," he says, "is no abstraction inherent in each separate individual. In its reality it is the ensemble (aggregate) of social relations."

(*Theses on Feuerbach*, VI, as translated by R. Pascal in the Appendix to *The German Ideology*, Parts I and III, by Karl Marx and Frederick Engels, London, Lawrence & Wishart, 1939.)

In the texts translated in the present volume, Marx frequently plays on the various meanings of *Wesen*, using it at times in two or even more of its senses in the one sentence. The English translator can only render the different senses by different English words, and explain their common equivalent in a note, as has been done in this volume.

Preface[1]

I have already given notice in the *Deutsch-Französische Jahrbücher*,[2] the critique of jurisprudence and political science in the form of a critique of the *Hegelian* Philosophy of Right. In the course of elaboration for publication, the intermingling of criticism directed only against speculation with criticism of the various subjects themselves proved utterly unsuitable, hampering the development of the argument and rendering comprehension difficult. Moreover the wealth and diversity of the subjects to be treated, could have been compressed into *one* work only in a purely aphoristic style; while an aphoristic presentation of this kind, for its part, would have given the *impression* of arbitrary systematizing. I shall therefore issue the critique of law, ethics, politics, etc., in a series of distinct, independent pamphlets, and at the end try in a special work to present them again as a connected whole showing the interrelationship of the separate parts, and finally, shall make a critique of the speculative elaboration of that material. For this reason it will be found that the interconnection between political economy and the state, law, ethics, civil life, etc., is touched on in the present work only to the extent to which political economy itself *exprofesso*[3] touches on these subjects.

It is hardly necessary to assure the reader conversant with political economy that my results have been won by means of a wholly empirical analysis based on a conscientious critical study of political economy.

[Whereas the uninformed reviewer who tries to hide his complete ignorance and intellectual poverty by hurling the *"utopian phrase"* at the positive critic's head, or again such phrases as "pure, resolute, utterly critical criticism," the "not merely legal but social—utterly social—society," the "compact, massy mass," the "oratorical orators of the massy mass,"[4] this reviewer has yet to furnish the first proof that besides his theological family-affairs he has anything to contribute to a discussion of *worldly* matters.][5]

It goes without saying that besides the French and English Socialists I have made use of German socialist works as well. The only *original* German works of substance in this science, however—other than Weitling's writings—are the essays by Hess published in *Einundzwanzig Bogen*,[6] and Engels's *Umrisse zu einer Kritik der* '[7] in the *Deutsch-Französische Jahrbücher*, where, likewise, I indicated in a very general way the basic elements of this work.

[Besides being indebted to these authors who have given critical attention to political economy, positive criticism as a whole—and therefore also German positive criticism of political economy—owes its true foundation to the discoveries of *Feuerbach*, against whose *Philosophie der Zukunft*[8] and *Thesen zur*

Reform der Philosophie[9] in the *Anecdotis,*[10] despite the tacit use that is made of them, the petty envy of some and the veritable wrath of others seem to have instigated a regular conspiracy of *silence.*]

It is only with *Feuerbach* that *positive*, humanistic and naturalistic criticism begins. The less noise they make, the more certain, profound, widespread and enduring is the effect of *Feuerbach's* writings, the only writings since Hegel's *Phänomenologie* and *Logik* to contain a real theoretical revolution.

In contrast to the *critical theologians*[11] of our day, I have deemed the concluding chapter of the present work—the settling of accounts with *Hegelian dialectic* and Hegelian philosophy as a whole—to be absolutely necessary, a task not yet performed. This *lack of thoroughness* is not accidental, since even the *critical* theologian remains a *theologian.* Hence, either he had to start from certain presuppositions of philosophy accepted as authoritative; or if in the process of criticism and as a result of other people's discoveries doubts about these philosophical presuppositions have arisen in him, he abandons them without vindication and in a cowardly fashion, *abstracts* from them showing his servile dependence on these presuppositions and his resentment at this dependence merely in a negative, unconscious and sophistical manner.

[In this connection the critical theologian is either forever repeating assurances about the *purity* of his own criticism, or tries to make it seem as though all that was left for criticism to deal with now was some other immature form of criticism outside itself—say eighteenth-century criticism—and the backwardness of the *masses,* in order to divert the observer's attention as well as his own from the *necessary* task of settling accounts between *criticism* and its point of origin—Hegelian *dialectic* and German philosophy as a whole—from this necessary raising of modern criticism above its own limitation and crudity. Eventually, however, whenever discoveries (such as *Feuerbach's)* are made about the nature of his own philosophic presuppositions, the critical theologian partly makes it appear as if he were the one who had accomplished this, producing that appearance by taking the results of these discoveries and, without being able to develop them, hurling them in the form of *catch-phrases* at writers still caught in the confines of philosophy; partly he even manages to acquire a sense of his own superiority to such discoveries by covertly asserting in a veiled, malicious and skeptical fashion elements of the Hegelian *dialectic* which he still finds lacking in the criticism of that dialectic (which have not yet been critically served up to him for his use) against such criticism—not having tried to bring such elements into their proper relation or having been capable of doing so, asserting, say, the category of mediating proof against the category of positive, self-originating truth, etc., in a way *peculiar* to Hegelian dialectic. For to the theological critic it seems quite natural that everything has to be *done* by philosophy, so that he can *chatter* away about purity, resoluteness, and utterly critical criticism; and he fancies himself the true *conqueror of philosophy* whenever he happens to *feel* some "moment" in Hegel[12] to be lacking in Feuerbach—for however much he practices the spiritual idolatry of *"self-consciousness"* and *"mind"* the theological critic does not get beyond feeling to consciousness.][13]

On close inspection *theological criticism*—genuinely progressive though it was at the inception of the movement—is seen in the final analysis to be nothing but the culmination and consequence of the *old philosophical,* and especially the *Hegelian, transcendentalism,* twisted into a *theological caricature.* This interesting example of the justice in history, which now assigns to theology, ever philosophy's spot of infection, the further role of portraying in itself the negative dissolution of philosophy— i.e., the process of its decay—this historical nemesis I shall demonstrate on another occasion.[14]

[How far, on the other hand, *Feuerbach's* discoveries about the nature of philosophy required still, for their *proof* at least, a critical settling of accounts with philosophical dialectic will be seen from my exposition itself.]

Footnotes

[1. *Economic and Philosophic Manuscripts of 1844* by Karl Marx has come down to us in the form of three manuscripts, each of which has its own pagination (in Roman figures). Just the last four pages have survived of the second manuscript (pp. XL-XLIII). Each of the 27 pages of the first manuscript is broken up into three columns with two vertical lines, and each of the columns on each page is supplied with a heading written in beforehand: *Wages of Labor. Profit of Capital. Rent of Land.* After p. XVII, inclusive, it is only the column headed *Rent of Land* which is filled in, and after p. XXII to the end of the first manuscript Marx wrote across the three columns, disregarding the headings. The text of these six pages (pp. XXII-XXVII) is given in the present book under the editor's title, *Estranged Labor.* The third manuscript contains 43 large pages divided into two columns and paginated by Marx himself. At the end of the third manuscript (pp. XXXIX-XL) is the "Introduction," which is given in the present volume at the beginning, preceding the text of the first manuscript.

The title of Marx's work and the headings of the various parts of the manuscripts, put in square brackets, were given by the Institute of Marxism-Leninism. The parts of the manuscripts are published in the sequence in which Marx put them down, save the "Introduction," which is given in the beginning, and the *Critique of Hegelian Dialectic and Philosophy as a Whole* which was put in the end in accordance with the reference made by Marx in the "Introduction."—Ed.]

[2. *Deutsch-Französische Jahrbücher* (*German-French Year-Books*) was edited by K. Marx and A. Ruge and published in German. The only issue was a double number which appeared in Paris in February 1844. In it were printed Marx's *Zur Judenfrage* (*On the Jewish Question*) and *Zur Kritik der Hegelschen Rechts Philosophie. Einleitung* (*Contribution to a Critique of Hegel's Philosophy of Right. Introduction*) and Engels's *Umrisse zu einer Kritik der '* (*Outlines of a Critique of Political Economy*) and *Die Lage Englands* (*The Position of England*). "Past and Present" by Thomas Carlyle. These works mark the final transition of Marx and Engels to materialism and communism. Differences of principle between Marx and the bourgeois radical Ruge were chiefly responsible for the discontinuation of the journal.—*Ed.*]

[3. Particularly.—*Ed.*]

[4. Marx refers here to Bruno Bauer who had published in *Allgemeine Literatur-Zeitung* two long reviews dealing with books, articles and pamphlets on the Jewish question. Most of the quoted phrases are taken from these reviews in *Allgemeine Literatur-Zeitung*, Heft I, Dezember 1843; Heft 4, März 1844. The expressions "utopian phrase" and "compact mass" can be found in B. Bauer's article "Was ist jetzt der Gegenstand der Kritik?" published in *Allgemeine Literatur-Zeitung*, Heft 8, Juli 1844.

Allgemeine Literatur-Zeitung (*General Literary Gazette*), a German monthly, was published by the young Hegelian B. Bauer in Charlottenburg from December 1843 to October 1844.

K. Marx and F. Engels gave a detailed critical appraisal of this monthly in their book *Die heilige Familie, oder Kritik der kritischen Kritik*. Cf. K. Marx and F. Engels, *The Holy Family, or Critique of Critical Critique*. Moscow, 1956.—*Ed.*]

[5. Passages enclosed in braces were crossed out by Marx in his manuscript.— *Ed.*]

[6. The full title of this collection of articles is *Einundzwanzig Bogen aus der Schweiz* (*Twenty-One Sheets from Switzerland*). Erster Teil, Zürich und Winterthur, 1843.— *Ed.*

[7. Engels's *Outlines*: See Appendix to present volume.—*Ed.*]

[8. Ludwig Feuerbach, *Grundsätze der Philosophie der Zukunft* (*Principles of the Philosophy of the Future*), Zürich und Winterthur, 1843.—*Ed.*]

[9. Ludwig Feuerbach, *Vorläufige Thesen zur Reformation der Philosophie* (*Preliminary Theses on the Reformation of Philosophy*) published in *Anekdota*. Bd. II.—*Ed.*]

[10. This is how Marx abbreviates *Anekdota zur neuesten deutschen Philosophie und Publicistik* (*Unpublished Materials Related to Modern German Philosophy and Writing*), a two-volume collection published by A. Ruge in Switzerland. It included Marx's *Notes on the Latest Prussian Instruction to Censors* and *Luther—the Arbiter Between Strauss and Feuerbach*, and articles by Bruno Bauer, Ludwig Feuerbach, Friedrich Köppen, Arnold Ruge. etc.—*Ed.*]

[11. Marx has in mind B. Bauer and his followers, who were associated with the *Allgemeine Literatur- Zeitung.—Ed.*]

[12. **"Moment" is a technical term in Hegelian philosophy meaning a vital element of thought. The term is used to stress that thought is a process, and thus that elements in a system of thought are also phases in a movement.—*Ed.*]**

[13. **In Hegel, "feeling" *(Empfindung)* denotes a relatively low form of mental life in which the subjective and the objective are still confused together. "Consciousness" *(Bewusstsein)*—the name given by Hegel to the first major section of his *Phenomenology of Mind*—denotes those forms of mental activity where a subject first seeks to comprehend an object. "Self-consciousness" and "mind" denote subsequent, higher phases in the evolution of "absolute knowledge" or "the absolute."—*Ed.*]**

[14. **Within a short time, Marx fulfilled this promise in *Die heilige Familie, oder Kritik der kritischen Kritik*, written in collaboration with Engels. See K. Marx and F. Engels, *The Holy Family or Critique of Critical Critique*, Moscow, 1956.—*Ed.*]**

Wages of Labor

Wages are determined through the antagonistic struggle between capitalist and worker. Victory goes necessarily to the capitalist. The capitalist can live longer without the worker than can the worker without the capitalist. Combination among the capitalists is customary and effective; workers' combination is prohibited and painful in its consequences for them.[1] Besides, the landowner and the capitalist can augment their revenues with the fruits of industry; the worker has neither ground-rent nor interest on capital to supplement his industrial income. Hence the intensity of the competition among the workers. Thus only for the workers is the separation of capital, landed property and labor an inevitable, essential and detrimental separation. Capital and landed property need not remain fixed in this abstraction, as must the labor of the workers.

The separation of capital, ground-rent and labor is thus fatal for the worker.

The lowest and the only necessary wage-rate is that providing for the subsistence of the worker for the duration of his work and as much more as is necessary for him to support a family and for the race of laborers not to die out. The ordinary wage, according to Smith, is the lowest compatible with common humanity (that is a cattle-like existence).[2]

The demand for men necessarily governs the production of men, as of every other commodity. Should supply greatly exceed demand, a section of the workers sinks into beggary or starvation. The worker's existence is thus brought under the same condition as the existence of every other commodity. The worker has become a commodity, and it is a bit of luck for him if he can find a buyer. And the demand on which the life of the worker depends, depends on the whim of the rich and the capitalists. Should the quantity in supply exceed the demand, then one of the constituent parts of the price—profit, ground-rent or wages—is paid below its *rate*,[3] a part of these factors is therefore withdrawn from this application, and thus the market-price gravitates towards the natural price as the center-point. But (i) where there is considerable division of labor it is most difficult for the worker to direct his labor into other channels; (ii) because of his subordinate relation to the capitalist, he is the first to suffer.

Thus in the gravitation of market-price to natural price it is the worker who loses most of all and necessarily. And it is just the capacity of the capitalist to direct his capital into another channel which renders destitute the worker who is restricted to some particular branch of labor, or forces him to submit to every demand of this capitalist.

The accidental and sudden fluctuations in market-price hit rent less than they do that part of the price which is resolved into profit and wages; but they hit profit less than they do wages. In most cases, for every wage that rises, one remains *stationary* and one *falls.*

The worker need not necessarily gain when the capitalist does, but he necessarily loses when the latter loses. Thus, the worker does not gain if the capitalist keeps the market-price above the natural price by virtue of some manufacturing or trading secret, or by virtue of monopoly or the favorable situation of his property.

Furthermore: *the prices of labor are much more constant than the prices of provisions,* often they stand in inverse proportion. In a dear year wages fall on account of the fall in demand, but rise on account of the rise in the prices of provisions—and thus balance. In any case, a number of workers are left without bread. In cheap years wages rise on account of the rise in demand, but fall on account of the fall in the prices of provisions—and thus balance.[4]

Another respect in which the worker is at a disadvantage: *The labor-prices of the various kinds of workers show much wider differences than the profits in the various branches in which capital is applied.* In labor all the natural, spiritual and social variety of individual activity is manifested and is variously rewarded, while dead capital always shows the same face and is indifferent to the *real* individual activity.

In general it has to be observed that in those cases where worker and capitalist equally suffer, the worker suffers in his very existence, the capitalist in the profit on his dead mammon.

The worker has to struggle not only for his physical means of subsistence: he has to struggle to get work, i.e., the possibility, the means, to perform his activity. Take the three chief conditions in which society can find itself and consider the situation of the worker in them:[5]

(1) If the wealth of society declines the worker suffers most of all, for: although the working class cannot gain so much as can the class of property-owners in a prosperous state of society, *no one suffers so cruelly from its decline as the working class.*[6]

(2) Take now a society in which wealth is increasing. This condition is the only one favorable to the worker. Here competition between the capitalists sets in. The demand for workers exceeds their supply, But:

In the first place, the raising of wages gives rise to *overwork* among the workers. The more they wish to earn, the more must they sacrifice their time and carry out slave-labor, in the service of avarice completely losing all their freedom, thereby they shorten their lives. This shortening of their life-span is a favorable circumstance for the working class as a whole, for as a result of it an ever-fresh supply of labor becomes necessary. This class has always to sacrifice a part of itself in order not to be wholly destroyed.

Furthermore: when does a society find itself in a condition of advancing wealth? When the capitals and revenues of a country are growing. But this is only possible

(a) as the result of the accumulation of much labor, capital being accumulated labor; as the result, therefore, of the fact that his products are being taken in ever-increasing degree from the hands of the workers, that to an increasing extent his own labor confronts him as another's property and that the means of his existence and his activity are increasingly concentrated in the hands of the capitalist.

(b) The accumulation of capital increases the division of labor, and the division of labor increases the numbers of the workers. Conversely, the workers' numbers increase the division of labor, just as the division of labor increases the accumulation of capitals. With this division of labor on the one hand and the accumulation of capitals on the other, the worker becomes ever more exclusively dependent on labor, and on a particular, very one-sided, machine-like labor. Just as he is thus depressed spiritually and physically to the condition of a machine and from being a man becomes an abstract activity and a stomach, so he also becomes ever more dependent on every fluctuation in market-price, on the application of capitals, and on the mood of the rich. Equally, the increase in the class of people wholly dependent on work intensifies competition among them, thus lowering their price. In the factory-system this situation of the worker reaches its climax.

(c) In an increasingly prosperous society it is only the very richest people who can go on living on money-interest. Everyone else has to carry on a business with his capital, or venture it in trade. As a result, the competition between capitals becomes more intense. The concentration of capitals increases, the big capitalists ruin the small, and a section of the erstwhile capitalists sinks into the working class, which as a result of this supply again suffers to some extent a depression of wages and passes into a still greater dependence on the few big capitalists. The number of capitalists having been diminished, their competition with respect to workers scarcely exists any longer; and the number of workers having been augmented, their competition among themselves has become all the more intense, unnatural and violent. Consequently, a section of the working class falls into the ranks of beggary or starvation just as necessarily as a section of the middle capitalists falls into the working class.

Hence, even in the condition of society most favorable to the worker, the inevitable result for the worker is overwork and premature death, decline to a mere machine, a bond servant of capital, which piles up dangerously over against him, more competition, and for a section of the workers starvation or beggary.

The raising of wages excites in the worker the capitalist's mania to get rich, which he, however, can only satisfy by the sacrifice of his mind and body. The raising of wages presupposes and entails the accumulation of capital, and thus sets the product of labor against the worker as something ever more alien to him. Similarly, the division of labor renders him ever more one-sided and dependent, bringing with it the competition not only of men but of machines. Since the worker has sunk to the level of a machine, he can be confronted by the machine as a competitor. Finally, as the amassing of capital increases the amount of industry and therefore the number of workers, it causes the same amount of industry to manufacture a *greater amount of product*, which leads to over-production and thus either ends by throwing a large section of workers out of work or by reducing their wages to the most miserable minimum. Such are the consequences of a condition of society most favorable to the worker—namely, of a condition of *growing, advancing wealth.*

Eventually, however, this state of growth must sooner or later reach its peak. What is the worker's position now?

(3) "In a country which had attained the utmost degree of its wealth, both wages of labor and interest of stock would be very low. The competition among the workers to obtain employment would be so great that wages would be reduced to a point sufficient for the maintenance of the given number of workers; and as the country would already be sufficiently populated, this number could not be increased."[7]

The surplus would have to die.

Thus in a declining state of society—increasing misery of the worker; in an advancing state—misery with complications; and in a fully developed state of society—static misery.

Since, however, (according to Smith, a society is not happy, of which the greater part suffers[8]—yet even the wealthiest state of society leads to this suffering of the majority—and since the *economic system*[9] (and in general a society based on private interest) leads to this wealthiest condition, it follows that the goal of the economic system is the *unhappiness* of society.

Concerning the relationship between worker and capitalist one should add that the capitalist is more than compensated for the raising of wages by the reduction in the amount of labor-time, and that the raising of wages and the raising of interest on capital operate on the price of commodities like simple and compound interest respectively.

Let us put ourselves now wholly at the standpoint of the political economist, and follow him in comparing the theoretical and practical claims of the workers.

He tells us that originally and in theory the *whole produce* of labor[10] belongs to the worker. But at the same time he tells us that in actual fact what the worker gets is the smallest and utterly indispensable part of the product—as much, only, as is necessary, for his existence, not as a man but as a worker, and for the propagation, not of humanity but of the slave-class of workers.

The political economist tells us that everything is bought with labor and that capital is nothing but accumulated labor; but at the same time he tells us that the worker, far from being able to buy everything, must sell himself and his human identity.

While the rent of the lazy landowner usually amounts to a third of the product of the soil, and the profit of the busy capitalist to as much as twice the interest on money, the "something more" which the worker himself earns at the best of times amounts to so little that of four children *of* his, two must starve and die. While according to the political economists it is solely through labor that man enhances the value of the products of nature, while labor is man's active property,[11] according to this same political economy the landowner and the capitalist, who *qua* landowner and capitalist are merely privileged and idle gods, are everywhere superior to the worker and lay down the law to him.

While according to the political economists labor is the sole constant price of things, there is nothing more contingent than the price of labor, nothing exposed to greater fluctuations.

While the division of labor raises the productive power of labor and increases the wealth and refinement of society, it impoverishes the worker and reduces him to a machine. While labor brings about the accumulation of capitals and with this the increasing prosperity of society, it renders the worker ever more dependent on the capitalist, leads him into competition of a new intensity, and drives him into the headlong rush of over-production, with its subsequent corresponding slump.

While the interest of the worker, according to the political economists, never stands opposed to the interest of society, society always and necessarily stands opposed to the interest of the worker.

According to the political economists, the interest of the worker is never opposed to that of society: 1) because the raising of wages is more than made up for by the reduction in the amount of labor-time, together with the other consequences set forth above; and 2) because in relation to society the whole gross product is the net product, and only in relation to the private individual has the "net product" any significance.

But that labor itself, not merely in present conditions but in general insofar as its purpose is the mere increase of wealth— that labor itself, I say, is harmful and pernicious—follows, without his being aware of it, from the political economist's line of argument.

*

In theory, ground-rent and profit on capital are *deductions* suffered by wages. In actual fact, however, wages are a deduction which land and capital allow to go to the worker, a concession from the product of labor to the workers, to labor.

When society is in a state of decline, the worker suffers most severely. The specific severity of his burden he owes to his position as a worker, but the burden as such to the position of society.

But when society is in a state of progress, the ruin and impoverishment of the worker is the product of his labor and of the wealth produced by him. The misery results, therefore, from the *essence* of present-day labor itself.

Society in a state of maximum wealth, an ideal, but one which is more or less attained, and which at least is the aim of political economy as of civil society, means for the workers *static misery*.

It goes without saying that the *proletarian*, i.e., the man who, being without capital and rent, lives purely by labor, and by a one-sided, abstract labor, is considered by political economy only as a *worker*. Political economy can therefore advance the proposition that the proletarian, the same as any horse, must get as much as will enable him to work. It does not consider him when he is not working, as a human being; but leaves such consideration to criminal law, to doctors, to religion, to the statistical tables, to politics and to the workhouse beadle.

Let us now rise above the level of political economy and try to answer two questions on the basis of the above exposition, which has been presented almost in the words of the political economists:

(1) What in the evolution of mankind is the meaning of this reduction of the greater part of mankind to abstract labor?

(2) What are the mistakes committed by the piecemeal reformers, who either want to *raise* wages and in this way to improve the situation of the working class, or regard *equality* of wages (as Proudhon does) the goal of social revolution?

In political economy *labor* occurs only in the form of *wage-earning activity*.

"It can be asserted that those occupations which presuppose specific talents or longer training have become on the whole more lucrative; while the proportionate reward for mechanically monotonous activity in which one person can be trained as easily and quickly as another has fallen with growing competition, and was inevitably bound to fall. And it is just *this* sort of work which in the present state of the organization of labor is still by far the commonest. If therefore a worker in the first category now earns seven times as much as he did, say, fifty years ago, while the earnings of another in the second category have remained unchanged, then of course both are earning *on the average* four times as much. But if the first category comprises only a thousand workers in a particular country, and the second a million, then 999,000 are no better off than fifty years ago—and they are *worse off* if at the same time the prices of the necessaries of life have risen. With such superficial *calculations of averages* people try to deceive themselves about the most numerous class of the population. Moreover, the size of the *wage* is only one factor in the estimation of the *worker's income*, because it is essential for the measurement of the latter to take into account the assurance of its *permanence*—of which there is obviously no possibility in the anarchy of so-called free competition, with its ever-recurring fluctuations and periods of stagnation. Finally, the *hours of work* customary formerly and now have to be considered. And for the English cotton-workers these have been raised, as a result of the entrepreneurs' mania for profit, to between twelve and sixteen hours a day during the past twenty-five years or so—that is to say, precisely during the period of the introduction of labor-saving machines; and this rise in one country and in one branch of industry inevitably asserted itself elsewhere to a greater or lesser degree for the right of the unlimited exploitation of the poor by the rich is still universally recognized." (Wilhelm Schulz, *Movement of Production*, p. 65.)[12]

"But even if it were as true as it is false that the average income of *every* class of society has increased, the income-differences and *relative* income-distances may nevertheless have become greater and the contrasts between wealth and poverty accordingly stand out more sharply. For just *because* total production rises—and in the same measure as it rises—needs, desires and claims also multiply and thus *relative* poverty can increase while absolute poverty diminishes. The Samoyed living on fish-oil and rancid fish is not poor for in his secluded society all have the same needs. But in a state *that is forging ahead*, which in the course of a decade, say, increased by a third its total production in proportion to the population, the worker who is getting as much at the end of ten years as at the beginning has not remained as well off, but has become poorer by a third." (Ibid., pp. 65-66.)

But political economy knows the worker only as a working-animal—as a beast reduced to the strictest bodily needs.

"To develop in greater spiritual freedom, a people must break their bondage to their bodily needs—they must cease to be the slaves of the body. They must, therefore, above all, have *time* at their disposal for spiritual creative activity and spiritual enjoyment. The developments in the labor-organism gain this time. Indeed with new motive-forces and improved machinery, a single worker in the cotton factories now not infrequently performs the work formerly requiring a hundred, or even 250 to 350 workers. Similar results can be observed in all branches of production, because external natural forces are being compelled to participate to an ever-greater degree in human labor. If the satisfaction of a given amount of material needs formerly required a certain expenditure of time and human effort which has later been reduced by half, then without any loss of material comfort the scope for spiritual activity and enjoyment has been simultaneously extended by as much. . . . But again the way in which the booty, that we win from old Kronos[13] himself in his most private domain, is shared out is still decided by the dice-throw of blind, unjust Chance. In France it has been calculated that at the present stage in the development of production an average working-period of five hours a day by every person capable of work could suffice for the satisfaction of all the material interests of society. . . . Notwithstanding the time saved by the perfecting of machinery, the duration of the slave-labor performed by a large population in the factories has only increased." (Ibid., pp. 67, 68.)

"The transition from compound manual labor rests on a breaking-down of the latter into its simple operations. At first, however, only *some* of the uniformly-recurring operations will devolve on machines, while some devolve on men. From the nature of things, and from confirmatory experience, it is clear that unendingly monotonous activity of this kind is as harmful to the mind as to the body; thus this *combination* of machinery with mere division of labor among a greater number of hands must inevitably show all the disadvantages of the latter. These disadvantages appear, among other things, in the greater mortality of factory-workers. . . . Consideration has not been given ... to this big distinction as to how far men work *through* machines or *as* machines." (Ibid., p. 69.)

"In the future life of the peoples, however, the inanimate forces of nature working in machines will be our slaves and servants." (Ibid., p. 74.)

"The English spinning-mills employ 196,818 females and only 158,818 men. For every 100 male workers in the cotton-factories of Lancashire there are 103 female workers, and in Scotland as many as 209. In the English flax-mills of Leeds, for every 100 male workers there were found to be 147 female workers. In Druden and on the East Coast of Scotland as many as 280. In the English silk-mills . . . many female workers; male workers predominate in the wool-mills where the work requires greater physical strength. In 1833, no fewer than 38,927 females were employed alongside 18,593 men in the North American cotton-mills. As a result of the changes in the labor organism, a wider sphere of gainful employment has thus fallen to the share of the female sex. . . . Women now occupying an economically more independent position. . . . The two sexes drawn closer together in their social conditions." (Ibid., pp. 71, 72.)

"Working in the English steam- and water-driven spinning-mills in 1835 were: 20,558 children between the ages of eight and twelve; 35,867 between the ages of twelve and thirteen; and, lastly, 108,208 children between the ages of thirteen and eighteen. . . . Admittedly, further advances in mechanization, by more and more removing all monotonous work from human hands, are operating in the direction of a gradual elimination of this social evil. But standing in the way of these more rapid advances is the very circumstance that the capitalists can, in the easiest and cheapest fashion, appropriate the energies of the lower classes down to the children, to be employed and used up *instead* of mechanical aids." (Ibid., pp. 70-71.)

"Lord Brougham's call to the workers—'Become capitalists'. . . . The evil that millions are only able to earn a bare pittance for themselves by strenuous labor which is shattering the body and crippling them morally and intellectually; that they are even obliged to consider the misfortune of finding *such* work a piece of good fortune." (Ibid., p. 60.)

"In order to live, then, the non-owners are obliged to place themselves, directly or indirectly, *at the service* of the owners—to put themselves, that is to say, into a position of dependence upon them." (Pecqueur, *Théorie nouvelle d'économie soc, etc.*, p. 409.)[14]

"*Servants—pay; workers—wages; employees—salary or emoluments.* "(Ibid., pp. 409, 410.)

"To hire out one's labor"; "To lend one's labor at interest"; "To work in another's place."

"To hire out the materials of labor"; "To lend the materials of labor at interest." "To make others work in one's place." (Ibid. p. 411.)

"Such an economic order condemns men to occupations so mean, to a degradation so devastating and bitter, that by comparison savagery seems like a kingly condition." (Ibid., pp. 417, 418.) "Prostitution of the non-owning class in all its forms." (Ibid., p. 421 f.) "Ragmen."

Loudon, in the book *Solution du problème de la population, etc.*, Paris, 1842,[15] declares the number of prostitutes in England to be between sixty and seventy thousand. The number of women of doubtful virtue is said to be equally large (p. 228).

"The average life of these unfortunate creatures on the streets, after they have embarked on their career of vice, is about six or seven years. To maintain the number of sixty to seventy thousand prostitutes, there must be in the three kingdoms at least eight to nine thousand women who commit themselves to this degrading profession each year, or about twenty-four new victims each day—in average of *one* per hour; and it follows that if the same proportion holds good over the whole surface of the globe, there must constantly be in existence one and half million unfortunate women of this kind." (Ibid., p. 229.)

"The population of the poverty-stricken grows with their poverty, and at the extreme limit of destitution human beings are crowded together in the greatest numbers contending with each other for the right to suffer. . . . In 1821 the population of Ireland was 6,801,827. In 1831 it had risen to 7,764,010— an increase of 14 per cent in ten years. In Leinster, the wealthiest province, the population increased by only 8 per cent; while in Connaught, the most poverty-stricken province, the increase reached 21 per cent. (*Extract from the Enquiries Published in England on Ireland*, Vienna, 1840.)" (Buret, *De la misère, etc.*, t.1, pp. 36, 37.)[16]

Political economy considers labor in the abstract as a thing; "labor is a commodity." If the price is high, then the commodity is in great demand; if the price is low, then the commodity is in great supply, "the price of labor as a commodity must fall lower and lower." This is made inevitable partly by the competition between capitalist and worker, and partly by the competition among the workers. "The working population, the seller of labor, is necessarily reduced to accepting the meagerest part of the product. ... Is the theory of labor as a commodity anything other than a theory of disguised bondage?" (Ibid., p. 43.) "Why then has nothing but an exchange-value been seen in labor?" (Ibid., p. 44.) The large workshops prefer to buy the labor of women and children, because this costs less than that of men. (Ibid.) "The worker is not at all in the position of a *free seller* vis-à-vis the one who employs him. . . . The capitalist is always free to use labor, and the worker is always forced to sell it. The value of labor is completely destroyed if it is not sold every instant. Labor can neither be accumulated nor even be saved, unlike true commodities. Labor is life, and if life is not each day exchanged for food, it suffers and soon perishes. To claim that human life is a commodity, one must, therefore, admit slavery." (Ibid., pp. 49, 50.) If, then, labor is a commodity, it is a commodity with the most unfortunate attributes. But even by the principles of political economy it is no commodity, for it is not the *free result of a free transaction*. The present economic regime simultaneously lowers the price and the remuneration of labor; it perfects the worker and degrades the man. (Ibid., pp. 52-53.) "Industry has become a war, and commerce a gamble." (Ibid., p. 62.)

The cotton-working machines (in England) alone represent 84,000,000 manual workers. (Ibid., p. 193.)

Up to the present, industry has been in a state of war— a war of conquest: "It has squandered the lives of the men who made up its army with the same indifference as the great conquerors. Its aim was the possession of wealth, not the happiness of men." (Buret, l.c., p. 20.) "These interests (that is, economic interests), freely left to themselves . . . must necessarily come into conflict; they have no other arbiter but war, and the decisions of war assign defeat and death to some, in order to give victory to the others. ... It is in the conflict of opposed forces that science seeks order and equilibrium: *perpetual war*, according to it, is the sole means of obtaining peace; that war is called competition." (Ibid., p. 23.)

"The industrial war, to be conducted with success, demands large armies which it can amass on one spot and profusely decimate. And it is neither from devotion nor from duty that the soldiers of this army bear the exertions imposed on them, but only to escape the hard necessity of hunger. They feel neither attachment nor gratitude towards their bosses, nor are these bound to their subordinates by any feeling of benevolence. They do not know them as men, but only as instruments of production which have to yield as much as possible with as little cost as possible. These populations of workers, ever more crowded together, have not even the assurance of always being employed. Industry, which has called them together, only lets them live while it needs them, and as soon as it can get rid of them it abandons them without the slightest scruple; and the workers are compelled to offer their persons and their powers for whatever price they can get. The longer, more painful and more disgusting the work they are given, the less they are paid. There are those who, with sixteen hours' work a day and unremitting exertion, scarcely buy the right not to die." (Ibid., pp. 68-69.)

"We are convinced ... as are the commissioners charged with the enquiry into the condition of the hand-loom weavers, that the large industrial towns would in short time lose their population of workers if they were not all the time receiving from the neighboring rural areas constant recruitments of healthy men, a constant flow of fresh blood." (Ibid., p. 362.)

Footnotes

[1. Compare what Marx says here about the determination of wages, combination among workers, etc., with *The Wealth of Nations*, by Adam Smith (Everyman Library edition, Vol. I, pp. 58-60). In the first three sections of this manuscript, Marx, as he himself points out later, is constantly drawing upon the words of the classical political economists, and particularly of Smith. This is often the case, as here, even where Marx does not explicitly indicate that he is quoting or paraphrasing. The text of *The Wealth of Nations* used by Marx was Garnier's French translation of 1802 (*Recherche sur la Nature et les Causes de la richesse des Nations; par Adam Smith. Traduction nouvelle avec les notes et observations; par Germain Garnier, Tomes I-V, Paris, 1802).–lid.]

[2. A. Smith, *Wealth of Nations*. Everyman edition, Vol. I, pp. 60-61.–Ed.]

[3. Ibid., pp. 71-72, and pp. 50-51.—Ed.]

[4. A. Smith, *Wealth of Nations*. Vol. I, p. 77.– Ed.]

[5. Cf. *Wealth of Nations,* Vol. I, p. 230; also pp. 61-65, where Smith illustrates these three possible conditions of society by referring to contemporary conditions in Bengal, China, and North America. *(The Wealth of Nations* was first published in 1776.)—Ed.]

[6. Cf. Smith, l.c., p. 230; in Marx's manuscript the last clause of this sentence is in French, being taken direct from Garnier's translation. Tome II, p. 162.—Ed.]

[7. Cf. A. Smith. *Wealth of Nations,* Vol. I. p. 84 (Garnier. T. I, p. 193). Despite Marx's quotation marks, this is not in fact an exact quotation from Smith but a condensed version of some sentences of his.—Ed.]

[8. Cf. A. Smith. *Wealth of Nations.* Vol. I, p. 70.—Ed.]

[9. In this sentence the phrase "economic system" has been used to render the German term *Nationalokönomie* the term used by Marx in these manuscripts for "Political Economy." Here, and occasionally elsewhere, Marx seems to use *Nationalokönomie* lo stand not simply for Political Economy as a body of theory, but for the economic system, the developing industrial capitalist system, portrayed and championed by the classical political economists. —Ed.]

[10. Cf. A. Smith. *Wealth of Nations.* Vol. I, p. 57.—Ed.]

[11. Property, that is, in the sense of "a possession." not "an attribute." The German term is *Eigentum.* not *Eigenschqft.*—Ed.]

[12. Die Bewegung der Produktion, eine geschichilich-statistische Abhandlung, von Wilhelm Schulz, Zürich and Winterthur, 1843.—Ed.]

[13. The god of Greek mythology identified with Time.—Ed.]

[14. *Théorie nouvelle d'économie sociale et politique, ou Etude sur l'organisation des Sociétés,* par C. Pecqueur, Paris, 1842. This and all succeeding quotations from Pecqueur, Buret and Loudon in this section are in French in Marx's manuscript.— Ed.]

[15. *Solution du problème de la population et de la subsistance, soumise a un médicin dans une série de lettres,* par Charles Loudon, Paris, 1842, p. 229. This work was a translation into French, slightly abridged, of an English manuscript which seems never to have been published. In 1836, however, Loudon did issue at Leamington a short pamphlet in English—*The Equilibrium of Population and Sustenance Demonstrated;* but the French work referred to is a substantial book of 336 pages.—Ed.]

[2. *De la misère des classes laborieuses en Angleterre et en France,* par Eugene Buret, T. I-II, Paris, 1840.—Ed.]

Profit of Capital

1. CAPITAL

1) What is the basis of *capital*, that is, of private property in the products of others' labor?

"For if capital itself does not merely amount to theft or fraud, it requires still the co-operation of legislation to sanctify inheritance." (Say, t.I, p. 136, footnote.)[1]

How does one become a proprietor of productive stock? How does one become owner of the products created by means of this stock?

By virtue of *positive law.* (Say, t. II, p. 4.)

What does one acquire with capital, with the inheritance of a large fortune, for instance?

"The person who either acquires, or succeeds to a great fortune, does not necessarily acquire or succeed to any political power. . . . The power which that possession immediately and directly conveys to him, is the *power of purchasing;* a certain command over all the labor, or over all the produce of labor, which is then is then in the market." *(The Wealth of Nations,* by Adam Smith, Vol. I, pp. 26-27.)

Capital is thus the *governing power* over labor and its products. The capitalist possesses this power, not on account of his personal or human qualities, but inasmuch as he is an *owner* of capital. His power is the *purchasing* power of his capital, which noting can withstand.

Later we shall see first how the capitalist, by means of capital, exercises his governing power over labor, then, however, we shall see the governing power of capital over the capitalist himself.

What is capital?

"A certain quantity of *labor stocked* and stored up to be employed." (Ibid., Vol. I, p. 295.)

Capital is *stored-up labor.*

2) *Funds,* or stock, is any accumulation of products of the soil or of manufacture. Stock is called *capital* only when it yields to its owner a revenue or profit. (Ibid., Vol. I, p. 243.)

2. THE PROFIT OF CAPITAL

The *profit or gain of capital* is altogether different from the *wages of labor*. This difference is manifested in two ways: in the first place, the profits of capital are regulated altogether by the value of the capital employed, although the labor of inspection and direction associated with different capitals may be the same. Moreover in large works the whole of this labor is committed to some principal clerk, whose salary bears no regular proportion to the capital of which he oversees the management. And although the labor of the proprietor is here reduced almost to nothing, he still demands profits in proportion to his capital. (Ibid., Vol. I, p. 43.)

Why does the capitalist demand this proportion between profit and capital?

He would have no *interest* in employing the workers, unless he expected from the sale of their work something more than is necessary to replace the stock advanced by him as wages; and he would have no *interest* in employing a great stock rather than a small one unless his profit were to bear some proportion to the extent of the stock employed. (Ibid., p. 42.)

The capitalist thus makes a profit, first, on the wages, and secondly on the raw materials advanced by him.

What proportion, then, does profit bear to capital?

If it is already difficult to determine the usual average level of wages at a particular place and at a particular time, it is even more difficult to determine the profit on capitals. A change in the price of the commodities in which the capitalist deals, the good or bad fortune of his rivals and customers, a thousand other accidents to which commodities are exposed both in transit and in the warehouses—all produce a daily, almost hourly variation in profit. (Ibid., pp. 78-79.) But although it is impossible to determine with precision what are the profits on capitals, some notion may be formed of them from the *interest of money*. Wherever a great deal can be made by the use of money, a great deal will be given for the use of it; wherever little can be made by it, little will be given. (Ibid., p. 79.) The proportion which the usual market-rate of interest ought to bear to the rate of clear profit, necessarily varies as profit rises or falls. Double interest is in Great Britain reckoned what the merchants call *un profit honnête, modéré, raisonnable,*[3] terms which mean no more than a *common and usual profit.* (Ibid., p. 87.)

What is the *lowest* rate of profit? And what the *highest*?

The *lowest rate* of ordinary profit on capitals must always be *something more* than what is necessary to compensate the occasional losses to which every employment of capital is exposed. It is this surplus only which is the neat or clear profit. The same holds for the lowest rate of interest. (Ibid., p. 86.)

The *highest rate* to which ordinary profits can rise is that which in the price of the greater part of commodities *eats up the whole of the rent of the land,* and reduces the wages of labor contained in the commodity supplied to the *lowest rate,* the bare subsistence of the laborer during his work. The worker must always be fed in some way or other while he is required to work; ground-rent can disappear entirely. For example: the servants of the East India Company in Bengal. (Ibid., pp. 86-87.)

Besides all the advantages of limited competition which the capitalist may *exploit* in this case, he can keep the market-price above the natural-price by quite decorous means.

For one thing, by keeping *secrets in trade* if the market is at a great distance from those who supply it, that is, by concealing a price change, its rise above the natural level. This concealment has the effect that other capitalists do not follow him in investing their capital in this branch of industry or trade.

Then again by keeping *secrets in manufacture,* which enable the capitalist to reduce the costs of production and supply his commodity at the same or even at lower prices than his competitors while obtaining a higher profit. (Deceiving by keeping secrets is not immoral? Dealings on the stock exchange.) *Furthermore,* where production is restricted to a particular locality (as in the case of a rare wine), and where the *effective demand* can never be satisfied. *Finally,* through *monopolies* exercised by individuals or companies. Monopoly-price is the highest possible. (Ibid., pp. 53-54.)

Other fortuitous causes which can raise the profit on capital: the acquisition of new territories, or of new branches of trade, often increases the profit on capitals even in a wealthy country, because they withdraw some of the capitals from the old branches of trade, reduce competition, and cause the market to be supplied with fewer commodities, the prices of which then rise: those who deal in these commodities can then afford to borrow at a higher rate of interest. (Ibid., p. 83.)

The more a commodity is worked up—the more it becomes a manufactured object—the greater becomes that part of the price which resolves itself into wages and profit in proportion to that which resolves itself into rent. In the progress of the manufacture of a commodity, not only the number of profits increases, but every subsequent profit is greater than the foregoing; because the capital from which it is derived must always be greater. The capital which employs the weavers, for example, must always be greater than that which employs the spinners; because it not only replaces that capital with its profits, but pays, besides, the wages of weavers; and the profits must always bear some proportion to the capital.

Thus the advance made by human labor in converting the product of nature into the manufactured product of nature increases, not the wages of labor, but in part the number of profitable capitals, and in part the size of every subsequent capital in comparison with the foregoing.

With regard to the advantage which the capitalist derives from the division of labor, more later.

He profits doubly—first, by the division of labor; and secondly, in general, by the advance which human labor makes on the natural product. The greater the human share in a commodity, the greater the profit of dead capital.

In one and the same society the average rate of capital profits is much more nearly on the same level than the wages of the different sorts of labor. (Ibid., p. 100.) In the different employments of capital, the ordinary rate of profit varies with the certainty or uncertainty of the returns. "The ordinary profit of stock, though it rises with the risk, does not always seem to rise in proportion to it." (Ibid., pp. 99-100.)

It goes without saying that profits also rise if the means of circulation become less expensive or easier available (e.g., paper money).

3. THE RULE OF CAPITAL OVER LABOR AND THE MOTIVES OF THE CAPITALIST

The consideration of his own private profit is the sole motive which determines the owner of any capital to employ it either in agriculture, in manufactures, or in some particular branch of the wholesale or retail trade. The different quantities of *productive labor* which it may put into motion, and the different values which it may add to the annual produce of the land and labor of his country, according as it is employed in one or other of those different ways, never enter into his thoughts. (Ibid., p. 335.)

The most useful employment of capital for the capitalist is that which, risks being equal, yields him the greatest profit. This employment is not always the most useful for society: the most useful employment is that which draws benefit from the productive powers of nature. (Say, t. II, pp. 130-31.)

The plans and projects of the employers of capitals regulate and direct all the most important operators of labor, and *profit* is the end proposed by all those plans and projects. But the rate of profit does not, like rent and wages, rise with the prosperity and fall with the declension of the society. On the contrary, it is naturally low in rich and high in poor countries, and it is always highest in the countries which are going fastest to ruin. The interest of this class, therefore, has not the same connection with the general interest of the society as that of the other two. . . . The particular interest of the dealers in any particular branch of trade or manufactures is always in some respects different from, and frequently even in sharp opposition to, that of the public. To widen the market and to narrow the sellers' competition is always the interest of the dealer. This is a class of people whose interest is never exactly the same as that of society, a class of people who have generally an interest to deceive and to oppress the public. (Smith, Vol. I, pp. 231-32.)

4. THE ACCUMULATION OF CAPITALS AND THE COMPETITION AMONG THE CAPITALISTS

The *increase of capitals*, which raises wages, tends to lower the capitalists' profit, because of the *competition* among the capitalists.

"If, for example, the capital which is necessary for the grocery trade of a particular town is divided between two different grocers, their competition will tend to make that which each of them sells cheaper than if it were in the hands of one only; and if it were divided among twenty, their competition would be just so much the greater, and the chance of their combining together, in order to raise the price, just so much less."

Since we already know that monopoly-prices are as high as possible, since the interest of the capitalists, even from the point of view commonly held by political economists, stands in hostile opposition to society, and since a rise of profit operates like compound interest on the price of the commodity (Ibid., pp. 87-88), it follows that the sole defense against the capitalists is *competition*, which according to the evidence of political economy acts beneficently by both raising wages and lowering the prices of commodities to the advantage of the consuming public.

But competition is only possible if capitals multiply, and are held in many hands. The formation of many capitals is only possible as a result of multilateral accumulation, since capital comes into being only by accumulation; and multilateral accumulation necessarily turns into unilateral accumulation. Competition among capitals increases accumulation of capitals.

Accumulation, where private property prevails, is the *concentration* of capital in the hands of a few, it is in general an inevitable consequence if capitals are left to follow their natural course, and it is precisely through competition that the way is cleared for this natural destination of capital.

We have been told that the profit on capital is in proportion to the size of the capital. A large capital therefore accumulates more quickly than a small capital in proportion to its size, even if we disregard for the time being deliberate competition.

Accordingly, the accumulation of large capital proceeds much more rapidly than that of smaller capital, quite irrespective of competition. But let us follow this process further.

With the increase of capitals the profits on the capitals diminish, because of competition. The first to suffer, therefore, is the small capitalist.

The increase of capitals and a large number of capitals presupposes, further, a condition of advancing wealth in the country.

"In a country which had acquired its full complement of riches, ... as the ordinary rate of clear profit would be very small, so the usual market-rate of interest which could be afforded out of it would be so low as to render it impossible for any but the very wealthiest people to live upon the interest of their money. All people of small or middling fortunes would be obliged to superintend themselves the employment of their own stocks."

This is the situation most dear to the heart of political economy.

"The proportion between capital and revenue, therefore, seems everywhere to regulate the proportion between industry and idleness; wherever capital predominates, industry prevails; wherever revenue, idleness."

What about the employment of capital, then, in this condition of increased competition?

"As stock increases, the quantity of stock to be lent at interest grows gradually greater and greater. As the quantity of stock to be lent at interest increases, the interest ... diminishes...."(i) because "the market-price of things commonly diminishes as their quantity increases. ..." and (ii) because with the *increase of capitals in any country*, "*it becomes gradually more and more difficult* to find within the country a profitable method of employing any new capital. There arises in consequence a competition between different capitals, the owner of one endeavoring to get possession of that employment which is occupied by another. But upon most occasions he can hope to jostle that other out of his employment by no other means but by dealing upon more reasonable terms. He must not only sell what he deals in somewhat cheaper, but in order to get it to sell, he must sometimes, too, buy it dearer. The demand for productive labor, by the increase of the funds which are destined for maintaining it, grows every day greater and greater. Laborers easily find employment, but the owners of capitals find it difficult to get laborers to employ. Their competition raises the wages of labor and sinks the profits of stock."

Thus the small capitalist has the choice: 1) either to consume his capital, since he can no longer live on the interest—and thus cease to be a capitalist; or: 2) to set up a business himself, sell his commodity cheaper, buy dearer than the wealthier capitalist, and pay increased wages—thus ruining himself, the market-price being already very low as a result of the intense competition presupposed. If, however, the big capitalist wants to squeeze out the smaller capitalist, he has all the advantages over him which the capitalist has as a capitalist over the worker. The larger size of his capital compensates him for the smaller profits, and he can even bear temporary losses until the smaller capitalist is ruined and he finds himself freed from this competition. In this way, he accumulates the small capitalist's profits.

Furthermore: the big capitalist always buys cheaper than the small one, because he buys bigger quantities. He can therefore well afford to sell cheaper.

But if a fall in the rate of interest turns the middle capitalists from rentiers into business men, the increase in business capitals and the smaller profit consequent thereon produce conversely a fall in the rate of interest.

"When the profits which can be made by the use of a capital are ... diminished, ... the price which can be paid for the use of it, ... must necessarily be diminished with them."

"As riches, improvement, and population have increased, interest has declined," and consequently the profit of capitals, "after these are diminished, stock may not only continue to increase, but to increase much faster than before. ... A great stock though with small profits, generally increases faster than a small stock with great profits. Money, says the proverb, makes money."

If, however, this large capital is opposed by small capitals with small profits, as it is under the presupposed condition of intense competition, it crushes them completely. The necessary result of this competition is a general deterioration of commodities, adulteration, fake-production and universal poisoning, evident in large towns.

An important circumstance in the competition of large and small capitals is, furthermore, the relationship between *fixed capital* and *circulating capital*.[4]

"*Circulating capital* is a capital which is employed in raising provisions, in manufacture or trade. The capital employed in this manner yields no revenue or profit to its employer while it either remains in his possession or continues in the same shape. It is continually going from him in one particular shape in order to return to him in another, and it is only by means of such circulation, or such successive exchanges and transformations that it yields any profit. *Fixed capital* consists of capital invested in the improvement of land, the purchase of useful machines, instruments of trade, and suchlike things."

"Every saving in the expense of supporting the fixed capital is an improvement of the net revenue of the society. The whole capital of the undertaker of every work is necessarily divided between his fixed and his circulating capital. While his whole capital remains the same, the smaller the one part, the greater must necessarily be the other. It is the circulating capital which furnishes the materials and wages of labor, and puts industry into motion. Every saving, therefore, in the expense of maintaining the fixed capital, which does not diminish the productive powers of labor, must increase the fund which puts industry into motion."

It is clear from the outset that the relationship of fixed capital and circulating capital is much more favorable to the big capitalist than to the smaller capitalist. The extra fixed capital required by a very big banker as against a very small one is insignificant. Their fixed capital amounts to nothing more than the office. The equipment of the bigger landowner does not increase in proportion to the size of his estate. Similarly, the credit which a big capitalist enjoys compared with a smaller one means for him all the greater saving in fixed capital—that is, in the amount of ready money he must always have at hand. Finally, it is obvious that where industrial labor has reached a high level, and where therefore almost all manual labor has become factory-labor, the entire capital of a small capitalist does not suffice to provide him even with the necessary fixed capital.[5]

The accumulation of large capitals is generally accompanied by a corresponding concentration and simplification of fixed capital relative to the smaller capitalists. The big capitalist introduces for himself some kind of organization of the instruments of labor.

"Similarly, in the sphere of industry every manufactory and mill is already a more comprehensive combination of a larger material fortune with numerous and varied intellectual capacities and technical skills serving the *common* purpose of production. . . . Where legislation preserves landed property in large units, the surplus of a growing population flocks into trades, and it is therefore as in Great Britain in the field of industry, principally, that proletarians aggregate in great numbers. Where, however, the law permits the continuous division of the land, the number of small, debt-encumbered proprietors increases, as in France; and the continuing process of fragmentation throws them into the class of the needy and the discontented. When eventually this fragmentation and indebtedness reaches a higher degree still, big landed property once more swallows up small property, just as large-scale industry destroys small industry. And as larger estates are formed again, large number of property-less workers not required for the cultivation of the soil are again driven into industry." (Schulz, *Bewegung der Produktion*, pp. 58, 59.)

"Commodities of a particular kind change in character as a result of changes in the method of production, and especially as a result of the use of machinery. Only by the exclusion of human power has it become possible to spin from a pound of cotton worth 3 shillings and 8 pence 350 hanks of a total length of 167 English miles (i.e., 36 German miles), and of a commercial value of 25 guineas."

"On the average the prices of cotton cloths have decreased in England during the past 45 years by eleven-twelfths, and according to Marshall's calculations the same amount of manufactured goods for which 16 shillings was still paid in 1814 is now supplied at 1 shilling and 10 pence. The greater cheapness of industrial products expands both consumption at home and the market abroad, and because of this the number of workers in cotton has not only not fallen in Great Britain after the introduction of machines but has risen from forty thousand to one and a half million. As to the earnings of industrial entrepreneurs and workers: the growing competition between the factory-owners has resulted in their profits necessarily falling relative to the amount of products supplied by them. In the years 1820-33 the Manchester manufacturer's gross profit on a piece of calico fell from four shillings 11/3 pence to one shilling 9 pence. But to make up for this loss, the volume of manufacture has been correspondingly increased. The consequence of this is ... that separate branches of industry experience over-production to some extent; that frequent bankruptcies occur causing property to fluctuate and vacillate unstably *within* the class of capitalists and masters of labor, thus throwing into the proletariat some of those who have been ruined economically; and that, frequently and suddenly, close-downs or cuts in employment become necessary, the painful effects of which are always bitterly felt by the class of wage-laborers." (Ibid., p. 63.)

"To hire out one's labor is to begin one's enslavement. To hire out the materials of labor is to establish one's freedom. . . . Labor is man; but the materials of labor, on the other hand, contain nothing human." (Pecqueur, *Théorie sociale*, etc., pp. 411-12.)

"The element of *matter*, which is quite incapable of creating wealth without the other element, *labor*, acquires the magical virtue of being fertile for them,[6] as if by their own action they had placed there this indispensable element" (Ibid.)

"Supposing that the daily labor of a worker brings him on the average four hundred francs a year and that this sum suffices for every adult to live some sort of crude life, then any proprietor receiving 2,000 francs in interest or rent, from a farm, a house, etc., compels indirectly five men to work for him; an income of 100,000 francs represents the labor of two hundred and fifty men, and that of 1,000,000 francs the labor of two thousand five hundred individuals (and 300 million [Louis Philippe] therefore the labor of 750,000 workers)." (Ibid., pp. 412-13.)

"The human law has given owners the right to use and abuse—that is to say, the right to do what they will with the materials of labor. . . . They are in no way obliged by law to provide work for the propertyless when required and at all times, or to pay them always an adequate wage, etc." (Ibid., p. 413.) "Complete freedom concerning the nature, the quantity, the quality and the opportunity of production; concerning the use and the disposal of wealth; and full command over the materials of all labor. Everyone is free to exchange what belongs to him as he thinks fit, without considering anything other than his own interest as an individual." (Ibid., p. 413.)

"Competition is merely the expression of the freedom to exchange, which itself is the immediate and logical consequence of the individual's right to use and abuse all the instruments of production. The right to use and abuse, freedom of exchange, and arbitrary competition—these three economic moments, which form one unit, entail the following consequences; each produces what he wishes, as he wishes, when he wishes, where he wishes, produces well or produces badly, produces too much or not enough, too soon or too late, at too high a price or too low a price; none knows whether he will sell, how he will sell, when he will sell, where he will sell, to whom he will sell. And it is the same with regard to purchases. The producer is ignorant of needs and resources, of demand and supply. He sells when he wishes, when he can, where he wishes, to whom he wishes, at the price he wishes. And he buys in the same way. In all this he is ever the plaything of chance, the slave of the law of the strongest, of the least harassed, of the richest. . . . While at one place there is scarcity, at another there is glut and waste. While one producer sells a lot or at a very high price, and at an enormous profit, the other sells nothing or sells at a loss. . . . The supply does not know the demand, and the demand does not know the supply. You produce, trusting to a taste, a fashion, which prevails among the consuming public. But by the time you are ready to deliver the commodity, the whim has already passed and has settled on some other kind of product. . . . The inevitable consequences: bankruptcies occurring permanently and universally; miscalculations, sudden ruin and unexpected fortunes, commercial crises, unemployment, periodic gluts or shortages; instability and depreciation of wages and profits, the loss or enormous waste of wealth, time and effort in the area of fierce competition." (Ibid., pp. 414-16.)

Ricardo in his book (Rent of Land): Nations are merely production-shops; man is a machine for consuming and producing; human life is a kind of capital; economic laws blindly rule the world. For Ricardo men are nothing, the product everything. In the 26th chapter of the French translation it says: "To an individual with a capital of £20,000 whose profits were £2,000 per annum, it would be a matter quite indifferent whether his capital would employ a hundred or a thousand men. ... Is not the real interest of the nation similar? Provided its net real income, its rent and profits be the same, it is of no importance whether the nation consists of ten or of twelve millions of inhabitants." "In fact," says M. Sismondi (t. II, p. 331), "nothing remains to be desired but that the King, living quite alone on the island, should by continuously turning a crank cause automata to do all the work of England."[7]

"The master who buys the worker's labor at such a low price that it scarcely suffices for the worker's most pressing needs is responsible neither for the inadequacy of the wage nor for the excessive duration of the labor: he himself has to submit to the law which he imposes. . . . Poverty is not so much caused by men as by the power of things." (Buret, l.c. p. 82.)

"The inhabitants of many different parts of Great Britain have not capital sufficient to improve and cultivate all their lands. The wool of the southern counties of Scotland is, a great part of it, after a long land carriage through very bad roads, manufactured in Yorkshire, for want of capital to manufacture it at home. There are many little manufacturing towns in Great Britain, of which the inhabitants have not capital sufficient to transport the produce of their own industry to those distant markets where there is demand and consumption for it. If there are any merchants among them, they are properly only the agents of wealthier merchants who reside in some of the greater commercial cities." (Smith, l.c., Vol. I, pp. 326-27.)

"The annual produce of the land and labor of any nation can be increased in its value by no other means but by increasing either the *number of its productive laborers* or *the productive powers of those laborers* who had before been employed. ... In either case an additional capital is almost always required." (Ibid., pp. 306-07.)

"As the *accumulation* of stock must, in the nature of things, be previous to the division of labor, so labor can be more and more subdivided in proportion only as stock is previously more and more accumulated. The quantity of materials which the same number of people can work up, increases in a great proportion as labor comes to be more and more subdivided; and as the operations of each workman are gradually reduced to a greater degree of simplicity, a variety of new machines comes to be invented for facilitating and abridging those operations. As the division of labor advances, therefore, in order to give constant employment to an equal number of workmen, an equal stock of provisions, and a greater stock of materials and tools than what would have been necessary in a ruder state of things, must be accumulated beforehand. But the number of workmen in every branch of business generally increases with the division of labor in that branch, or rather it is the increase of their number which enables them to class and subdivide themselves in this manner." (Ibid., pp. 241-42.)

"As the accumulation of stock is previously necessary for carrying on this great improvement in the productive powers of labor, so that accumulation naturally leads to this improvement. The person who employs his stock in maintaining labor, necessarily wishes to employ it in such a manner as to produce as great a quantity of work as possible. He endeavors, therefore, both to make among his workmen the most proper distribution of employment, and to furnish them with the best machines which he can either invent or afford to purchase. His abilities in both these respects are generally in proportion to the extent of his stock, or to the number of people whom it can employ. The quantity of industry, therefore, not only increases in every country with the *increase of the stock* which employs it, but, in consequence of that increase, the same quantity of industry produces a much greater quantity of work." (Ibid., p. 242.) Hence *overproduction*.

"More comprehensive combinations of productive forces ... in industry and trade by uniting more numerous and more diverse, human and natural powers in larger-scale enterprises. Already here and there, closer association of the chief branches of production. Thus, big manufacturers will try to acquire also large estates in order to become independent of others for at least a part of the raw materials required for their industry; or they will go into trade in conjunction with their industrial enterprises, not only to sell their own manufactures, but also to purchase other kinds of products and to sell these to their workers. In England, where a single factory-owner sometimes employs ten to twelve thousand workers ... it is already not uncommon to find such combinations of various branches of production controlled by *one* brain, such smaller states or provinces within the state. Thus, the mine-owners in the *Birmingham* area have recently taken over the *whole* process of iron production, which was previously distributed among various entrepreneurs and owners. See 'Der Bergmännische Distrikt bei Birmingham,' *Deutsche Vierteljahrs-schrift*, No. 3, 1838. Finally in the larger joint-stock enterprises which have become so numerous, we see far-reaching combinations of the financial resources of *many* participants with the scientific and technical knowledge and skills of others to whom the carrying-out of the work is handed over. The capitalists are thereby enabled to apply their savings in more diverse ways and perhaps even to employ them simultaneously in agriculture, industry and commerce; as a consequence their interest becomes more comprehensive, and the contradictions between agricultural, industrial and commercial interests are reduced and disappear. But this increased possibility of applying capital profitably in the most diverse ways cannot but intensify the antagonism between the propertied and the non-propertied classes." (Schulz, l.c, pp. 40-41.)

The enormous profit which the landlords of houses make out of poverty. House-rent stands in inverse proportion to industrial poverty. [The lower the standard of living, the higher the house-rent.]

So does the interest obtained from the vices of the ruined proletarians. (Prostitution, drunkenness; the pawnbroker.) The accumulation of capitals increases and the competition between them decreases, when capital and landed property are united in the same hand, also when capital is enabled by its size to combine different branches of production.

Indifference towards men. Smith's twenty lottery-tickets.[8] Say's net and gross revenue.

Footnotes

[1. *Traité d'économie politique*, par Jean-Baptiste *Say* (*Treatise on Political Economy*, by Jean-Baptiste Say). 3ᵉᵐᵉ edition, t. I-II, Paris, 1817.– Ed.]

[2. *De la misère des classes laborieuses en Angleterre et en France*, par Eugene Buret, T. I-II, Paris, 1840.—Ed.]

[3. Smith has "good, moderate, reasonable profit."—Ed.]

[4. Marx uses the French terms *capital fixe* and *capital circulant*.—Ed.]

[5. Marx has made here the following note in French: "As is well known, large-scale cultivation usually provides employment only for a small number of hands."– Ed.]

[6. For those who own this matter, this object of labor.—Ed.]

[7. The whole paragraph (including the quotation from Ricardo's book on the *Principles of Political Economy and Taxation* and from Sismondi's *Nouveaux principes d'économie politique*) is an except from E. Buret's book *De la misère des classes laborieuses en Angleterre et en France*, T. 1, Paris, 1840, pp. 6-7.—Ed.]

[8. Marx alludes to the following passage: "In a perfectly fair lottery, those who draw the prizes ought to gain all that is lost by those who draw the blanks. In a profession where twenty fail for one that succeeds, that one ought to gain all that should have been gained by the unsuccessful twenty." (Smith, l.c, Vol. I, Bk. I, p. 94)—Ed.]

Rent of Land

Landlords' right has its origin in robbery. (Say, t. I, p. 136, footnote.) The landlords, like all other men, love to reap where they never sowed, and demand a rent even for the natural produce of the earth. (Smith, I .c, p. 44.)

"The rent of land, it may be thought, is frequently no more than a reasonable profit or interest for the stock laid out by the landlord upon its improvement. This, no doubt, may be partly the case upon some occasions; . . . The landlord demands 1) a rent even for unimproved land, and the supposed interest or profit upon the expense of improvement is generally an addition to this original rent. 2) Those improvements, besides, are not always made by the stock of the landlord, but sometimes by that of the tenant. When the lease comes to be renewed, however, the landlord commonly demands the same augmentation of rent as if they had all been made by his own. He sometimes demands rent for what is altogether incapable of human improvement." (Ibid., p. 131.)

Smith cites as an instance of the last case kelp, a species of seaweed which, when burned, yields an alkaline salt, useful for making glass, soap, etc. It grows in several parts of Great Britain, particularly in Scotland, upon such rocks only as lie within the high water mark, which are twice every day covered with the sea, and of which the produce, therefore, was never augmented by human industry. The landlord, however, whose estate is bounded by a kelp shore of this kind, demands a rent for it as much as for his corn fields. The sea in the neighborhood of the Islands of Shetland is more than commonly abundant in fish, which makes a great part of the subsistence of their inhabitants. But in order to profit by the produce of the water they must have a habitation upon the neighboring land. The rent of the landlord is in proportion, not to what the farmer can make by the land, but to what he can make both by the land and by the water. (Ibid., p. 131.)

"This rent may be considered as the produce of those *powers of nature*, the use of which the landlord lends to the farmer. It is greater or smaller according to the supposed extent of those powers, or in other words, according to the supposed natural or improved fertility of the land. It is the work of nature which remains after deducting or compensating everything which can be regarded as the work of man." (Ibid., p. 324-25.)

"*The rent of land*, therefore, considered as the price paid for the use of land, is naturally a *monopoly price*. It is not at all proportioned to what the landlord may have laid out upon the improvement of the land, or to what he can afford to take; but to what the farmer can afford to give." (Ibid., p. 131.)

Of the three original classes, that of the landlords is the one "whose revenue costs them neither labor nor care, but comes to them, as it were, of its own accord, and independent of any plan or project of their own." (Ibid., p. 230.)

We have already learned that the size of the rent depends on the degree of *fertility* of the land.

Another factor in its determination is *situation*.

"The rent of land not only varies with its *fertility*, whatever be its produce, but with its *situation*, whatever be its fertility." (Ibid., p. 133.)

"The produce of land, mines and fisheries, when their natural fertility is equal, is in proportion to the extent and proper application of the capitals employed about them. When the capitals are equal and equally well applied, it is in proportion to their natural fertility." (Ibid., p. 249.)

These propositions of Smith are important, because, given equal costs of production and capital of equal size, they reduce the rent of land, to the greater or lesser fertility of the soil. Thereby showing clearly the perversion of concepts in political economy, which turns the fertility of the land into an attribute of the landlord.

Now, however, let us consider the rent of land as it is formed in real life.

The rent of land is established as a result of the *struggle between tenant and landlord*. We find that the hostile antagonism of interests, the struggle, the war is recognized throughout political economy as the basis of social organization.

Let us see now what the relations are between landlord and tenant.

"In adjusting the terms of the lease, the landlord endeavors to leave him no greater share of the produce than what is sufficient to keep up the stock from which he furnishes the seed, pays the labor, and purchases and maintains the cattle and other instruments of husbandry, together with the ordinary profits of farming stock in the neighborhood. This is evidently the smallest share with which the tenant can content himself without being a loser, and the landlord seldom means to leave him any more. Whatever part of the produce, or, what is the same thing, whatever part of its price is over and above this share, he naturally endeavors to reserve to himself as the rent of his land, which is evidently the highest the tenant can afford to pay in the actual circumstances of the land. . . . This portion, however, may still be considered as the natural rent of land, or the rent for which it is naturally meant that land should for the most part be let." (Ibid., pp. 130-31.)

"The landlords," says Say, "operate a certain kind of monopoly against the tenants. The demand for their commodity, site and soil, can go on expanding indefinitely; but there is only a given, limited about of their commodity. . . . The bargain struck between landlord and tenant is always advantageous to the former in the greatest possible degree. . . . Besides the advantage he derives from the nature of the case, he derives a further advantage from his position, his larger fortune and greater credit and standing. But the first by itself suffices to enable him and him *alone* to profit from the favorable circumstances of the land. The opening of a canal, or a road; the increase of population and of the prosperity of a district, always raise the rent. . . . Indeed, the tenant himself may improve the ground at his own expense; but he only derives the profit from this capital for the duration of his lease, with the expiry of which it remains with the proprietor of the land; henceforth it is the latter who reaps the interest thereon, without having made the outlay, for there is now a proportionate increase in the rent." (Say, t. II, pp. 142-43.)

"Rent considered as the price paid for the use of land, is naturally the highest which the tenant can afford to pay in the actual circumstances of the land." (Smith, l.c, p. 130.)

"The rent of an estate above ground commonly amounts to what is supposed to be a third of the gross produce; and it is generally a rent certain and independent of the occasional variations in the crop." (Ibid., p. 153.) This rent "is seldom less than a fourth ... of the whole produce." (Ibid., p. 325.)

Ground-rent cannot be paid on all commodities. For instance, in many districts no rent is paid for stones.

"Such parts only of the produce of land can commonly be brought to market of which the ordinary price is sufficient to replace the stock which must be employed in bringing them thither, together with its ordinary profits. If the ordinary price is more than this, the surplus part of it will naturally go to the rent of the land. If it is not more, though the commodity may be brought to market, it can afford no rent to the landlord. Whether the price is or is not more depends upon the demand." (Ibid., p. 132.)

"Rent, it is to be observed, therefore, enters into the composition of the *price of commodities* in a *different way* from wages and profit. *High or low wages and profit are the causes of high or low prices; high or low rent is the effect of it.*" (Ibid., p. 132.)

Food belongs to the *products* which always yield a *ground-rent.*

"As men, like all other animals, naturally multiply in proportion to the means of their subsistence, food is always, more or less, in demand. It can always purchase or command a greater or smaller quantity of labor, and somebody can always be found who is willing to do something in order to obtain it. The quantity of labor, indeed, which it can purchase is not always *equal* to what it could maintain, if managed in the most economical manner, on account of the high wages which are sometimes given to labor. But it can always purchase such a quantity of labor as it can maintain, according to the rate at which the sort of labor is commonly maintained in the neighborhood. But land, in almost any possible situation, produces a greater quantity of food than what is sufficient to maintain all the labor necessary for bringing it to market in the most liberal way in which that labor is ever maintained. The surplus, too, is always more than sufficient to replace the stock which employed that labor, together with its profits. Something, therefore, always remains for a rent to the landlord." (Ibid., pp. 132-33.)

"Food is in this manner not only the original source of rent, but every other part of the produce of land which afterwards affords rent derives that part of its value from the improvement of the powers of labor in producing food by means of the improvement and cultivation of land." (Ibid., p. 150.)

"Human food seems to be the only produce of land which always and necessarily affords some rent to the landlord." (Ibid., p. 147.)

"Countries are populous not in proportion to the number of people whom their produce can clothe and lodge, but in proportion to that of those whom it can feed." (Ibid., p. 149.)

"After food, clothing and lodging are the two great wants of mankind." (Ibid., p. 147.) They usually yield a rent, but not inevitably.

Let us now see how the landlord exploits everything from which society benefits.

(1) The rent of land increases with population. (Ibid., p. 146.)

(2) We have already learned from Say how the rent of land increases with railways, etc., with the improvement, safety, and multiplication of the means of communication.

(3) "Every improvement in the circumstances of the society tends either *directly* or *indirectly* to raise the real rent of land, to increase the real wealth of the landlord, his power of purchasing the labor, or the produce of the labor of other people. . . . The extension of improvement and cultivation tends to raise it directly. The landlord's share of the produce necessarily increases with the increase of the produce. The rise in the real price of those parts of the rude produce of land, ... the rise in the price of cattle, for example, tends too to raise

the rent of land directly, and in a still greater proportion. The real value of the landlord's share, his real command of the labor of other people, not only rises with the real value of the produce, but the proportion of his share to the whole produce rises with it. That produce, after the rise in its real price, requires no more labor to collect it than before. A smaller proportion of it will, therefore, be sufficient to replace, with the ordinary profit, the stock which employs that labor. A greater proportion of it must, consequently, belong to the landlord." (Ibid., pp. 228-29.)

The greater demand for raw produce, and therefore the rise in value, may in part result from the increase of population and from the increase of their needs. But every new invention, every new application in manufacture of a previously unused or little-used raw material, augments the rent of the land. Thus, for example, there was a tremendous rise in the rent of coal-mines with the advent of the railways, steamships, etc.

Besides this advantage which the landlord derives from manufacture, discoveries, and labor, there is yet another, as we shall presently see.

"All those improvements in the productive powers of labor, which tend directly to reduce the real price of manufactures, tend indirectly to raise the real rent of land. The landlord exchanges that part of his rude produce, which is over and above his own consumption, or what comes to the same thing, the price of that part of it, for manufactured produce. Whatever reduces the real price of the latter, raises that of the former. An equal quantity of the former becomes thereby equivalent to a greater quantity of the latter; and the landlord is enabled to purchase a greater quantity of the conveniences, ornaments, or luxuries, which he has occasion for." (Ibid., p. 229.)

But it is absurd to conclude, as Smith does, that since the landlord exploits every benefit which comes to society, the interest of the landlord is always identical with that of society. (Ibid., p. 230.) In the economic system, under the rule of private property, the interest which an individual has in society is in precisely inverse proportion to the interest society has in him—just as the interest of the money-lender in the spendthrift is by no means identical with the interest of the spendthrift.

We shall mention only in passing the landlord's obsession with monopoly directed against the landed property of foreign countries, from which the corn-laws, for instance, originate. Likewise, we shall here pass over medieval serfdom, the slavery in the colonies, and the miserable condition of the country folk, the day-laborers, in Great Britain. Let us confine ourselves to the propositions of political economy itself.

(1) The landlord being interested in the welfare of society means, according to the principles of political economy, that he is interested in the growth of its population, production, in the expansion of its needs—in short, in the increase of wealth; and the increase of wealth is, as we have already seen, identical with the increase of poverty and slavery. The relation between increasing house-rent and increasing poverty is an example of the landlord's interest in society, for the ground-rent, the interest obtained from the land on which the house stands, goes up with the rent of the house.

(2) According to the political economists themselves, the landlord's interest is the antagonistic opposite of the interest of the tenant farmer—and thus already of a significant section of society.

(3) As the landlord can demand all the more rent from the tenant farmer the less wages the farmer pays, and as the farmer forces down wages all the lower the more rent the landlord demands, it follows that the interest of the landlord is just as hostile to that of the farm workers as is that of the manufacturers to their workers. It forces down wages to the minimum in just the same way.

(4) Since a real reduction in the price of manufactured products raises the rent of land, the landowner has a direct interest in lowering the wages of industrial workers, in competition among the capitalists, in over-production, in all the misery associated with industrial production.

(5) While, thus, the landlord's interest, far from being identical with the interest of society, stands in antagonistic opposition to the interest of tenant farmers, farm laborers, factory-workers and capitalists, on the other hand, the interest of one landlord is not even identical with that of another, on account of competition, which we will now consider.

In general the relationship of large and small landed property is like that of big and small capital. But in addition, there are special circumstances which lead inevitably to the accumulation of large landed property and to the absorption of small property by it.

(1) Nowhere does the relative number of workers and implements decrease more with increases in the size of the stock than in landed property. Likewise, the possibility of all-round exploitation, of economizing production costs, and of effective division of labor, increases nowhere more with the size of the stock than in landed property. However small a field may be, it requires for its working a certain irreducible minimum of implements (plough, saw, etc.), while the size of a piece of landed property can be reduced far below this minimum.

(2) The big landed property accumulates to itself the interest on the capital which the tenant farmer has employed to improve the land. The small landed

property has to employ its own capital, and therefore does not get this profit at all.

(3) While every social improvement benefits the big estate, it harms small property, because it increases its need for ready cash.

(4) Two important laws relating to this competition remain to be considered:

(a) The rent of the of the cultivated land, of which the produce is human food, regulates the rent of the greater part of other cultivated land. (Ibid., p. 144.)

Ultimately, only the big estate can produce such food as cattle, etc.. Therefore it regulates the rent of other land and can force it down to a minimum.

The small landed proprietor working on his own account stands then to the big landowner in the same relation as an artisan possessing his *own* tool to the factory-owner. Small property in land has become a mere instrument of labor. Rent of land entirely disappears for the small proprietor; there remains to him at the most the interest on his capital, and his wages. For ground-rent can be driven down by competition till it is nothing more than the interest on capital not invested by the proprietor.

(b) In addition, we have already learned that with equal fertility and equally efficient exploitation of lands, mines and fisheries, the produce is proportionate to the size of the capital. Hence the victory of the big landowner. Similarly, where equal capitals are employed the product is proportionate to the fertility. Hence, where capitals are equal victory goes to the proprietor of the more fertile soil.

(c) "A mine of any kind may be said to be either fertile or barren, according as the quantity of mineral which can be brought from it by a certain quantity of labor is greater or less than what can be brought by an equal quantity from the greater part of other mines of the same kind." (Ibid., p. 151.)

"The most fertile coal-mine, too, regulates the price of coals at all other mines in its neighborhood. Both the proprietor and the undertaker of the work find, the one that he can get a greater rent, the other that he can get a greater profit, by somewhat underselling all their neighbors. Their neighbors are soon obliged to sell at the same price, though they cannot so well afford it, and though it always diminishes, and sometimes takes away altogether both their rent and their profit. Some works are abandoned altogether; others can afford no rent, and can be wrought only by the proprietor." (Ibid., pp. 152-53.) "After the discovery of the mines of Peru, the silver mines of Europe were, the greater part of them, abandoned. . . . This was the case, too, with the mines of Cuba and St. Domingo, and even with the ancient mines of Peru, after the discovery of those of Potosi." (Ibid., p. 154.)

What Smith here says of mines applies more or less to landed property generally.

(d) "The ordinary market-price of land, it is to be observed, depends everywhere upon the ordinary market rate of interest. ... If the rent of land should fall short of the interest of money by a greater difference, nobody would buy land, which would soon reduce its ordinary price. On the contrary, if the advantages should much more than compensate the difference, everybody would buy land, which again would soon raise its ordinary price." (Ibid., p. 320.)

From this relation of ground-rent to interest on money it follows that rent must fall more and more, so that eventually only the wealthiest people can live on rent. Hence the ever greater competition between landowners who do not lease their land to tenants. Ruin of some of these—further accumulation of large landed property.

This competition has the further consequence that a large part of landed property falls into the hands of the capitalists and that capitalists thus become simultaneously landowners, just as the smaller landowners, are on the whole already nothing more than capitalists. Similarly, a section of large landowners become simultaneously industrialists.

The final consequence is thus the abolishment of the distinction between capitalist and landowner, so that there remain altogether only two classes of the population—the working class and the class of capitalists. This huckstering with landed property, the transformation of landed property into a commodity, constitutes the final overthrow of the old and the final consummation of the money aristocracy.)

(1)We will not join in the sentimental tears wept over this by romanticism. Romanticism always confuses the shamefulness of *huckstering the land* with the perfectly rational consequence, inevitable and desirable within the realm of private property, of the *huckstering of private property* in land. In the first place, feudal landed property is already by its very nature huckstered land—the earth which is estranged from man and hence, confronts him in the shape of a few great lords. The domination of the land as an alien power over men is already inherent in feudal landed property. The serf is the adjunct of the land. Likewise, the lord of an entailed estate, the firstborn son, belongs to the land. It inherits him. Indeed, the dominion of private property begins with property in land—that is its basis. But in feudal landed property the lord at least *appears* as the king of the estate. Similarly, there still exists the semblance of a more intimate connection between the proprietor and the land than that of mere *material* wealth. The estate is individualized with its lord: it has his rank, is baronial or ducal with him, has his privileges, his jurisdiction, his political position, etc. It appears as the inorganic body of its lord. Hence the proverb *nulle terre sans maître*,[1] which expresses the fusion of nobility and landed property. Similarly, the rule of landed property does not appear directly as the rule of mere capital. For those belonging to it, the estate is more like their fatherland. It is a constricted sort of nationality.

In the same way, feudal landed property gives its name to its lord, as does a kingdom to its king. His family history, the history of his house, etc.—all this individualizes the estate for him and makes it literally his house, personifies it. Similarly those working on the estate have not the position of *day-laborers;* but they are in part themselves his property, as are serfs; and in part they are bound to him by ties of respect, allegiance and duty. His relation to them is therefore directly political, and has likewise a human, *intimate* side. Customs, character, etc., vary from one estate to another and seem to be one with the land to which they belong; later, on the other hand, a man is bound to his land, not by his character or his individuality, but only by his purse strings. Finally, the feudal lord does not try to extract the utmost advantage from his land. Rather, he consumes what is there and calmly leaves the worry of producing to the serfs and the tenants. Such is *nobility*'s relationship to landed property, which casts a romantic glory on its lords.

It is necessary that this appearance be abolished—that landed property, the root of private property, be dragged completely into the movement of private property and that it become a commodity; that the rule of the proprietor appear as the undisguised rule of private property, of capital, freed of all political tincture; that the relationship between proprietor and worker be reduced to the economic relationship of exploiter and exploited; that all personal relationship between the proprietor and his property cease, property becoming merely *objective*, material wealth; that the marriage of convenience should take the place of the marriage of honor with the land; and that the land should likewise sink to the status of a commercial value, like man. It is essential that that which is the root of landed property—filthy self-interest—make its appearance, too, in its cynical form. It is essential that the immovable monopoly turn into the mobile and restless monopoly, into competition; and that the idle enjoyment of the products of the other peoples' blood and toil turn into a bustling commerce in the same commodity. Lastly, it is essential that in this competition landed property, in the form of capital, manifest its dominion over both the working class and the proprietors themselves who are either being ruined or raised by the laws governing the movement of capital. The medieval proverb *nulle terre sans seigneur*[2] is thereby replaced by that other proverb, *l'argent n'a pas de maître*[3] wherein is expressed the complete domination of dead matter over men.

(2) Concerning the argument of division or non-division of landed property, the following is to be observed.

The division of landed property negates the *large-scale monopoly* of property in land—abolishes it; but only by *generalizing* this monopoly. It does not abolish the source of monopoly, private property. It attacks the existing form but not the essence, of monopoly. The consequence is that it falls victim to the laws of private property. For the division of landed property corresponds to the movement of competition in the sphere of industry. In addition to the economic disadvantages of such a dividing-up of the instruments of labor, and of separated labor (to be clearly distinguished from the division of labor: in separated labor the work is not shared out among many, but each carries on the same work by himself, it is a multiplication of the same work) this division of land, like competition in industry, necessarily turns again into accumulation.

Therefore, where the division of landed property takes place, there remains nothing for it but to return to monopoly in a still more malignant form, or to negate, to abolish the division of landed property itself. To do that, however, is not to return to feudal ownership, but to abolish private property in the soil altogether. The first abolition of monopoly is always its generalization, the broadening of its existence. The abolition of monopoly once it has come to exist in its utmost breadth and inclusiveness is its total annihilation. Association, applied to land, shares the economic advantage of large-scale landed property, and first brings to realization the original tendency inherent in land-division, namely, equality. In the same way association reestablishes, now on a rational basis, no longer mediated by serfdom, overlordship and the silly mysticism of property, the intimate ties of man with the earth, for the earth ceases to be an object of huckstering, and through free labor and free enjoyment becomes once more a true personal property of man. A great advantage of the division of landed property is that its masses, who can no longer resign themselves to servitude perish through property in a different way than in industry.

As for large landed property, its defenders have always sophistically identified the economic advantages offered by large-scale agriculture with large-scale landed property, as if it were not precisely as a result of the abolition of property, that this advantage, for one thing, received its greatest possible extension, and, for another, only then would be of social benefit. In the same way, they have attacked the huckstering spirit of small landed property, as if large landed property did not contain huckstering latent within it, even in its feudal form—not to speak of the modern English form, which combines the landlord's feudalism with the tenant farmer's huckstering and industry.

Just as large landed property can throw back the reproach of monopoly leveled against it by partitioned land, for partitioned land is also based on the monopoly of private property, partitioned landed property can likewise throw back to large landed property the reproach of partition, since partition also prevails there, though in a rigid and crystallized form. Indeed, private property rests altogether on partitioning. Moreover, just as division of the land leads back to large landed property as a form of capital wealth, feudal landed property must necessarily lead to partitioning or at least fall into the hands of the capitalists, turn and twist as it may.

For large landed property, as in England, drives the overwhelming majority of the population into the arms of industry and reduces its own workers to utter wretchedness. Thus, it engenders and enlarges the power of its enemy, capital, industry, by throwing poor people and an entire activity of the country on to the other side. It makes the majority of the people of the country industrial, and thus opponents of large landed property. Where industry has attained to great power, as in England at the present time, it progressively forces large landed property to discard its monopolies against foreign countries and throws them into competition with landed property abroad. For under the sway of industry landed property could keep its feudal grandeur secure only by means of monopolies against foreign countries, thereby protecting itself against the general laws of trade, which are incompatible with its feudal character. Once thrown into competition, landed property obeys the laws of competition, like every other commodity subjected to competition. It begins thus to fluctuate, to decrease and to increase, to fly from one hand to another; and no law can keep it any longer in a few pre-destined hands. The immediate consequence is the splitting up of the land among many hands, and in any case subjection to the power of industrial capitals.

Finally, large landed property which has been forcibly preserved in this way and which has begotten by its side a tremendous industry leads even more quickly to crisis than the partitioning of land, by whose side the power of industry remains constantly of second rank.

Large landed property, as we see in England, has already cast off its feudal character and adopted an industrial character insofar as it is aiming to make as much money as possible. To the owner it yields the utmost possible rent, to the tenant farmer the utmost possible profit on his capital. The workers on the land, in consequence, have already been reduced to the minimum, and the class of tenant farmers already represent within landed property the power of industry and capital. As a result of foreign competition, rent of land can in most cases form no longer an independent income. A large number of landowners have to displace farmers, some of whom in this way sink into the proletariat. On the other hand, many farmers will take over landed property; for the big proprietors who with their comfortable incomes have mostly given themselves over to extravagance are for the most part, not competent to conduct large-scale agriculture, and in some cases possess neither the capital nor the ability for the exploitation of the land. Hence a section of this class, too, is completely ruined. Eventually wages, which have already been reduced to a minimum, must be reduced yet further, to meet the new competition. This then necessarily leads to revolution.

Landed property had to develop in each of these two ways so as to experience in both its necessary eclipse, just as industry both in the form of monopoly and in that of competition had to ruin itself so as to learn to believe in man.

Footnotes
[1.There is no land without its master.—Ed.]
[2. There is no land without its lord.—Ed.]
[3. Money knows no master.—Ed.]

Estranged Labor[1]

We have proceeded from the premises of political economy. We have accepted its language and its laws. We presupposed private property, the separation of labor, capital and land, and of wages, profit of capital and rent of land—likewise division of labor, competition, the concept of exchange-value, etc. On the basis of political economy itself, in its own words, we have shown that the worker sinks to the level of a commodity and becomes indeed the most wretched of commodities; that the wretchedness of the worker is in inverse proportion to the power and magnitude of his production; that the necessary result of competition is the accumulation of capital in a few hands, and thus th' restoration of monopoly in a more terrible form; that finally the distinction between capitalist and land-rentier, like that between the tiller of the soil and the factory-worker, disappears and that the whole of society must fall apart into the two classes—the property-*owners* and the propertyless *workers*.

Political economy proceeds from the fact of private property, but it does not explain it to us. It expresses in general, abstract formulae the *material* process through which private property actually passes, and these formulae it then takes for *laws*. It does not *comprehend* these laws—i.e., it does not demonstrate how they arise from the very nature of private property. Political economy does not disclose the source of the division between labor and capital, and between capital and land. When, for example, it defines the relationship of wages to profit, it takes the interest of the capitalists to be the ultimate cause; i.e., it takes for granted what it is supposed to evolve. Similarly, competition comes in everywhere. It is explained from external circumstances. As to how far these external and apparently fortuitous circumstances are but the expression of a necessary course of development, political economy teaches us nothing. We have seen how, to it, exchange itself appears to be a fortuitous fact. The only wheels which political economy sets in motion are *avarice* and the *war among the avaricious—competition*.

Precisely because political economy does not grasp the connections within the movement, it was possible to counterpose, for instance, the doctrine of competition to the doctrine of monopoly, the doctrine of craft-liberty to the doctrine of the corporation, the doctrine of the division of landed property to the doctrine of the big estate—for competition, craft-liberty and the division of landed property were explained and comprehended only as fortuitous, premeditated and violent consequences of monopoly, the corporation, and feudal property, not as their necessary, inevitable and natural consequences.

Now, therefore, we have to grasp the essential connection between private property, avarice, and the separation of labor, capital and landed property; between exchange and competition, value and the devaluation of men, monopoly and competition, etc.; the connection between this whole estrangement and the *money-system*.

Do not let us go back to a fictitious primordial condition as the political economist does, when he tries to explain. Such a primordial condition explains nothing. He merely pushes the question away into a gray nebulous distance. He assumes in the form of fact, of an event, what he is supposed to deduce—namely, the necessary relationship between two things—between, for example, division of labor and exchange. Theology in the same way explains the origin of evil by the fall of man; that is, it assumes as a fact, in historical form, what has to be explained.

We proceed from an *actual* economic fact.

The worker becomes all the poorer the more wealth he produces, the more his production increases in power and range. The worker becomes an ever cheaper commodity the more commodities he creates. With the *increasing value* of the world of things proceeds in direct proportion the *devaluation* of the world of men. Labor produces not only commodities: it produces itself and the worker as a *commodity*—and does so in the proportion in which it produces commodities generally.

This fact expresses merely the object which labor produces— labor's product—confronts it as *something alien*, as a *power independent* of the producer. The product of labor is labor which has been congealed in an object, which has become material: it is the *objectification* of labor. Labor's realization is its objectification. In the conditions dealt with by political economy this realization of labor appears as *loss of reality* for the workers; objectification as *loss of the object* and *object-bondage*; appropriation as *estrangement*, as *alienation*.[2]

So much does labor's realization appear as loss of reality that the worker loses reality to the point of starving to death. So much does objectification appear as loss of the object that the worker is robbed of the objects most necessary not only for his life but for his work. Indeed, labor itself becomes an object which he can get hold of only with the greatest effort and with the most irregular interruptions. So much does the appropriation of the object appear as estrangement that the more objects the worker produces the fewer can he possess and the more he falls under the dominion of his product, capital.

All these consequences are contained in the definition that the worker is related to the *product of his labor* as to an *alien* object. For on this premise it is clear that the more the worker spends himself, the more powerful the alien objective world becomes which he creates over-against himself, the poorer he himself— his inner world—becomes, the less belongs to him as his own. It is the same in religion. The more man puts into God, the less he retains in himself. The worker puts his life into the object; but now his life no longer belongs to him but to the object. Hence, the greater this activity, the greater is the worker's lack of objects. Whatever the product of his labor is, he is not. Therefore the greater this product, the less is he himself. The *alienation* of the worker in his product means not only that his labor becomes an object, an *external* existence, but that it exists *outside him*, independently, as something alien to him, and that it becomes a power on its own confronting him; it means that the life which he has conferred on the object confronts him as something hostile and alien.

Let us now look more closely at the *objectification*, at the production of the worker, and therein at the *estrangement*, the *loss* of the object, his product.

The worker can create nothing without *nature*, without the *sensuous external world*. It is the material on which his labor is manifested, in which it is active, from which and by means of which it produces.

But just as nature provides labor with the *means of life* in the sense that labor cannot *live* without objects on which to operate, on the other hand, it also provides the *means of life* in the more restricted sense—i.e., the means for the physical subsistence of the *worker* himself.

Thus the more the worker by his labor *appropriates* the external world, sensuous nature, the more he deprives himself of *means of life* in the double respect: first, that the sensuous external world more and more ceases to be an object belonging to his labor—to be his labor's *means of life*; and secondly, that it more and more ceases to be *means of life* in the immediate sense, means for the physical subsistence of the worker.

Thus in this double respect the worker becomes a slave of his object, first, in that he receives an *object of labor*, i.e., in that he receives *work*; and secondly, in that he receives *means of subsistence*. Therefore, it enables him to exist, first, as a *worker*; and, second, as a *physical subject*. The extremity of this bondage is that it is only as a *worker* that he continues to maintain himself as a *physical subject*, and that it is only as a *physical subject* that he is a *worker*.

(The laws of political economy express the estrangement of the worker in his object thus: the more the worker produces, the less he has to consume; the more values he creates, the more valueless, the more unworthy he becomes; the better formed his product, the more deformed becomes the worker, the more civilized his object, the more barbarous becomes the worker, the mightier labor becomes, the more powerless becomes the worker, the more ingenious labor becomes, the duller becomes the worker and the more he becomes nature's bondsman.)

Political economy conceals the estrangement inherent in the nature of labor by not considering the direct relationship between the worker (labor) *and production. It is true* that labor produces for the rich wonderful things—but for the worker it produces privation. It produces palaces—but for the worker, hovels. It produces beauty—but for the worker, deformity. It replaces labor by machines—but some of the workers it throws back to a barbarous type of labor, and the other workers it turns into machines. It produces intelligence—but for the worker idiocy, cretinism.

The direct relationship of labor to its produce is the relationship of the worker to the objects of his production. The relationship of the man of means to the objects of production and to production itself is only a *consequence* of the first relationship— and confirms it. We shall consider this other aspect later.

When we ask, then, what is the essential relationship of labor we are asking about the relationship of the *worker* to production.

Till now we have been considering the estrangement, the alienation of the worker only in one of its aspects, i.e., the worker's *relationship to the products of his labor*. But the estrangement is manifested not only in the result but in the *act of production*— within the *producing activity* itself. How would the worker come to face the product of his activity as a stranger, were it not that in the very act of production he was estranging himself from himself? The product is after all but the summary of the activity, of production. If then the product of labor is alienation, production itself must be active alienation, the alienation of activity, the activity of alienation. In the estrangement of the object of labor is merely summarized the estrangement, the alienation, in the activity of labor itself.

What, then, constitutes the alienation of labor?

First, the fact that labor is *external* to the worker, i.e., it does not belong to his essential being; that in his work, therefore, he does not affirm himself but denies himself, does not feel content but unhappy, does not develop freely his physical and mental energy but mortifies his body and ruins his mind. The worker therefore only feels himself outside his work, and in his work feels outside himself. He is at home when he is not working, and when he is working he is not at home. His labor is therefore not voluntary, but coerced; it is *forced labor*. It is therefore not the satisfaction of a need; it is merely a *means* to satisfy needs external to it. Its alien character emerges clearly in the fact that as soon as no physical or other compulsion exists, labor is shunned like the plague. External labor, labor in which man alienates himself, is a labor of self-sacrifice, of mortification. Lastly, the external character of labor for the worker appears in the fact that it is not his own, but someone else's, that it does not belong to him, that in it he belongs, not to himself, but to another. Just as in religion the spontaneous activity of the human imagination, of the human brain and the human heart, operates independently of the individual— that is, operates on him as an alien, divine or diabolical activity— in the same way the worker's activity is not his spontaneous activity. It belongs to another, it is the loss of his self.

As a result, therefore, man (the worker) no longer feels himself to be freely active in any but his animal functions—eating, drinking, procreating, or at most in his dwelling and in dressing-up, etc.; and in his human functions he no longer feels himself to be anything but an animal. What is animal becomes human and what is human becomes animal.

Certainly drinking, eating, procreating, etc., are also genuinely human functions. But in the abstraction which separates them from the sphere of all other human activity and turns them into sole and ultimate ends, they are animal.

We have considered the act of estranging practical human activity, labor, in two of its aspects. (1) The relation of the worker to the *product of labor* as an alien object exercising power over him. This relation is at the same time the relation to the sensuous external world, to the objects of nature as an alien world antagonistically opposed to him. (2) The relation of labor to the *act of production* within the *labor* process. This relation is the relation of the worker to his own activity as an alien activity not belonging to him; it is activity as suffering, strength as weakness, begetting as emasculating, the worker's *own* physical and mental energy, his personal life or what is life other than activity—as an activity which is turned against him, neither depends on nor belongs to him. Here we have *self-estrangement*, as we had previously the estrangement of the *thing*.

We have yet a third aspect of *estranged labor* to deduce from the two already considered.

Man is a species being, not only because in practice and in theory he adopts the species as his object (his own as well as those of other things), but—and this is only another way of expressing it—but also because he treats himself as the actual, living species; because he treats himself as a *universal* and therefore a free being.

The life of the species, both in man and in animals, consists physically in the fact that man (like the animal) lives on inorganic nature; and the more universal man is compared with an animal, the more universal is the sphere of inorganic nature on which he lives. Just as plants, animals, stones, the air, light, etc., constitute a part of human consciousness in the realm of theory, partly as objects of natural science, partly as objects of art—his spiritual inorganic nature, spiritual nourishment which he must first prepare to make it palatable and digestable—so too in the realm of practice they constitute a part of human life and human activity. Physically man lives only on these products of nature, whether they appear in the form of food, heating, clothes, a dwelling, or whatever it may be. The universality of man is in practice manifested precisely in the universality which makes all nature his *inorganic* body—both inasmuch as nature is (1) his direct means of life, and (2) the material, the object, and the instrument of his life-activity. Nature is man's *inorganic body*— nature, that is, insofar as it is not itself the human body. Man *lives* on nature—means that nature is his *body*, with which he must remain in continuous intercourse if he is not to die. That man's physical and spiritual life is linked to nature means simply that nature is linked to itself, for man is a part of nature.

In estranging from man (1) nature, and (2) himself, his own active functions, his life-activity, estranged labor estranges the *species* from man. It turns for him the *life of the species* into a means of individual life. First it estranges the life of the species and individual life, and secondly it makes individual life in its abstract form the purpose of the life of the species, likewise in its abstract and estranged form.

For in the first place labor, *life-activity, productive life* itself, appears to man merely as a *means* of satisfying a need—the need to maintain the physical existence. Yet the productive life is the life of the species. It is life-engendering life. The whole character of a species—its species character—is contained in the character of its life-activity; and free, conscious activity is man's species character. Life itself appears only as a *means to life*.

The animal is immediately identical with its life-activity. It does not distinguish itself from it. It is *its life-activity*. Man makes his life-activity itself the object of his will and of his consciousness. He has conscious life-activity. It is not a determination with which he directly merges. Conscious life-activity directly distinguishes man from animal life-activity. It is just because of this that he is a species being. Or it is only because he is a species being that he is a Conscious Being, i.e., that his own life is an object for him. Only because of that is his activity free activity. Estranged labor reverses this relationship, so that it is just because man is a conscious being that he makes his life-activity, his *essential* being, a mere means to his *existence*.

In creating an *objective world* by his practical activity, in *working-up* inorganic nature, man proves himself a conscious species being, i.e., as a being that treats the species as its own essential being, or that treats itself as a species being. Admittedly animals also produce. They build themselves nests, dwellings, like the bees, beavers, ants, etc. But an animal only produces what it immediately needs for itself or its young. It produces one-sidedly, while man produces universally. It produces only under the dominion of immediate physical need, while man produces even when he is free from physical need and only truly produces in freedom therefrom. An animal produces only itself, while man reproduces the whole of nature. An animal's product belongs immediately to its physical body, while man freely confronts his product. An animal forms things in accordance with the standard and the need of the species to which it belongs, while man knows how to produce in accordance with the standard of every species, and knows how to apply everywhere the inherent standard to the object. Man therefore also forms things in accordance with the laws of beauty.

It is just in the working-up of the objective world, therefore, that man first really proves himself to be a *species being*. This production is his active species life. Through and because of this production, nature appears as *his* work and his reality. The object of labor is, therefore, the *objectification of man's species life:* for he duplicates himself not only, as in consciousness, intellectually, but also actively, in reality, and therefore he contemplates himself in a world that he has created. In tearing away from man the object of his production, therefore, estranged labor tears from him his *species life*, his real species objectivity, and transforms his advantage over animals into the disadvantage that his inorganic body, nature, is taken from him.

Similarly, in degrading spontaneous activity, free activity, to a means, estranged labor makes man's species life a means to his physical existence.

The consciousness which man has of his species is thus transformed by estrangement in such a way that the species life becomes for him a means.

Estranged labor turns thus:

(3) Man's *species being*, both nature and his spiritual species property, into a being *alien* to him, into a *means* to his *individual existence*. It estranges man's own body from him, as it does external nature and his spiritual essence, his *human being*.

(4) An immediate consequence of the fact that man is estranged from the product of his labor, from his life-activity, from his species being is the *estrangement of man* from *man*. If a man is confronted by himself, he is confronted by the *other* man. What applies to a man's relation to his work, to the product of his labor and to himself, also holds of a man's relation to the other man, and to the other man's labor and object of labor.

In fact, the proposition that man's species nature is estranged from him means that one man is estranged from the other, as each of them is from man's essential nature.[3]

The estrangement of man, and in fact every relationship in which man stands to himself, is first realized and expressed in the relationship in which a man stands to other men.

Hence within the relationship of estranged labor each man views the other in accordance with the standard and the position in which he finds himself as a worker.

We took our departure from a fact of political economy— the estrangement of the worker and his production. We have formulated the concept of this fact—*estranged, alienated* labor. We have analyzed this concept—hence analyzing merely a fact of political economy.

Let us now see, further, how in real life the concept of estranged, alienated labor must express and present itself.

If the product of labor is alien to me, if it confronts me as an alien power, to whom, then, does it belong?

To a being *other* than me.

Who is this being?

The *gods?* To be sure, in the earliest times the principal production (for example, the building of temples, etc., in Egypt, India and Mexico) appears to be in the service of the gods, and the product belongs to the gods. However, the gods on their own were never the lords of labor. No more was *nature.* And what a contradiction it would be if, the more man subjugated nature by his labor and the more the miracles of the gods were rendered superfluous by the miracles of industry, the more man were to renounce the joy of production and the enjoyment of the produce in favor of these powers.

The *alien* being, to whom labor and the produce of labor belongs, in whose service labor is done and for whose benefit the produce of labor is provided, can only be *man* himself.

If the product of labor does not belong to the worker, if it confronts him as an alien power, this can only be because it belongs to some *other man than the worker.* If the worker's activity is a torment to him, to another it must be *delight* and his life's joy. Not the gods, not nature, but only man himself can be this alien power over man.

We must bear in mind the above-stated proposition that man's relation to himself only becomes *objective* and *real* for him through his relation to the other man. Thus, if the product of his labor, his labor *objectified,* is for him an *alien,* hostile, powerful object independent of him, then his position towards it is such that someone else is master of this object, someone who is alien, hostile, powerful, and independent of him. If his own activity is to him an unfree activity, then he is treating it as activity performed in the service, under the dominion, the coercion and the yoke of another man.

Every self-estrangement of man from himself and from nature appears in the relation in which he places himself and nature to men other than and differentiated from himself. For this reason religious self-estrangement necessarily appears in the relationship of the layman to the priest, or again to a mediator, etc., since we are here dealing with the intellectual world. In the real practical world self-estrangement can only become manifest through the real practical relationship to other men. The medium through which estrangement takes place is itself *practical.* Thus through estranged labor man not only engenders his relationship to the object and to the act of production as to powers that are alien and hostile to him; he also engenders the relationship in which other men stand to his production and to his product, and the relationship in which he stands to these other men. Just as he begets his own production as the loss of his reality, as his punishment; just as he begets his own product as a loss, as a product not belonging to him; so he begets the dominion of the one who does not produce over production and over the product. Just as he estranges from himself his own activity, so he confers to the stranger activity which is not his own.

Till now we have only considered this relationship from the standpoint of the worker and later we shall be considering it also from the standpoint of the non-worker.

Through *estranged, alienated labor*, then, the worker produces the relationship to this labor of a man alien to labor and standing outside it. The relationship of the worker to labor engenders the relation to it of the capitalist, or whatever one including the fact that it would be by force, too, that the higher wages, being an anomaly, could be maintained) would therefore be nothing but *better payment for the slave*, and would not conquer either for the worker or for labor their human statues and dignity.

Indeed, even the *equality of wages* demanded by Proudhon only transforms the relationship of the present-day worker to his labor into the relationship of all men to labor. Society is then conceived as an abstract capitalist.

Wages are a direct consequence of estranged labor, and estranged labor is the direct cause of private property. The downfall of the one aspect must therefore mean the downfall of the other.

(2) From the relationship of estranged labor to private property it further follows that the emancipation of society from private property, etc., from servitude, is expressed in the *political* form of the *emancipation of the workers*; not that *their* emancipation alone was at stake but because of the emancipation of the workers contains universal human emancipation—and it contains this, because the whole of human servitude is involved in the relation of the worker to production, and every relation of servitude is but a modification and consequence of this relation.

Just as we have found the concept of *private property* from the concept of *estranged, alienated labor* by analysis, in the same way every *category* of political economy can be evolved with the help of these two factors; and we shall find again in each category, e.g., trade, competition, capital, money, only a *definite* and *developed expression* of the first foundations.

Before considering this configuration, however, let us try to solve two problems.

(1) To define the *general nature of private property*, as it has arisen as a result of estranged labor, in its relations to *truly human, social property*.

(2) We have accepted the *estrangement of labor*, its *alienation*, as a fact, and we have analyzed this fact. How, we now ask, does *man* come to *alienate*, to

estrange, *his labor?* How is this estrangement rooted in the nature of human development? We have already gone a long way to the solution of this problem by *transforming* the question as to the *origin of private property* into the question as to the relation of *alienated labor* to the course of humanity's development. For when one speaks of *private property,* one thinks of being concerned with something external to man. When one speaks of labor, one is directly concerned with man himself. This new formulation of question already contains its solution.

As to (1): The general nature of private property and its relation to truly human property.

Alienated labor has resolved itself for us into two elements which mutually condition one another, or which are but different expressions of one and the same relationship. *Appropriation* appears as *estrangement,* as *alienation;* and *alienation* appears as *appropriation, estrangement* as true *enfranchisement.*

We have considered the one side—*alienated* labor in relation to the *worker* himself, i.e., the *relation of alienated labor to itself.* The *property-relation of the non-worker to the worker and to labor* we have found as the product, the necessary outcome of this relation of alienated labor. *Private property,* as the material, summary expression of alienated labor, embraces both relations—the *relation of the worker to work, to the product of his labor and to the non-worker,* and the relation of the *non-worker to the worker and to the product of his labor.*

Having seen that in relation to the worker who *appropriates* nature by means of his labor, this appropriation appears as estrangement, his own spontaneous activity as activity for another and as an activity of another, vitality as a sacrifice of life, production of the object as loss of the object to an alien power, to an *alien* person—we shall now consider the relation to the worker, to labor and its object of this person who is *alien* to labor and the worker.

First it has to be noted, that everything which appears in the worker as an *activity of alienation, of estrangement,* appears in the non-worker as a *state of alienation, of estrangement.*

Secondly, that the worker's *real, practical attitude* in production and to the product (as a state of mind) appears in the non-worker confronting him as a *theoretical* attitude.

Thirdly, the non-worker does everything against the worker which the worker does against himself; but he does not do against himself what he does against the worker.

Let us look more closely at these three relations.[4]

Footnotes

[1. Estranged Labor—Die *Entfremdet Arbeit:* re-"estranged," see *Entfremdung* in "Translator's Note on Terminology."—Ed.]

[2. Alienation—*Entäusserung*: See *Entäusserung* in "Translator's Note on Terminology."—*Ed.*]

[3. Species nature (and earlier species being)—*Gattungswesen*: man's essential nature—*menschlichen Wesen*: see *Wesen* in Translator's Note on Terminology."

The following short passages from Feuerbach's *Essence of Christianity* may help readers to understand the ideological background to this part of Marx's thought, and, incidentally, to see how Marx accepted but infused with new content concepts made current by Feuerbach as well as by Hegel and the political economists:

"What is this essential difference between man and the brute? . . . Consciousness— but consciousness in the strict sense; for the consciousness implied in the feeling of self as an individual, in discrimination by the senses, in the perception and even judgment of outward things according to definite sensible signs, cannot be denied to the brutes. Consciousness in the strictest sense is present only in a being to whom his species, his essential nature, is an object of thought. The brute is indeed conscious of himself as an individual—and he has accordingly the feeling of self as the common center of successive sensations—but not as a species. ... In practical life we have to do with individuals; in science, with species. ... But only a being to whom his own species, his own nature, is an object of thought, can make the essential nature of other things or beings an object of thought. . . . The brute has only a simple, man a twofold life; in the brute, the inner life is one with the outer. Man has both an inner and an outer life. The inner life of man is the life which has relation to his species—to his general, as distinguished from his individual nature. . . . The brute can exercise no function which has relation to its species without another individual external to itself; but man can perform the functions of thought and speech, which strictly imply such a relation, apart from another individual. . . . Man is in fact at once I and Thou; he can put himself in the place of another, for this reason, that to him his species, his essential nature, and not merely his individuality, is an object of thought. ... An object to which a subject essentially, necessarily relates, is nothing else than this subject's own, but objective nature. . . .

"The relation of the sun to the earth is, therefore, at the same time a relation of the earth to itself, or to its own nature, for the measure of the size and of the intensity of light which the sun possesses as the object of the earth, is the measure of the distance, which determines the peculiar nature of the earth.... In the object which he contemplates, therefore, man becomes acquainted with himself. . . . The power of the object over him is therefore the power of his own nature."

(*The Essence of Christianity*, by Ludwig Feuerbach, translated from the second German edition by Marian Evans, London, 1854, pp. 1-5.)—*Ed.*]

[4. At this point the first manuscript breaks off unfinished.—*Ed.*]

Antithesis of Capital and Labor Landed Property and Capital

. . . forms the interest on his capital.[1] The worker is the subjective manifestation of the fact that capital is man wholly lost to himself, just as capital is the objective manifestation of the fact that labor is man lost to himself. But the *worker* has the misfortune to be a *living* capital, and therefore a capital *with needs*—one which loses its interest, and hence its livelihood, every moment it is not working. The *value* of the worker as capital rises according to demand and supply, and even *physically* his *existence*, his *life*, was and is looked upon as a supply of a *commodity* like any other. The worker produces capital, capital produces him— hence he produces himself, and man as *worker*, as a *commodity*, is the product of the entire cycle. To the man who is nothing more than a *worker*—and to him as a worker—his human qualities only exist in so far as they exist for capital *alien* to him. Because man and capital are foreign to each other, however, and thus stand in an indifferent, external and fortuitous relationship to each other, it is inevitable that this foreignness should also appear as something *real*. As soon, therefore, as it occurs to capital (whether from necessity or caprice) no longer to be for the worker, he himself is no longer for himself: he has *no* work, hence *no* wages, and as he has no existence as a *human being* but only as a *worker*, he can go and bury himself, starve to death, etc. The worker exists as a worker only when he exists *for himself* as capital; and he exists as capital only when some *capital* exists *for him*. The existence of capital is *his* existence, his *life*; as it determines the tenor of his life in a manner indifferent to him.

Political economy, therefore, does not recognize the unoccupied worker, the workman, in so far as he happens to be outside this labor-relationship. The cheat-thief, swindler, beggar, and unemployed man; the starving, wretched and criminal working-man—these are *figures* who do not exist for *political economy* but only for other eyes, those of the doctor, the judge, the grave-digger and bum-bailiff, etc.; such figures are specters outside the domain of political economy. For it, therefore, the worker's needs are but the one *need*—to maintain him *while he is working* insofar as may be necessary to *prevent the race of laborers from dying out*. The wages of labor have thus exactly the same significance as the *maintenance* and *servicing* of any other productive instrument, or as the *consumption of a capital*, required for its reproduction with interest; or as the oil which is applied to wheels to keep them turning. Wages, therefore, belong to capital's and the capitalist's necessary *costs*, and must not exceed the bounds of this necessity. It was therefore quite logical for the English factory-owners to deduct from the wages of the worker the public charity which he was receiving out of the Poor Rate before the Amendment Bill of 1834, and to consider this to be an integral part of the wage.

Production does not simply produce man as a *commodity*, the *commodity-man*, man in the role of *commodity*; it produces him in keeping with this role as a *spiritually* and physically *dehumanized* being.—Immorality, deformity, and hebetation of the workers and the capitalists.—Its product is the *self-conscious and self-acting commodity.. . . .* The commodity-man.. . . . Great advance of Ricardo, Mill, etc., on Smith and Say, to declare the *existence* of the human being—the greater or lesser human productivity of the commodity—to be a matter of *indifference* and even *harmful.* Not how many workers are maintained by a given capital, but rather how much interest it brings in, the sum-total of the annual *saving*, is said to be the true purpose of production.

It was likewise a great and logical advance of modern English political economy, that, while elevating *labor* to the position of its *sole* principle, it should at the same time expound with complete clarity the *inverse* relation between wages and interest on capital, and the fact that the capitalist could normally *only* gain by pressing down wages, and vice versa. Not the doing-down of the consumer, but the capitalist and the worker doing-down each other, is shown to be the *normal* relationship.

The relations of private property contain latent within them the relations of private property as *labor*, the same relations as *capital*, and the *mutual* relation of these two to one another. There is the production of human activity as *labor*—that is, as an activity quite alien to itself, to man and to nature, and therefore to consciousness and the flow of life—the *abstract* existence of man as a mere *workman* who may therefore daily fall from his filled void into the absolute void—into his social, and therefore actual, non-existence. On the other hand there is the production of the object of human activity as *capital*— in which all the natural and social determinateness of the object is *extinguished*; in which private property has lost its natural and social quality (and therefore every political and social illusion, and is unmixed with any *seemingly* human relationships); in which the *selfsame* capital remains the *same* in the most diverse social and natural manifestations, totally indifferent to its *real* content. This contradiction, driven to the limit, is of necessity the limit, the culmination, and the downfall of the whole private-property relationship.

It is therefore another great achievement of modern English political economy to have declared rent to be the difference in the interest yielded by the worst and the best land under cultivation; to have exposed the landowner's romantic illusions— his alleged social importance and identity of his interest with the interest of society, still maintained by *Adam Smith* after the physiocrats; and to have anticipated and prepared the movement of the real world which will transform the landowner into an ordinary, prosaic capitalist, and thus simplify and sharpen the antithesis between labor and capital and hasten its resolution. *Land as land*, and *rent as rent*, have lost their *distinction of rank* and become dumb *capital* and *interest*—or rather, become capital and interest that only talk money.

The *distinction* between capital and land, between profit and rent, and between both and wages, and *industry*, and *agriculture*, and *immovable* and *movable* private property—this distinction is not an inherently essential one, but a *historical* distinction, a *fixed* moment in the formation and development of the antithesis between capital and labor. Industry, etc., as opposed to immovable landed property, is only the expression of the way industry came into being and of the contradiction to agriculture in which industry developed. This distinction of industry only continues to exist as a *special* sort of work—as an *essential, important* and *life-embracing* distinction—so long as industry (town life) develops *over-against* landed property (aristocratic feudal life) and itself continues to bear the feudal character of its opposite in the form of monopoly, craft, guild, corporation, etc., within which labor still has a *seemingly social* signficance, still the significance of *real community-life*, and has not yet reached the stage of *indifference* to its content, of complete being-for-self, i.e., of abstraction from all other being, and hence has not yet become *liberated* capital.

But liberated industry, *industry* constituted for itself as such, and *liberated capital*, are a necessary *development* of labor. The power of industry over its opposite is at once revealed in the emergence of *agriculture* as a real industry, most of the work having previously been left to the soil and to the *slave* of the soil, through whom the land cultivated itself. With the transformation of the slave into *a free* worker—i.e., into a *hireling*—the landlord himself is transformed into a captain of industry, into a capitalist—a transformation which takes place at first through the intermediacy of the *tenant farmer*. The *farmer*, however, is the landowner's representative—the landowner's revealed *secret*: it is only through him that the landowner has his *economic* existence—his existence as a private proprietor— for the rent of his land only exists due to the competition between the farmers. Thus, in the person of the *tenant farmer* the landlord has already become in essence a *common* capitalist. And thus must work itself out, too, in actual fact: the capitalist engaged in agriculture—the farmer—must become a landlord, or vice versa. The farmer's *industrial trade* is the *landowner's* industrial trade, for the being of the former postulates the being of the latter.

But mindful of their contrasting origin—of their line of descent—the landowner knows the capitalist as his insolent, liberated slave of yesterday now become rich, and sees himself as a *capitalist* who is threatened by him. The capitalist knows the landowner as the idle, cruel and egotistical master of yesterday; he knows that he injures him as a capitalist, and yet that it is to industry that he, the landowner, owes all his present social significance, his possessions and his pleasures; he sees in him an antithesis to *free* industry and to *free* capital—to capital independent of every natural determination. This contradiction between landowner and capitalist is extremely bitter, and each side gives the truth about the other. One need only read the attacks of immovable on movable property and vice versa to obtain a clear picture of their respective worthlessness. The landowner lays stress on the noble lineage of his property, on feudal mementoes, reminiscences, the poetry of recollections, on his romantic disposition, on his political importance, etc.; and when he talks economics, it is *only* agriculture that he holds to be productive. At the same time he depicts his adversary as a sly, haggling, deceitful, greedy, mercenary, rebellious, heart-and soul-less cheapjack—extorting, pimping, servile, smooth, flattering, fleecing, dried-up twister without honor, principles, poetry, substance, or anything else—a person estranged from the community who freely trades it away and who breeds, nourishes and cherishes competition, and with it pauperism, crime, and the dissolution of all social bonds. (Among others see the physiocrat *Bergasse*, whom Camille Desmoulins flays in his journal, *Revolutions de France et de Brabant*;[2] see von Vincke, Lancizolle, Haller, Leo, Kosegarten[3] and also *Sismondi*.)

Movable property for its part points to the miracles of industry and progress. It is the child of the modern time and its legitimate, native-born son. It pities its adversary as a simpleton, *unenlightened* about his own nature (and in this it is completely right), who wants to replace moral capital and free labor by brute, immoral force and serfdom. It depicts him as a Don Quixote who under the guise of *bluntness, decency, the general interest, and stability*, conceals incapacity for progress, greedy self-indulgence, selfishness, sectional interest and evil intent. It declares him for an artful *monopolist*; it pours cold water on his reminiscences, his poetry, and his romanticism by a historical and sarcastic enumeration of the baseness, cruelty, degradation, prostitution, infamy, anarchy and rebellion, of which romantic castles were the workshops.

It claims to have obtained political freedom for the people; to have loosed the chains binding civil society; to have linked together different worlds; to have created trade promoting friendship between the peoples; to have created pure morality and an agreeable degree of culture; to have given the people civilized in place of their crude needs, and the means of satisfying them. Meanwhile, it claims, the landowner—this idle, troublesome, parasitic grain-jobber—puts up the price of the people's basic necessities and so forces the capitalist to raise wages without being able to increase productivity, thus impeding and eventually cancelling the nation's annual income, the accumulation of capital, and therefore the possibility of providing work for the people and wealth for the country, and producing in consequence a general decline—while he parasitically exploits *every* advantage of modern civilization without doing the least thing for it, and without even abating in the slightest his feudal prejudices. Finally, let him—for whom the cultivation of the land and the land itself exist only as a source of money, which comes to him as a present—let him just take a look at his *tenant farmer* and say whether he himself is not a *"decent," deluded sly* scoundrel who in his heart and in actual fact has for a long time belonged to *free* industry and to *beloved* trade, however much he may protest and prattle about historical memories and ethical or political goals. Everything which he can really advance to justify himself is true only of the *cultivator of the land* (the capitalist and the laborers), of whom the *landowner* is rather the *enemy*. Thus he gives evidence against himself. *Without* capital landed property is dead, worthless matter. Movable property's civilized victory has precisely been to discover and make human labor the source of wealth in place of the dead thing. (See Paul Louis Courier, Saint-Simon, Ganilh, Ricardo, Mill, MacCulloch and Destutt de Tracy and Michel Chevalier.)

The *real* course of development (to be inserted at this point) results in the necessary victory of the *capitalist* over the *landowner*—that is to say, of developed over undeveloped immature private property—just as generally movement must triumph over immobility—open, self-conscious baseness over hidden, unconscious baseness; *avarice* over *self-indulgence*; the avowedly restless, adroit self-interest of *enlightenment* over the parochial, worldwise, naive, idle and deluded *self-interest of superstition*; and *money* over the other forms of private property.

Those states which divine something of the danger attaching to fully-developed free industry, to fully-developed pure morality and to the full development of trade promoting friendship between the peoples, try, but in vain, to hold in check the capitalization of landed property.

Landed property in its distinction from capital is private property—capital—still afflicted with *local* and political prejudices; it is capital which has not yet regained itself from its entanglement with the world—capital not yet *fully-developed*. It must in the course of its *world-wide development* achieve its abstract, that is, its *pure*, expression.

The relations of *private property* are labor, capital, and the relations between these two.

The movement through which these constituents have to pass is:

[*First*] *Unmediated* or *mediated unity of the two.* Capital and labor at first still united. Then, though separated and estranged, they reciprocally develop and foster each other as *positive* conditions.

[*Second*] *The two in opposition,* mutually excluding each other. The worker knows the capitalist as his non-existence, and vice versa: each tries to rob the other of his existence.

[*Third*] *Opposition* of each *to* itself. Capital—stored-up labor—labor. Capital as such—splitting into capital *itself* and into its *interest,* and this latter again into *interest* and *profit.* The capitalist completely sacrificed. He falls into the working class, while the worker (but only exceptionally) becomes a capitalist. Labor as a moment of capital—its *costs.* Thus the wages of labor—a sacrifice of capital.

Splitting of labor into *labor itself* and the *wages of labor.* The worker himself a capital, a commodity.

Inimical mutual opposition. [4]

Footnotes

[1. The XL page of Marx's second manuscript opens with these words. The beginning of the sentence is unknown, because the first 39 pages of the manuscript are missing.— Ed.]

[2. *Revolutions de France et de Brabant,* par Camille Desmoulins. Second Trimestre, contenant Mars, Avril et Mai. Paris, l'an l'ier. No. 16, p. 139 f.; No. 23 p. 425 f.; No. 26, p. 580 f.—Ed.]

[3. See the garrulous, old-Hegelian theologian Funke who tells after Herr Leo with tears in his eyes how a slave had refused, when serfdom was abolished, to cease being the *property of the gentry.* See also the *Patriotic Visions* of Justus Möser, which distinguish themselves by never for a moment abandoning the ingenious, petty-bourgeois "home-baked," *ordinary,* narrow, horizon of the philistine, and which nevertheless remain *pure* fancy. This contradiction has made them so plausible in the German disposition.]

[4. Here ends the second manuscript.—Ed.]

Private Property and Labor Views of the Mercantile System and Physiocracy, Adam Smith, Ricardo and His School

Re. p. XXXVI. The *subjective essence* of private property— *private property* as activity for itself,[1] as *subject*, as *person*— is *labor*. It is therefore self-evident that only the political economy which acknowledged *labor* as its principle (Adam Smith), and which therefore no longer looked upon private property as a mere *condition* external to man—that it is this political economy which has to be regarded on the one hand as a product of the real *energy* and the real *movement* of private property[2]— as a product of modern *industry*—and, on the other hand, as a force which has quickened and glorified the energy and development of modern *industry* and made it a power in the realm of *consciousness*. To this enlightened political economy, which has discovered within private property the *subjective essence* of wealth, the adherents of the money and mercantile system, who look upon private property *only as an objective* substance[3] confronting men, seem therefore to be *idolators, fetishists, Catholics. Engels* was therefore right to call *Adam Smith the Luther of Political Economy.*[4] Just as Luther recognized *religion—faith*—as the substance of the external *world* and in consequence stood opposed to Catholic paganism—just as he superseded[5] *external* religiosity by making religiosity the *inner* substance of man—just as he negated the priests outside the layman because he transplanted the priest into laymen's hearts, just so with wealth: wealth as something outside man and independent of him, and therefore as something to be maintained and asserted only in an external fashion, is done away with; that is, this *external, mindless objectivity* of wealth is done away with, with private property being incorporated in man himself and with man himself being recognized as its essence. But as a result man is brought within the orbit of private property, just as in Luther he is brought within the orbit of religion. Under the semblance of recognizing man, the political economy whose principal is labor is really no more than consistent implementation of the denial of man, since man himself no longer stands in an external relation of tension to the external substance of private property, but has himself become this tensed essence of private property. What was previously being *external* to oneself—man's externalization in the thing—has merely become the act of externalizing—the process of alienating.[6] If then this political economy begins by seeming to acknowledge man (his independence, spontaneity, etc.); and if, locating private property in man's own being, it can no longer be conditioned by the local, national or other *characteristics of private property* as of *something existing outside itself;* and if this political economy consequently displays a *cosmopolitan*, universal energy which overthrows every restriction and bond so as to establish itself instead as the *sole* politics, the sole universality, the sole limit and sole bond, then it must throw aside this *hypocrisy* in the course of its further development and come out *in its complete cynicism*. And this it does—untroubled by all the apparent contradictions in which it becomes involved—by developing the idea of *labor* much *more one-sidedly*, and therefore *more sharply* and *more consistently*, as the sole *essence of wealth*; by proving the implications of this theory to be *anti-human* in character, in contrast to the other, original approach; and finally, by dealing the deathblow to *rent*—that last, *individual, natural* mode of private property and source of wealth existing independently of the movement of labor, that expression of feudal property, an expression which has already become wholly economic in character and therefore incapable of resisting political economy. (The *Ricardo* school.) There is not merely a relative growth in the *cynicism* of political economy from Smith through Say to Ricardo, Mill, etc., inasmuch as the implications of *industry* appear more developed and more contradictory in the eyes of the last-named; these later economists also constantly and consciously advance further than their predecessors in a positive sense in their estrangement from man. They do so, however, *only* because their science develops more consistently and genuinely. Because they make private property in its active form the subject, thus simultaneously making man—and man as something unessential—the essence, the contradiction of actuality corresponds completely to the contradictory essence which they accept as their principle. Far from refuting it, the ruptured *world of industry* confirms their *internally-ruptured* principle. Their principle is, after all, the principle of this rupture.

The physiocratic doctrine of Dr. *Quesnay* forms the transition from the mercantile system to Adam Smith. *Physiocracy* is directly the dissolution of feudal property in *political economy*, but it is therefore just as directly its *metamorphosis* and restoration in *political economy*, save that now its language is no longer feudal but economic. All wealth is resolved into *land* and *cultivation* (agriculture). Land is not yet *capital*: it is still a *special* mode of its existence, the validity of which is supposed to lie in, and to *derive from*, its natural peculiarity. Yet land is a general natural *element*, while the mercantile system admits the existence of wealth only in the form of *precious metal*. Thus the *object* of wealth—its *matter*— has straightaway obtained the highest degree of generality within the *bounds of nature*, insofar as it is immediately objective wealth even as *nature*. And land only exists for *man* through labor, through agriculture. Thus the subjective essence of wealth has already been transferred to labor. But at the same time agriculture is the *only productive* labor. Hence, labor is not yet grasped in its generality and abstraction: it is still bound to a particular *natural element as its matter*, and it is therefore only recognized in a *particular mode of existence determined by nature*. It is therefore still only a *specific, particular* alienation of man, just as its product is conceived only as a specific form of wealth, due more to nature than to labor itself. The land is here still recognized as a phenomenon of nature independent of man— not yet as capital, i.e., as an aspect of labor itself. Labor appears, rather, as an aspect of the *land*. But since the fetishism of the old external wealth, of wealth existing only as an object, has been reduced to a very simple natural element, and since—even if only partially and in a particular form—its essence has been recognized within its subjective existence, there is the necessary step forward in that the *general nature* of wealth has been revealed and that *labor* has therefore in its total absoluteness (i.e., its abstraction) been raised and established as the *principle*. It is argued against Physiocracy that *agriculture*, from the economic point of view—that is to say, from the only valid point of view, does not differ from any other industry; and that the *essence* of wealth, therefore, is not a *specific* form of labor bound to a particular element—a particular expression of labor—but *labor in general*.

Physiocracy denies *particular*, external, merely objective wealth by declaring labor to be the *essence* of wealth. But for Physiocracy labor is from the outset only the *subjective essence* of landed property. (It takes its departure from the type of property which historically appears as the dominant acknowledged type.) It only turns landed property into *alienated man*. It annuls its feudal character by declaring *industry* (agriculture) to be its *essence*. But its attitude to the world of industry is one of denial; it acknowledges the feudal system by declaring *agriculture* to be the *only* industry.

It is clear that if the *subjective essence* of industry is now grasped (of industry in opposition to landed property, i.e., of industry constituting itself as industry), this essence encompasses this its opposite. For just as industry incorporates annulled landed property, the *subjective essence* of industry at the same time incorporates the subjective essence of *landed property*.

Just as landed property is the first form of private property, with industry at first confronting it historically merely as a special kind of property—or, rather, as landed property's liberated slave—so this process repeats itself at the level of the scientific comprehension of the *subjective* essence of private property, *labor*. Labor appears at first only as *agricultural labor*; but then asserts itself as *labor* in general.

All wealth has become *industrial* wealth, the wealth of *labor*; and *industry* is accomplished labor, just as the *factory-system* is the essence of *industry—of* labor—brought to its maturity, and just as *industrial capital* is the accomplished objective form of private property.

We can now see how it is only at this point that private property can consummate its dominion over man and become in its most general form a world-historical power.

Footnotes

[1. "For itself"—*fuer sich*: a Hegelian term used in antithesis with "In itself"—*an sich*. "In itself" means roughly "implicit" or even "unconscious"; "For itself," similarly, can be read as "present to itself," or "consciously)."—*Ed.*]

[2. It is a movement of private property become independent for itself in consciousness—the modern industry as Self.]

[3. Substance—*Wesen*. Elsewhere on this page *Wesen* is rendered as "essence." See "Translator's Note on Terminology."— *Ed.*]

[4. See F. Engels, *Outlines of a Critique of Political Economy*, p. 9.—*Ed.*]

[5. Superseded—*aufhob* (rendered below "done away with"). See under *Aufheben* in "Translator's Note on Terminology."—*Ed.*]

[6. Man's externalization in the thing—*reale Entäusserung des Menschen*: the process of alienating—*Verässerung*: See under *Entäusserung* in "Translator's Note on Terminology."—*Ed.*]

Private Property and Communism Various Stages of Development of Communist Views. Crude, Equalitarian Communism and Communism as Socialism Coinciding with Humaneness

Re. p. XXXIX. The antithesis of *propertylessness* and *property*, so long as it is not comprehended as the antithesis of *labor* and *capital*, still remains an antithesis of indifference, not grasped in its *active connection*, its *internal* relation—an antithesis not yet grasped as a *contradiction*. It can find expression in this *first* form even without the advanced development of private property (as in ancient Rome, Turkey, etc.). It does not yet *appear* as having been established by private property itself. But labor, the subjective essence of private property as exclusion of property, and capital, objective labor as exclusion of labor, constitute *private property* as its developed state of contradiction—hence a dynamic relationship moving inexorably to its resolution.

Re. the same page. The transcendence[1] of self-estrangement follows the same course as self-estrangement. *Private property* is first considered only in its objective aspect—but nevertheless with labor as its essence. Its form of existence is therefore *capital*, which is to be annulled "as such" (Proudhon). Or a *particular form* of labor—labor leveled down, parceled, and therefore unfree—is conceived as the source of private property's *perniciousness* and of its existence in estrangement from men; for instance, *Fourier*, who, like the physiocrats, also conceived *agricultural labor* to be at least the *exemplary* type, while *Saint-Simon* declares in contrast that *industrial labor* as such is the essence, and now also aspires to the *exclusive* rule of the industrialists and the improvement of the workers' condition. Finally, *communism* is the *positive* expression of annulled private property—at first as *universal* private property. By embracing this relation as a *whole*, communism is:

(1) In its first form only a *generalization* and *consummation* of this relationship. It shows itself as such in a twofold form: on the one hand, the dominion of *material* property bulks so large that it wants to destroy *everything* which is not capable of being possessed by all as *private property*. It wants to abstract *by force* from talent, etc. For if the sole purpose of life and existence is direct, physical *possession.* The category of laborer is not done away with, but extended to all men. The relationship of private property persists as the relationship of the community to the world of things. Finally, this movement of counterposing

universal private property to private property finds expression in the bestial form of counterposing to *marriage* (certainly *a form of exclusive private property*) the *community of women*, in which a woman becomes a piece of *communal* and *common* property. It may be said that this idea of the *community of women* gives away the *secret* of this as yet completely crude and thoughtless communism. Just as the woman passes from marriage to general prostitution,[2] so the entire world of wealth (that is, of man's objective substance) passes from the relationship of exclusive marriage with the owner of private property to a state of universal prostitution with the community. In negating the *personality* of man in every sphere, this type of communism is really nothing but the logical expression of private property, which is this negation. General *envy* constituting itself as a power is the disguise in which *avarice* re-establishes itself and satisfies itself, only in *another* way. The thoughts of every piece of private property— inherent in each piece as such—are *at least* turned against all *wealthier* private property in the form of envy and the urge to reduce to a common level, so that this envy and urge even constitute the essence of competition. The crude communism is only the consummation of this envy and of this leveling-down proceeding from the *preconceived* minimum. It has a *definite, limited* standard. How little this annulment of private property is really an appropriation is in fact proved by the abstract negation of the entire world of culture and civilization, the regression to the *unnatural* simplicity of the *poor and undemanding* man who has not only failed to go beyond private property, but has not yet even attained to it.

The community is only a community of *labor*, and an equality of *wages* paid out by the communal capital—the *community* as the universal capitalist. Both sides of the relationship are raised to an *imagined* universality—*labor* as a state in which every person is put, and *capital* as the acknowledged universality and power of the community.

In the approach to *woman* as the spoil and handmaid of communal lust is expressed the infinite degradation in which man exists for himself, for the secret of this approach has its *unambiguous*, decisive, *plain* and undisguised expression in the relation of *man* to *woman* and in the manner in which the *direct* and *natural* procreative relationship is conceived. The direct, natural, and necessary relation of person to person is the *relation of map to woman*. In this *natural* relationship of the sexes man's relation to nature is immediately his relation to man, just as his relation to man is immediately his relation to nature—his own *natural* function. In this relationship, therefore, is *sensuously manifested*, reduced to an observable *fact*, the extent to which the human essence has become nature to man, or to which nature has to him become the human essence of man. From this relationship one can therefore judge man's whole level of development. It follows from the character of this relationship how much man as a *species being,* as *man,* has come to be himself and to comprehend himself; the relation of man to woman is *the most natural* relation of human being to human being. It therefore reveals the extent to which man's *natural* behavior has become *human,* or the extent to which the *human* essence in him has become a *natural* essence—the extent to which his *human nature* has come to be *nature to him.* In this relationship is revealed, too, the extent to which man's *need* has become a *human* need; the extent to which, therefore, the *other* person as a person has become for him a need—the extent to which he in his individual existence is at the same time a social being. The first positive annulment of private property—*crude* communism—is thus merely one *form* in which the vileness of private property, which wants to set itself up as the *positive community, comes to the surface.*

(2) Communism (*a*) of a political nature still—democratic or despotic; (*b*) with the annulment of the state, yet still incomplete, and being still affected by private property (i.e., by the estrangement of man). In both forms communism already knows itself to be re-integration or return of man to himself, the transcendence of human self-estrangement; but since it has not yet grasped the positive essence of private property, and just as little the *human* nature of need, it remains captive to it and infected by it. It has, indeed, grasped its concept, but not its essence.

(3) *Communism* as the *positive* transcendence of *private property,* as *human self-estrangement,* and therefore as the real *appropriation of the human* essence by and for man; communism therefore as the complete return of man to himself as a *social* (i.e., human) being—a return become conscious, and accomplished within the entire wealth of previous development. This communism, as fully-developed naturalism, equals humanism, and as fully-developed humanism equals naturalism; it is the *genuine* resolution of the conflict between man and nature and between man and man—the true resolution of the strife between existence and essence, between objectification and self-confirmation, between freedom and necessity, between the individual and the species. Communism is the riddle of history solved, and it knows itself to be this solution.

The entire movement of history is, therefore, both its *actual* act of genesis (the birth act of its empirical existence) and also for its thinking consciousness the *comprehended* and *known* process of its *coming-to-be.* That other, still immature communism, meanwhile, seeks *a historical proof* for itself—a proof in the realm of the existent—among disconnected historical phenomena opposed to private property, tearing single phases from the historical process and focusing attention on them as proofs of its historical pedigree (a horse ridden hard especially by Cabet, Villegardelle, etc.). By so doing it simply makes clear that by far the greater part of this process contradicts its claims, and that, if it has once been, precisely its being in the *past* refutes its pretension to being *essential.*

That the entire revolutionary movement necessarily finds both its empirical and its theoretical basis in the movement *of private property*—in that of the economy, to be precise—is easy to see.

This *material,* immediately *sensuous* private property is the material sensuous expression of *estranged human* life. Its movement—production and consumption—is the *sensuous* revelation of the movement of all production hitherto—i.e., the realization or the reality of man. Religion, family, state, law, morality, science, art, etc., are only *particular* modes of production, and fall under its general law. The positive transcendence *of private property* at the appropriation of *human* life is, therefore, the positive transcendence of all estrangement—that is to say, the return of man from religion, family, state, etc., to his *human,* i.e., *social* mode of existence. Religious estrangement as such occurs only in the realm of *consciousness,* of man's inner life, but economic estrangement is that of *real life;* its transcendence therefore embraces both aspects. It is evident that the *initial* stage of the movement among the various peoples depends on whether the true and for them *authentic* life of the people manifests itself more in consciousness or in the external world—is more ideal or real. Communism begins from the outset (*Owen*) with atheism; but atheism is at first far from being *communism;* indeed, it is still mostly an abstraction.

The philanthropy of atheism is therefore at first only *philosophical,* abstract, philanthropy, and that of communism is at once *real* and directly bent on *action.*

We have seen how on the premise of positively annulled private property man produces man—himself and the other man; how the object, being the direct embodiment of his individuality, is simultaneously his own existence for the other man, the existence of the other man, and that existence for him. Likewise, however, both the material of labor and man as the subject, are the point of departure as well as the result of the movement (and precisely in this fact, that they must constitute the *point of departure,* lies the historical *necessity* of private property). Thus the *social* character is the general character of the whole movement: *just as* society itself produces *man as man,* so is society *produced* by him. Activity and consumption, both in their content and in their *mode of existence,* are *social: social* activity and *social* consumption; the *human* essence of nature first exists only for *social* man; for only here does nature exist for him as a *bond* with *man*—as his existence for the other and the other's existence for him—as the life-element of the human world; only here does nature exist as the *foundation* of his own *human* existence. Only here has what is to him his *natural* existence become his *human* existence, and nature become man for him. Thus *society* is the consummated oneness in substance of man and nature—the true resurrection of nature—the naturalism of man and the humanism of nature both brought to fulfillment.

Social activity and social consumption exist by no means *only* in the form of some *directly* communal activity and directly *communal* consumption, although *communal* activity and *communal* consumption—i.e., activity and consumption which are manifested and directly confirmed in *real association* with other men—will occur wherever such a *direct* expression of sociality stems from the true character of the activity's content and is adequate to the nature of consumption.

But again when I am active *scientifically*, etc.,—when I am engaged in activity which I can seldom perform in direct community with others—then I am *social*, because I am active as a *man*. Not only is the material of my activity given to me as a social product (as is even the language in which the thinker is active): my *own* existence *is* social activity, and therefore that which I make of myself, I make of myself for society and with the consciousness of myself as a social being.

My *general* consciousness is only the *theoretical* shape of that of which the *living* shape is the *real* community, the social fabric, although at the present day *general* consciousness is an abstraction from real life and as such antagonistically confronts it. Consequently, too, the *activity* of my general consciousness, as an activity, is my *theoretical* existence as a social being.

What is to be avoided above all is the re-establishing of "Society" as an abstraction *vis-à-vis* the individual. The individual is *the social being*. His life, even if it may not appear in the direct form of a *communal* life carried out together with others— is therefore an expression and confirmation of *social life*. Man's individual and species life are not *different*, however much—and this is inevitable—the mode of existence of the individual is a more *particular*, or more *general* mode of the life of the species, or the life of the species is a more *particular* or more *general* individual life.

In his *consciousness of species* man confirms his real *social life* and simply repeats his real existence in thought, just as conversely the being of the species confirms itself in species-consciousness and is for *itself* in its generality as a thinking being.

Man, much as he may therefore be a *particular* individual (and it is precisely his particularity which makes him an individual, and a real *individual* social being), is just as much the *totality*— the ideal totality—the subjective existence of thought and experienced society present for itself; just as he exists also in the real world as the awareness and the real enjoyment of social existence, and as a totality of human life-activity.

Thinking and being are thus no doubt *distinct*, but at the same time they are in *unity* with each other.

Death seems to be a harsh victory of the species over the *definite* individual and to contradict their unity. But the determinate individual is only a *determinate species being*, and as such mortal.

(4) Just as *private property* is only the sensuous expression of the fact that man becomes *objective* for himself and at the same time becomes to himself a strange and inhuman object; just as it expresses the fact that the assertion of his life is the alienation of his life, that his realization is his loss of reality, is an *alien* reality: conversely, the positive transcendence of private property—i.e., the *sensuous* appropriation for and by man of the human essence and of human life, of objective man, of human *achievements*—is not to be conceived merely in the sense of *direct*, one-sided *gratification*—merely in the sense of *possessing*, of *having*. Man appropriates his total essence in a total manner, that is to say, as a whole man. Each of his *human* relations to the world—seeing, hearing, smelling, tasting, feeling, thinking, being aware, sensing, wanting, acting, loving—in short, all the organs of his individual being, like those organs which are directly social in their form, are in their *objective* orientation or in their *orientation to the object*, the appropriation of that object, the appropriation of the *human* world; their orientation to the object is the *manifestation of the human world;*[3] it is human *efficaciousness* and human *suffering*, for suffering, apprehended humanly, is an enjoyment of self in man.

Private property has made us so stupid and one-sided that an object is only *ours* when we have it—when it exists for us as capital, or when it is directly possessed, eaten, drunk, worn, inhabited, etc.,—in short, when it is *used* by us. Although private property itself again conceives all these direct realizations of possession as *means of life*, and the life which they serve as means is the *life of private property*—labor and conversion into capital.

In place of *all* these physical and mental senses there has therefore come the sheer estrangement of *all* these senses—the sense of *having*. The human being had to be reduced to this absolute poverty in order that he might yield his inner wealth to the outer world. (On the category of "*having*," see Hess in the *Twenty-One Sheets.*[4])

The transcendence of private property is therefore the complete *emancipation* of all human senses and attributes; but it is this emancipation precisely because these senses and attributes have become, subjectively and objectively, *human*. The eye has become a *human* eye, just as its *object* has become a social, *human* object—an object emanating from man for man. The *senses* have therefore become directly in their practice *theoreticians*. They relate themselves to the *thing* for the sake of the thing, but the thing itself is an *objective human* relation to itself and to man,[5] and vice versa Need or enjoyment have consequently lost their *egotistical* nature, and nature has lost its mere *utility* by use becoming *human* use.

In the same way, the senses and enjoyments of other men have become my *own* appropriation. Besides these direct organs, therefore, *social* organs develop in the *form* of society; thus, for instance, activity in direct association with others, etc., has become an organ for *expressing* my own *life*, and a mode of appropriating *human* life.

It is obvious that the *human* eye gratifies itself in a way different from the crude, non-human eye; the human *ear* different from the crude ear, etc.

To recapitulate: man is not lost in his object only when the object becomes for him a *human* object or objective man. This is possible only when the object becomes for him a *social* object, he himself for himself a social being, just as society becomes a being for him in this object.

On the one hand, therefore, it is only when the objective world becomes everywhere for man in society the world of man's essential powers[6]—human reality, and for that reason the reality of his *own* essential powers—that all *objects* become for him the *objectification of himself*, become objects which confirm and realize his individuality, become *his* objects: that is, *man himself* becomes the object. The manner in which they become *his* depends on the *nature of the objects* and on the nature of the *essential power* corresponding *to it*; for it is precisely the *determinateness* of this relationship which shapes the particular, *real* mode of affirmation. To the *eye* an object comes to be other than it is to the *ear*, and the object of the eye is another object than the object of the *ear*. The peculiarity of each essential power is precisely its *peculiar essence*, and therefore also the peculiar mode of its objectification, of its *objectively actual* living being. Thus man is affirmed in the objective world not only in the act of thinking, but with *all* his senses.

On the other hand, looking at this in its subjective aspect: just as music alone awakens in man the sense of music, and just as the most beautiful music has *no* sense for the unmusical ear—is no object for it, because my object can only be the confirmation of one of my essential powers and can therefore only be so for me as my essential power is present for itself as a subjective capacity, because the sense of an object for me goes only so far as *my* senses go (has only sense for a sense corresponding to that object)—for this reason the *senses* of the social man are *other* senses than those of the non-social man. Only through the objectively unfolded richness of man's essential being is the richness of subjective *human* sensibility (a musical ear, an eye for beauty of form—in short, *senses* capable of human gratifications, senses confirming themselves as essential powers of *man*) either cultivated or brought into being. For not only the five senses but also the so-called mental senses —the practical senses (will, love, etc.)—in a word, *human sense*—the humanness of the senses—comes to be by virtue of its object, by virtue of *humanized* nature. The *forming* of the five senses is a labor of *humanized* nature. The *forming* of the five senses is a labor of the entire history of the world down to the present.

The *sense* caught up in crude practical need has only a *restricted* sense. For the starving man, it is not the human form of food that exists, but only its abstract being as food; it could just as well be there in its crudest form, and it would be impossible to say wherein this feeding-activity differs from that of *animals*. The care-burdened man in need has no sense for the finest play; the dealer in minerals sees only the mercantile value but not the beauty and the unique nature of the mineral: he has no mineralogical sense. Thus, the objectification of the human essence both in its theoretical and practical aspects is required to make man's *sense human*, as well as to create the *human sense* corresponding to the entire wealth of human and natural substance.

Just as resulting from the movement of *private property*, of its wealth as well as its poverty—or of its material and spiritual wealth and poverty—the budding society finds to hand all the material for this *development*: so *established* society produces man in this entire richness of his being—produces the *rich* man *profoundly endowed with all the senses*—as its enduring reality.

It will be seen how subjectivism and objectivism, spiritualism and materialism, activity and suffering, only lose their antithetical character, and thus their existence, as such antitheses in the social condition; it will be seen how the resolution of the *theoretical* antitheses is *only* possible in *a practical* way, by virtue of the practical energy of men. Their resolution is therefore by no means merely a problem of knowledge, but a *real* problem of life, which *philosophy* could not solve precisely because it conceived this problem as *merely* a theoretical one.

It will be seen how the history of *industry* and the established *objective* existence of industry are the *open* book of *man's essential powers*, the exposure to the senses of human *psychology*. Hitherto this was not conceived in its inseparable connection with man's *essential being*, but only in an external relation of utility, because, moving in the realm of estrangement, people could only think man's general mode of being—religion or history in its abstract—of man's essential powers and *man's species-activity*. We have before us the *objectified essential powers* of man in the form of *sensuous, alien, useful objects*, in the form of estrangement, displayed in *ordinary material industry* (which can be conceived as a part of that general movement, just as that movement can be conceived as a particular part of industry, since all human activity hitherto has been labor—that is, industry—activity estranged from itself).

A *psychology* for which this, the part of history most contemporary and accessible to sense, remains a closed book, cannot become a genuine, comprehensive and *real* science. What indeed are we to think of a science which *airily* abstracts from this large part of human labor and which fails to feel its own incompleteness, while such a wealth of human endeavor unfolded before it means nothing more to it than, perhaps, what can be expressed in one word—"*need*," "*vulgar need*"?

The *natural sciences* have developed an enormous activity and have accumulated a constantly growing mass of material. Philosophy, however, has remained just as alien to them as they remain to philosophy. Their momentary unity was only a *chimerical illusion*. The will was there, but the means were lacking. Even historiography pays regard to natural science only occasionally, as a factor of enlightenment and utility arising from individual great discoveries. But natural science has invaded and transformed human life all the more *practically* through the medium of industry; and has prepared human emancipation, however directly and much it had to consummate dehumanization. *Industry* is the *actual*, historical relation of nature, and therefore of natural science, to man. If, therefore, industry is conceived as the *exoteric* revelation of man's *essential powers*, we also gain an understanding of the *human* essence of nature or the *natural* essence of man. In consequence, natural science will lose its abstractly material—or rather, its idealistic—tendency, and will become the basis of *human* science, as it has already become the basis of actual human life, albeit in an estranged form. *One* basis for life and another basis for *science* is *a priori* a lie. The nature which comes to be in human history—the genesis of human nature which comes to be in human history—the genesis of human society—is man's *real* nature; hence nature as it comes to be through industry, even though in an *estranged form, is true anthropological* nature.

Sense-perception (see Feuerbach) must be the basis of all science. Only when it proceeds from sense-perception in the twofold form both of *sensuous* consciousness and of *sensuous* need—that is, only when science proceeds from nature—is it *true* science. All history is the preparation for "*man*" to become the object of *sensuous* consciousness, and for the needs of "man as man" to become [natural, sensuous] needs. History itself is a *real part of natural history—of nature's* coming to be man. Natural science will in time subsume under itself the science of man, just as the science of man will subsume under itself natural science: there will be *one* science.

Man is the immediate object of natural science: for immediate, *sensuous nature* for man is, immediately, human sensuousness (the expressions are identical)—presented immediately in the form of the *other* man sensuously present for him. For his own sensuousness first exists as human sensuousness for himself through the *other* man. But *nature* is the immediate object of the *science of man*: the first object of man—man—is nature, sensuousness; and the particular human sensuous essential powers can only find their self-knowledge in the science of the natural world in general, since they can find their objective realization in *natural* objects only. The element of thought itself—the element of thought's living expression—*language*—is of a sensuous nature. The *social* reality of nature, and *human* natural science, or the *natural science about man*, are identical terms.

It will be seen how in place of the *wealth* and *poverty* of political economy come the *rich human being* and rich *human* need. The *rich* human being is simultaneously the human being *in need of* a totality of human life-activities—the man in whom his own realization exists as an inner necessity, as *need*. Not only *wealth*, but likewise the *poverty* of man—given socialism— receives in equal measure a *human* and therefore social significance. Poverty is the passive bond which causes the human being to experience the need of the greatest wealth—the *other* human being. The dominion of the objective being in me, the sensuous outburst of my essential activity, is *emotion*, which thus becomes here the *activity* of my being.

(5) A *being* only considers himself independent when he stands on his own feet; and he only stands on his own feet when he owes his *existence* to himself. A man who lives by the grace of another regards himself as a dependent being. But I live completely by the grace of another if I owe him not only the sustenance of my life, but if he has, moreover, *created* my *life*— if he is the *source* of my life; and if it is not of my own creation, my life has necessarily a source of this kind outside it. The *Creation* is therefore an idea very difficult to dislodge from popular consciousness. The self-mediated being of nature and of man is *incomprehensible* to it, because it contradicts everything *palpable* in practical life.

The creation of the *earth* has received a mighty blow from *geogeny*—i.e., from the science which presents the formation of the earth, the coming-to-be of the earth, as a process, as self-generation. *Generatio aequivoca*[7] is the only practical refutation of the theory of creation.

Now it is certainly easy to say to the single individual what Aristotle has already said. You have been begotten by your father and your mother, therefore in you the mating of two human beings—a species-act of human beings—has produced the human being. You see, therefore, that even physically, man owes his existence to man. Therefore you must not only keep sight of the *one* aspect—the *infinite* progression which leads you further to enquire: "Who begot my father? Who his grandfather?", etc. You must also hold on to the *circular movement* sensuously perceptible in that progression, by which *man* repeats himself in procreation, thus always remaining the subject. You will reply, however: I grant you this circular movement; now grant me the progression which drives me ever further until I ask: Who begot the first man, and nature as a whole? I can only answer you: Your question is itself a product of abstraction. Ask yourself how you arrived at that question. Ask yourself whether your question is not posed from a standpoint to which I cannot reply, because it is a perverse one. Ask yourself whether that progression as such exists for a reasonable mind. When you ask about the creation of nature and man, you are abstracting, in so doing, from man and nature. You postulate them as *non-existent*, and yet you want me to prove them to you as *existing*. Now I say to you: Give up your abstraction and you will also give up your question. Or if you want to hold on to your abstraction, then be consistent, and if you think of man and nature as non-existent, then think of yourself as non-existent, for you too are surely nature and man. Don't think, don't ask me, for as soon as you think and ask, your *abstraction* from the existence of nature and man has no meaning. Or are you such an egoist that you postulate everything as nothing, and yet want yourself to be?

You can reply: I do not want to postulate the nothingness of nature. I ask you about *its genesis*, just as I ask the anatomist about the formation of bones, etc.

But since for the socialist man the *entire so-called history of the world* is nothing but the begetting of man through human labor, nothing but the coming-to-be of nature for man, he has the visible, irrefutable proof of his *birth* through himself, of his *process of coming-to-be*. Since the *real existence* of man and nature has become practical, sensuous and perceptible—since man has become for man as the being of nature, and nature for man as the being of man—the question about an *alien* being, about a being above nature and man—a question which implies the admission of the inessentiality of nature and of man—has become impossible in practice. *Atheism*, as the denial of this inessentiality, has no longer any meaning, for atheism is a *negation of God*, and postulates the *existence of man* through this negation; but socialism as socialism no longer stands in any need of such a mediation. It proceeds from the *practically and theoretically sensuous consciousness* of man and of nature as the *essence*. Socialism is man's *positive self-consciousness*, no longer mediated through the annulment of religion, just as *real life* is man's positive reality, no longer mediated through the annulment of private property, through *communism*. Communism is the position as the negation of the negation, and is hence the *actual* phase necessary for the next stage of historical development in the process of human emancipation and recovery. *Communism* is the necessary pattern and the dynamic principle of the immediate future, but communism as such[8] is not the goal of human development—the structure of human society.

Footnotes

[1. Transcended . . . annulled . . . done away with:—see *Aufheben* in Translator's Note on Terminology."—Ed.]

[2. Prostitution is only a *specific* expression of the *general* prostitution of the *laborer*, and since it is a relationship in which not the prostitute alone, but also the one who prostitutes, fall—and the latter's abomination is still greater—the capitalist, etc., also comes under this head.]

[3. For this reason it is just as highly varied as the *determinations* of human *essence* and *activities.*]

[4. *Einundzwanzig Bogen aus der Schweiz*, Erste Teil, Zürich und Winterthur, 1843, p. 329.—Ed.]

[5. In practice I can relate myself to a thing humanly only if the thing relates itself to the human being humanly.]

[6. Essential powers   *Wesenskräfte*: i.e., powers belonging to me as part of my essential nature, my very being. See *Wesen* in "Translator's Note on Terminology."—Ed.]

[7. The spontaneous generation.—Ed.]

[8. Under "communism as such" Marx here means crude, equalitarian communism, such as that propounded by Babeuf and his followers.—Ed.]

The Meaning of Human Requirements Where There Is Private Property and under Socialism. The Difference between Extravagant Wealth and Industrial Wealth. Division of Laborin Bourgeois Society

(7) We have seen what significance, given socialism, the *wealth* of human needs has, and what significance, therefore, both a *new mode of production* and a new *object* of production have: a new manifestation of the forces of *human* nature and a new enrichment of *human* nature.[1] Under private property their significance is reversed: every person speculates on creating a *new* need in another, so as to drive him to a fresh sacrifice, to place him in a new dependence and to seduce him into a new mode of *gratification* and therefore economic ruin. Each tries to establish over the other an *alien* power, so as thereby to find satisfaction of his own selfish need. The increase in the quantity of objects is accompanied by an extension of the realm of the alien powers to which man is subjected, and every new product represents a new *potency* of mutual swindling and mutual plundering. Man becomes ever poorer as man; his need for *money* becomes ever greater if he wants to overpower hostile being; and the power of his *money* declines exactly in inverse proportion to the increase in the volume of production: that is, his neediness grows as the *power* of money increases.

The need for money is therefore the true need produced by the modern economic system, and it is the only need which the latter produces. The *quantity* of money becomes to an ever greater degree its sole *effective* attribute: just as it reduces everything to its abstract form, so it reduces itself in the course of its own movement to something merely *quantitative*. *Excess* and *intemperance* come to be its true norm. Subjectively, this is even partly manifested in that the extension of products and needs falls into *contriving* and *ever-calculating* subservience to inhuman, refined, unnatural and *imaginary* appetites. Private property does not know how to change crude need into *human* need. Its *idealism* is *fantasy, caprice* and *whim*; and no eunuch flatters his despot more basely or uses more despicable means to stimulate his dulled capacity for pleasure in order to sneak a favor for himself than does the industrial eunuch—the producer—in order to sneak for himself a few pennies—in order to charm the golden birds out of the pockets of his Christianly beloved neighbours. He puts himself at the service of the other's most depraved fancies, plays the pimp between him and his need, excites in him morbid appetites, lies in wait for each of his weaknesses—all so that he can then demand the cash for this service of love. (Every product is a bait with which to seduce away the other's very being, his money; every real and possible need is a weakness which will lead the fly to the gluepot. General exploitation of communal human nature, just as every imperfection in man, is a bond with heaven—an avenue giving the priest access to his heart; every need is an opportunity to approach one's neighbor under the guise of the utmost amiability and to say to him: Dear friend, I give you what you need, but you know the *conditio sine qua non*; you know the ink in which you have to sign yourself over to me; in providing for your pleasure, I fleece you.)

And partly, this estrangement manifests itself in that it produces refinement of needs and of their means on the one hand, and a bestial barbarization, a complete, unrefined, abstract simplicity of need, on the other; or rather in that it merely resurrects itself in its opposite. Even the need for fresh air ceases for the worker. Man returns to living in a cave, which is now, however, contaminated with the mephitic breath of plague given off by civilization, and which he continues to occupy only *precariously*, it being for him an alien habitation which can be withdrawn from him any day—a place from which, if he does not pay, he can be thrown out any day. For this mortuary he has to *pay*. A dwelling in the *light*, which Prometheus in Aeschylus designated as one of the greatest boons, by means of which he made the savage into a human being, ceases to exist for the worker. Light, air, etc.—the simplest *animal* cleanliness—ceases to be a need for man. *Dirt*—this stagnation and putrefaction of man—the *sewage* of civilization (speaking quite literally)—comes to be the *element of life* for him. Utter, *unnatural* neglect, putrefied nature, comes to be his *life-element*. None of his senses exist any longer, and not only in his human fashion, but in an *inhuman* fashion, and therefore not even in an animal fashion. The crudest *modes* (and *instruments*) of human labor are coming back: the *treadmill* of the Roman slaves, for instance, is the means of production, the means of existence, of many English workers. It is not only that man has no human needs—even his *animal* needs are ceasing to exist. The Irishman no longer knows any need now but the need to *eat*, and indeed only the need to eat *potatoes*—and *scabby potatoes* at that, the worst kind of potatoes. But in each of their industrial towns England and France have already a *little* Ireland. The savage and the animal have at least the need to hunt, to roam, etc.—the need of companionship. Machine labor is simplified in order to make a worker out of the human being still in the making, the completely immature human being, the *child*—while the worker has become a neglected child. The machine accommodates itself to the *weakness* of the human being in order to make the *weak* human being into a machine.

How the multiplication of needs and of the means of their satisfaction breeds the absence of needs and of means is demonstrated by the political economist (and the capitalist: it should be noted that it is always *empirical* businessmen we are talking about when we refer to political economists—their *scientific* confession and mode of being). This he shows:

(1) By reducing the worker's need to the barest and most miserable level of physical subsistence, and by reducing his activity to the most abstract mechanical movement. Hence, he says: Man has no other need either of activity or of enjoyment. For he calls *even* this life *human* life and existence.

(2) By *counting* the *lowest* possible level of life (existence) as the standard, indeed as the general standard—general because it is applicable to the mass of men. He changes the worker into an insensible being lacking all needs, just as he changes his activity into a pure abstraction from all activity. To him, therefore, every *luxury* of the worker seems to be reprehensible, and everything that goes beyond the most abstract need—be it in the realm of passive enjoyment, or a manifestation of activity—seems to him a luxury. Political economy, this science of *wealth*, is therefore simultaneously the science of denial, of want, of *thrift, of saving*—and it actually reaches the point where it *spares* man the *need* of either fresh *air* or physical *exercise*. This science of marvelous industry is simultaneously the science of *asceticism*, and its true ideal is the *ascetic* but *extortionate* miser and the *ascetic* but *productive* slave. Its moral ideal is the *worker* who takes part of his wages to the savings-bank, and it has even found ready-made an abject *art* in which to clothe this its pet idea: they have presented it, bathed in sentimentality, on the stage. Thus political economy—despite its worldly and wanton appearance—is a true moral science, the most moral of all the sciences. Self-denial, the denial of life and of all human needs, is its cardinal doctrine. The less you eat, drink and read books; the less you go to the theater, the dance hall, the public-house; the less you think, love, theorize, sing, paint, fence, etc., the more you *save*—the *greater* becomes your treasure which neither moths nor dust will devour—your *capital.* The less you *are*, the more you *have*; the less you express your own life, the greater is your *alienated* life—the greater is the store of your estranged being. Everything which the political economist takes from you in life and in humanity, he replaces for you in *money* and in *wealth*; and all the things which you cannot do, your money can do. It can eat and drink, go to the dance hall and the theater; it can travel, it can appropriate art, learning, the treasures of the past, political power—all this it *can* appropriate for you—it can buy all this for you: it is the true *endowment.* Yet being all this, it is *inclined* to do nothing but create itself, buy itself; for everything else is after all its servant. And when I have the master I have the servant and do not need his servant. All passions and all activity must therefore be submerged in *avarice*. The

worker may only have enough for him to want to live, and may only want to live in order to have [enough].

Of course a controversy now arises in the field of political economy. The one side (Lauderdale, Malthus, etc.) recommends *luxury* and execrates thrift. The other (Say, Ricardo, etc.) recommends thrift and execrates luxury. But the former admits that it wants luxury in order to produce *labor* (i.e., absolute thrift); and the latter admits that it recommends thrift in order to produce *wealth* (i.e., luxury). The Lauderdale-Malthus school has the *romantic* notion that avarice alone ought not to determine the consumption of the rich, and it contradicts its own laws in advancing *extravagance* as a direct means of enrichment. Against it, therefore, the other side very earnestly and circumstantially proves that I do not increase but reduce my *possessions* by being extravagant. The Say-Ricardo school, however, is hypocritical in not admitting that it is precisely whim and caprice which determine production. It forgets the "refined needs"; it forgets that there would be no production without consumption; it forgets that as a result of competition production can only become more extensive and luxurious. It forgets that it is use that determines a thing's value, and that fashion determines use. It wishes to see only "useful things" produced, but it forgets that production of too many useful things produces too large a *useless* population. Both sides forget that extravagance and thrift, luxury and privation, wealth and poverty are equal.

And you must not only stint the immediate gratification of your senses, as by stinting yourself of food, etc.: you must also spare yourself all sharing of general interest, all sympathy, all trust, etc.; if you want to be economical, if you do not want to be ruined by illusions.

You must make everything that is yours *salable*, i.e., useful. If I ask the political economist: Do I obey economic laws if I extract money by offering my body for sale, by surrendering it to another's lust? (The factory workers in France call the prostitution of their wives and daughters the xth working hour, which is literally correct.)—Or am I not acting in keeping with political economy if I sell my friend to the Moroccans? (And the direct sale of men in the form of a trade in conscripts, etc., takes place in all civilized countries.)—then the political economist replies to me: You do not transgress my laws; but see what Cousin Ethics and Cousin Religion have to say about it. My *political economic* ethics and religion have nothing to reproach you with, but—But whom am I now to believe, political economy or ethics? The ethics of political economy is *acquisition*, work, thrift, sobriety—but political economy promises to satisfy my needs. The political economy of ethics is the opulence of a good conscience, of virtue, etc.; but how can I live virtuously if I do not live? And how can I have a good conscience if I am not conscious of anything? It stems from the very nature of estrangement that each sphere applies to me a different and opposite yardstick—ethics one and political economy another; for each is a specific estrangement of man and focuses attention on a particular round of estranged essential activity, and each stands in an estranged relation to the other. Thus M. *Michel Chevalier* reproaches Ricardo with having abstracted from ethics. But Ricardo is allowing political economy to speak its own language, and if it does not speak ethically, this is not Ricardo's fault. M. Chevalier abstracts from political economy insofar as he moralizes, but he really and necessarily abstracts from ethics insofar as he practices political economy. The reference of political economy to ethics, if it is other than an arbitrary, contingent and therefore unfounded and unscientific reference, if it is not being put up as a *sham* but is meant to be *essential,* can only be the reference of the laws of political economy to ethics. If there is no such connection, or if the contrary is rather the case, can Ricardo help it? Besides, the opposition between political economy and ethics is only a *sham* opposition and just as much no opposition as it is an opposition. All that happens is that political economy expresses moral laws *in its own way.*

Needlessness as the principle of political economy is *most brilliantly* shown in its *theory of population.* There are *too many* people. Even the existence of men is a pure luxury; and if the worker is *"ethical,"* he will be *sparing* in procreation. (Mill suggests public acclaim for those who prove themselves continent in their sexual relations, and public rebuke for those who sin against such barrenness of marriage. ... Is not this the ethics, the teaching of asceticism?) The production of people appears in the form of public misery.

The meaning which production has in relation to the rich is seen *revealed* in the meaning which it has for the poor. At the top the manifestation is always refined, veiled, ambiguous— a sham; lower, it is rough, straightforward, frank—the real thing. The worker's *crude* need is a far greater source of gain than the *refined* need of the rich. The cellar-dwellings in London bring more to those who let them than do the palaces; that is to say, with reference to the landlord they constitute *greater wealth,* and thus (to speak the language of political economy) greater *social* wealth.

Industry speculates on the refinement of needs, but it speculates just as much on their *crudeness,* but on their artificially produced crudeness, whose true enjoyment, therefore, is *self-stupefaction*—this *seeming* satisfaction of need—this civilization contained *within* the crude barbarism of need; the English gin-shops are therefore the *symbolical embodiments* of private property. Their *luxury* reveals the true relation of industrial luxury and wealth to man. They are therefore rightly the only Sunday pleasures of the people, dealt with at least mildly by the English police.

We have already seen how the political economist establishes the unity of labor and capital in a variety of ways: (1) Capital is *accumulated labor*. (2) The purpose of capital within production—partly, reproduction of capital with profit, partly, capital as raw material (material of labor), and partly, as itself a *working instrument* (the machine is capital directly equated with labor)—is *productive labor*. (3) The worker is a capital. (4) Wages belong to costs of capital. (5) In relation to the worker, labor is the reproduction of his life-capital. (6) In relation to the capitalist, labor is an aspect of his capital's activity.

Finally, (7) the political economist postulates the original unity of capital and labor in the form of the unity of the capitalist and the worker; this is the original state of paradise. The way in which these two aspects in the form of two persons leap at each other's throats is for the political economist a *contingent* event, and hence only to be explained by reference to external factors. (See Mill.)[2]

The nations which are still dazzled by the sensuous splendor of precious metals, and are therefore still fetish-worshippers of metal money, are not yet fully developed money-nations.— Contrast of France and England. The extent to which the solution of theoretical riddles is the task of practice and effected through practice, just as true practice is the condition of a real and positive theory, is shown, for example, in *fetishism*. The sensuous consciousness of the fetish-worshipper is different from that of the Greek, because his sensuous existence is still different. The abstract enmity between sense and spirit is necessary so long as the human feeling for nature, the human sense of nature, and therefore also the *natural* sense *of man*, are not yet produced by man's own labor.

Equality is nothing but a translation of the German "Ich=Ich" into the French, i.e., political form. Equality as the *groundwork* of communism is its *political* justification, and it is the same as when the German justifies it by conceiving man as *universal self-consciousness*. Naturally, the transcendence of the estrangement always proceeds from that form of the estrangement which is the *dominant* power: in Germany, *self-consciousness*; in France, *equality*, because politics; in England, real, material, *practical* need taking only itself as its standard. It is from this standpoint that Proudhon is to be criticized and appreciated.

If we characterize *communism* itself because of its character as negation of the negation, as the appropriation of the human essence which mediates itself with itself through the negation of private property—as being not yet the *true*, self-originating position but rather a position originating from private property, [. . .][3]

Since in that case[4] the real estrangement of the life of man remains, and remains all the more, the more one is conscious of it as such, it may accomplished solely by putting communism into operation.

In order to abolish the *idea* of private property, the *idea* of communism is completely sufficient. It takes *actual* communist action to abolish actual private property. History will come to it; and this movement, which in *theory* we already know to be a self-transcending movement, will constitute in *actual fact* a very severe and protracted process. But we must regard it as a real advance to have gained beforehand a consciousness of the limited character as well as of the goal of this historical movement—and a consciousness which reaches out beyond it.

When communist *workmen* associate with one another, theory, propaganda, etc., is their first end. But at the same time, as a result of this association, they acquire a new need—the need for society—and what appears as a means becomes an end. You can observe this practical process in its most splendid results whenever you see French socialist workers together. Such things as smoking, drinking, eating, etc., are no longer means of contact or means that bring together. Company, association, and conversation, which again has society as its end, are enough for them; the brotherhood of man is no mere phrase with them, but a fact of life, and the nobility of man shines upon us from their work-hardened bodies.

When political economy claims that demand and supply always balance each other, it immediately forgets that according to its own claim (theory of population) the supply of *people* always exceeds the demand, and that, therefore, in the essential result of the whole production process—the existence of man—the disparity between demand and supply gets its most striking expression.

The extent to which money, which appears as a means, constitutes true *power* and the sole *end*—the extent to which in general that means which gives me substance, which gives me possession of the objective substance of others, is an *end in itself*—can be clearly seen from the facts that landed property wherever land is the source of life, and *horse* and *sword* wherever these are the *true means of life*, are also acknowledged as the true political powers in life. In the middle ages a social class is emancipated as soon as it is allowed to carry the *sword*. Among nomadic peoples it is the *horse* which makes me a free man and a participant in the life of the community.

We have said above that man is regressing to the *cave dwelling*, etc.—but that he is regressing to it in an estranged, malignant form. The savage in his cave—a natural element which freely offers itself for his use and protection—feels himself no more a stranger, or rather feels himself to be just as much at home as a *fish* in water. But the cellar-dwelling of the poor man is a hostile dwelling, "an alien, restraining power which only gives itself up to him in so far as he gives up to it his blood and sweat"—a dwelling which he cannot look upon as his own home where he might at last exclaim, "Here I am at home," but where instead he finds himself in *someone else's* house, in the house of a *stranger* who daily lies in wait for him and throws him out if he does not pay his rent. Similarly, he is also aware of the contrast in quality between his dwelling and a human dwelling—a residence in that *other* world, the heaven of wealth.

Estrangement is manifested not only in the fact that *my* means of life belong to someone else, that *my* desire is the inaccessible possession of *another*, but also in the fact that everything is in itself something *different* from itself—that my activity is *something else* and that, finally (and this applies also to the capitalist), all is under the sway of *inhuman* power. There is a form of inactive, extravagant wealth given over wholly to pleasure, the enjoyer of which on the one hand *behaves* as a mere *ephemeral* individual frantically spending himself to no purpose, knows the slave-labor of others (human *sweat and blood)* as the prey of his cupidity, and therefore knows man himself, and hence also his own self, as a sacrificed and empty being. With such wealth the contempt of man makes its appearance, partly as arrogance and as the throwing-away of what can give sustenance to a hundred human lives, and partly as the infamous illusion that his own unbridled extravagance and ceaseless, unproductive consumption is the condition of the other's *labor* and therefore of his *subsistence*. He knows the realization of the *essential powers* of man only as the realization of his own excesses, his whims and capricious, bizarre notions. This wealth which, on the other hand, again knows wealth as a mere means, as something that is good for nothing but to be annihilated and which is therefore at once slave and master, at once generous and mean, capricious, presumptuous, conceited, refined, cultured and witty—this wealth has not yet experienced *wealth* as an utterly *alien power* over itself: it sees in it, rather, only its own power, and not wealth but *gratification* [is its][5] final aim and end.

This bright illusion about the nature of wealth, blinded by sensuous appearances, is confronted by the *working, sober, economical, prosaic* industrialist who is quite enlightened about the nature of wealth, and who, while providing a wider sphere for the other's self-indulgence and saying fulsome flatteries to him in his product (for his products are just so many base compliments to the appetites of the spendthrift), knows how to appropriate for himself in the only *useful* way the other's waning power. If, therefore, industrial wealth appears at first to be the result of extravagant fantastic wealth, its motion, the motion inherent in it, ousts the latter also in an active way. For the fall in the *interest on money* is a necessary consequence and result of industrial development. The extravagant rentier's means therefore dwindle day by day in *inverse* proportion to the increasing possibilities and pitfalls of pleasure. Consequently, he must either consume his capital himself, thus ruining himself, or must become an industrial capitalist. On the other hand, there is of course a direct, constant rise in the *rent of land* as a result of the course of industrial development; nevertheless, as we have already seen,[6] there must come a time when landed property, like every other kind of property, is bound to fall within the category of profitably self-reproducing capital—and this in fact results from the same industrial development. Thus the extravagant landowner, too, must either consume his capital, and thus be ruined, or himself become the farmer of his own estate—an agricultural industrialist.

The diminution in the interest on money, which Proudhon regards as the annulling of capital and as the tendency to socialize capital, is really and immediately, therefore, only a symptom of the total victory of working capital over extravagant wealth— i.e., the transformation of all private property into industrial capital. It is a total victory of private property over all those of its qualities which are still in *appearance* human, and the complete subjection of the owner of private property to the essence of private property—*labor*. To be sure, the industrial capitalist also takes his pleasures. He does not by any means return to the unnatural simplicity of need; but his pleasure is only a side-issue—recuperation—something subordinated to production: at the same time it is a *calculated* and, therefore, itself an *economical* pleasure. For he debits it to his capital's expense-account, and what is squandered on his pleasure must therefore amount to no more than will be replaced with profit through the reproduction of capital. Pleasure is therefore subsumed under capital, and the pleasure-taking individual under the capital-accumulating individual, while formerly the contrary was the case. The decrease in the interest-rate is therefore a symptom of the annulment of capital only inasmuch as it is a symptom of the rule of capital in the process of perfecting itself—of the estrangement in the process of becoming fully-developed and therefore of hastening to its annulment. This is indeed the only way in which that which exists affirms its opposite.

The quarrel between the political economists about luxury and thrift is, therefore, only the quarrel between that political economy which has achieved clarity about the nature of wealth, and that political economy which is still afflicted with romantic, anti-industrial memories. Neither side, however, knows how to reduce the subject of the controversy to its simple terms, and neither therefore can make short work of the other.

Moreover, *rent of land qua* rent of land has been overthrown, since, contrary to the argument of the physiocrats which maintains that the landowner is the only true producer, modern political economy has proved that the landowner as such is in fact the only completely unproductive rentier. According to it, agriculture is the business of the capitalist, who applies his capital in it provided he can expect from it the usual profit. The claim of the physiocrats that landed property, as the sole productive property, should alone pay state taxes and therefore should alone sanction them and participate in the affairs of state, is transformed into the opposite position that the tax on the rent of land is the only tax on unproductive income, and is therefore the only tax not detrimental to national production. It goes without saying that from this point of view the political prerogative of landowners no longer follows from their position as principal tax-payers.

Everything which Proudhon conceives as a movement of labor against capital is only the movement of labor in the form of capital, of *industrial capital,* against capital not consumed *as* capital—i.e., not consumed industrially. And this movement is proceeding along its triumphant road—the road to victory of *industrial* capital. It is clear, therefore, that only when *labor* is grasped as the essence of private property, can the economic process as such be penetrated in its actual concreteness.

Society, as it appears to the political economist, is *civil society,* in which every individual is a totality of needs and only exists for the other person, as the other exists for him, insofar as each becomes a means for the other. The political economist reduces everything (just as does politics in its *Rights of Man)* to man, i.e., to the individual whom he strips of all determinateness so as to class him as capitalist or worker.

The *division of labor* is the expression in political economy of the *social character of labor* within the estrangement. Or, since *labor* is only an expression of human activity within alienation, of the living of life as the alienating of life, the *division of labor,* too, is therefore nothing else but the *estranged, alienated* positing of human activity as *a real activity of the species* or as *activity of man as a species being.*

As for *the essence of the division of labor*—and of course the division of labor had to be conceived as a major driving force in the production of wealth as soon as *labor* was recognized as *the essence of private property*—i.e., about *the estranged and alienated form of human activity as an activity of the species*— the political economists are very unclear and self-contradictory about it.

Adam Smith:[7] "The *division of labor* is not originally the effect of any human wisdom. It is the necessary, slow and gradual consequence of the propensity to exchange and barter one product for another. This propensity to trade is probably a necessary consequence of the use of reason and of speech. It is common to all men, and to be found in no animal. The animal, when it is grown up, is entirely independent. Man has constant occasion for the help of others, and it is in vain for him to expect it from their benevolence only. He will be more likely to prevail if he can appeal to their personal interest and show them that it is for their own advantage to do for him what he requires of them. We address ourselves not to other men's *humanity* but to their *self-love*, and never talk to them of our *own necessities* but of *their advantages*.

"As it is by treaty, by barter, and by purchase that we obtain from one another the greater part of those mutual good offices which we stand in need of, so it is this same *trucking* disposition which originally gives occasion to the *division of labor*. In a tribe of hunters or shepherds a particular person makes bows and arrows, for example, with more readiness and dexterity than any other. He frequently exchanges them for cattle or for venison with his companions; and he finds at last that he can in this manner get more cattle and venison than if he himself went to the field to catch them. From a regard to his own interest, therefore, the making of bows, etc., grows to be his chief business.

The difference of *natural talents* in different individuals is not so much the *cause* as the *effect* of the division of labor. . . . Without the disposition to truck and exchange, every man must have procured to himself every necessary and conveniency of life. All must have had the *same work* to do, and there could have been no such *difference of employment* as could alone give occasion to any great difference of talents.

"As it is this disposition which forms that difference of talents among men, so it is this same disposition which renders that difference useful. Many tribes of animals of the same species derive from nature a much more remarkable distinction of genius than what, antecedent to custom and education, could be observed among men. By nature a philosopher is not in talent and in intelligence half so different from a street-porter, as a mastiff is from a greyhound, or a greyhound from a spaniel, or this last from a shepherd's dog. Those different tribes of animals, however, though all of the same species, are of scarce any use to one another. The mastiff cannot add to the advantages of his strength by making use of the swiftness of the greyhound, etc. The effects of these different talents or grades of intelligence, for want of the power or disposition to barter and exchange, cannot be brought into a common *stock*, and do not in the least contribute to the better *accommodation and conveniency of the species*. Each animal is still obliged to support and defend itself, separately and independently, and derives no sort of advantage from that variety of talents with which nature has distinguished its fellows. Among men, on the contrary, the most dissimilar geniuses are of use to one another; the *different produces* of their respective talents, by the general disposition to truck, barter and exchange, being brought, as it were, into a common stock, where every man may purchase whatever part of the produce of other men's industry he has occasion for.

"As it is the power of *exchanging* that gives occasion to the *division of labor*, so the *extent* of this *division* must always be limited by the *extent of that power*, or in other words, by the *extent of the market*. When the market is very small, no person can have any encouragement to dedicate himself entirely to one employment, for want of the power to exchange all that surplus part of the produce of his own labor, which is over and above his own consumption, for such parts of the produce of other men's labor as he has occasion for. ..."

In an *advanced* state of society "Every man lives by exchanging and becomes in some measure a *merchant*, and the *society itself grows* to be what is properly a *commercial* society."[8](See Destutt de Tracy:[9] "Society is a series of reciprocal exchanges; *commerce* contains the whole essence of society.") The accumulation of capitals mounts with the division of labor, and vice versa.—So much for *Adam Smith*.

"If every family produced all that it consumed, society could keep going although no exchange of any sort took place; without being *fundamental*, exchange is indispensable in our advanced state of society. The division of labor is a skillful deployment of man's powers; it increases society's production—its power and its pleasures—but it plunders and reduces the ability of every person taken individually. Production cannot take place without exchange."—Thus *J. B. Say*.[10]

"The powers inherent in man are his intelligence and his physical capacity for work. Those which arise from the condition of society consist of the capacity to *divide up labor* and to *distribute different jobs among different people* required to obtain means of subsistence, and the *power* to exchange *mutual services* and the products which constitute these means. The motive which impels a man to give his services to another is self-interest—he requires a reward for the services rendered. The right of exclusive private property is indispensable to the establishment of exchange among men." "Exchange and division of labor reciprocally condition each other." Thus Skarbek.[11]

Mill presents developed exchange—*trade*—as a *consequence of the division of labor*.

"The agency of man can be traced to very simple elements. He can, in fact, do nothing more than produce motion. He can move things towards one another, and he can separate them from one another: the properties of matter perform all the rest." "In the employment of labor and machinery, it is often found that the effects can be increased by skillful distribution, by separating all those operations which have any tendency to impede one another, and by bringing together all those operations which can be made in any way to aid one another. As men in general cannot perform many different operations with the same quickness and dexterity with which they can by practice learn to perform a few, it is always an advantage to limit as much as possible the number of operations imposed upon each. For dividing labor, and distributing the powers of men and machinery, to the greatest advantage, it is in most cases necessary to operate upon a large scale; in other words, to produce the commodities in greater masses. It is this advantage which gives existence to the great manufactories; a few of which, placed in the most convenient situations, frequently supply not one country, but many countries, with as much as they desire of the commodity produced."

Thus Mill.[12]

The whole of modern political economy agrees, however, that division of labor and wealth of production, division of labor and accumulation of capital, are mutually interrelated; just as it agrees that *liberated* private property alone—private property left to itself—can produce the most useful and comprehensive division of labor.

Adam Smith's argument can be summed up as follows: Division of labor bestows on labor infinite production capacity. It stems from the *propensity to exchange* and *barter*, a specifically human propensity which is probably not fortuitous but is conditioned by the use of reason and speech. The motive of those who engage in exchange is not *humanity* but *egoism*. The diversity of human talents is more the effect than the cause of the division of labor—i.e., of exchange. Besides, it is only the latter which makes such diversity useful. The differences between the particular attributes to which nature gives rise within a species of animal are much more marked than the degrees of difference in human aptitude and activity. But because animals are unable to engage in *exchange*, no individual animal benefits from the difference in the attributes of animals of the same species but of different breeds. Animals are unable to combine the different attributes of their species, and are unable to contribute anything to the *common* advantage and comfort of the species. It is otherwise with *men*, among whom the most dissimilar talents and forms of activity are of use to one another, *because* they can bring their *different* products together into a common stock, from which each can purchase. As the division of labor springs from the propensity to *exchange*, it grows and is limited by the *extent of exchange*—by the *extent of the market*. In advanced conditions, every man is a *merchant*, and society is a *commercial society*. *Say* regards *exchange* as accidental and not fundamental. Society could exist without it. It becomes indispensable in the advanced state of society. Yet *production* cannot take place *without it*. Division of labor is a *convenient, useful* means—a skillful deployment of human powers for social wealth; but it reduces the *ability of each person* taken *individually*. The last remark is a step forward for Say.

Skarbek distinguishes the *individual powers inherent in man*—intelligence and the physical capacity for work—from the powers *derived* from society—*exchange* and *division of labor*, which mutually condition one another. But the necessary premise of exchange is *private property*. Skarbek here expresses in an objective form what Smith, Say, Ricardo, etc., say when they designate *egoism* and *self-interest* as the basis of exchange, and *buying and selling* as the *essential* and *adequate* form of exchange.

Mill presents *trade* as the consequence of the *division of labor*. With him *human* activity is reduced to *mechanical motion*. Division of labor and use of machinery promote wealth of production. Each person must be entrusted with as small a sphere of operations as possible. Division of labor and use of machinery for their part require the production of wealth, and therefore of the product, in large quantities. This is the reason for large manufactories.

The examination of *division of labor* and *exchange* is of extreme interest, because these are *perceptibly alienated* expressions of human *activity* and of *essential human power* as a *species* activity and power.

To assert that *division of labor* and *exchange* rest on *private property* is nothing short of asserting that labor is the essence of private property—an assertion which the political economist cannot prove and which we wish to prove for him. Precisely in the fact that *division of labor* and *exchange* are embodiments of private property lies the twofold proof, on the one hand that *human* life required *private property* for its realization, and on the other hand that it now requires the supersession of private property.

Division of labor and *exchange* are the two *phenomena* in connection with which the political economist boasts of the social character of his science and in the same breath gives expression to the contradiction in his science—the establishment of society through unsocial, particular interests.

The factors we have to consider are: the *propensity to exchange*—the basis of which is found in egoism—regarded as the cause or reciprocal effect of the division of labor. Say regards exchange as not *fundamental* to the nature of society. Wealth— production—is explained by division of labor and exchange. The impoverishment of individual activity, and its loss of character as a result of the division of labor, are admitted. Exchange and division of labor are acknowledged as the sources of the great *diversity of human talents*—a diversity which in its turn becomes *useful* as a result of exchange. Skarbek divides man's essential powers of production—or productive powers— into two parts: (1) those which are individual and inherent in him—his intelligence and his special disposition, or capacity, for work; and (2) those *derived from* society and not the actual individual—division of labor and exchange. Furthermore, the division of labor is limited by the *market*. Human labor is simple *mechanical motion*: the main work is done by the material properties of the objects. The fewest possible operations must be apportioned to any one individual. Splitting up of labor and concentration of capital; the nothingness of individual production and the production of wealth in large quantities. Meaning of free private property within the division of labor.[13]

Footnotes

[1. Forces of human nature—*menschlichen Wesenskraft*; . . . human nature—*menschlichen Wesens*.—Ed.]

[2. James Mill, *Elements of Political Economy.*—Ed.]

[3. In the manuscript the lower left corner of the page is torn off. Just the right-hand endings of the last six lines remain, making restoration of the text impossible. It is possible to surmise, however, that Marx here criticizes Hegel's idealistic "transcending" of estrangement (the words that have survived are cited in the next footnote).—Ed.]

[4. In "transcending" estrangement "in the old German manner—the manner of the Hegelian phenomenology," i.e., in transcending it exclusively in the "consciousness" of the subject.—Ed.]

[5. The bottom of the page is torn. Three or four lines are missing.—Ed.]

[6. See "Rent of Land" above.—Ed.]

[7. *Wealth of Nations,* Book I, chs. II and III (but quoted with omissions, transpositions, etc.).—Ed.]

[8. Adam Smith, Vol. I, p. 20.—Ed.]

[9. Destutt de Tracy: *Elements d'Idiologie. Traité de la Volonté et de ses Effets (Elements of Ideology. Treatise on the Will and its Effects).* Paris, 1826, pp. 68, 78.— Ed.]

[10. Say, op. cit., p. 300 and p. 76 f.—Ed.]

[11. F. Skarbek, *Théorie des Richesses socialês, suivi d'une Biographie de l'Économie Politique (Theory of Social Wealth, Followed by an Account of the Development of Political Economy),* t. I-II, Paris, 1829, t. I, p. 25 f.—Ed.]

[12. *Elements of Political Economy,* by James Mill (London, 1821), pp. 5-9.—Ed.]

[13. That part of the third manuscript which serves as a supplement to p. XXXIX of the second manuscript breaks off at this point on the left side of p. XXXVIII. The right-hand side of p. XXXVIII is empty. Then follows the "Introduction" (pp. XXXIX-XL) and a passage on money (pp. XLI-XLIII).—Ed.]

The Power of Money in Bourgeois Society

If man's *feelings*, passions, etc., are not merely anthropological phenomena in the [narrower][1] sense, but truly *ontological* affirmations of essential being (of nature), and if they are only really affirmed because their *object* exists for them as an object of *sense*, then it is clear:

(1) That they have by no means merely one mode of affirmation, but rather that the distinctive character of their existence, of their life, is constituted by the distinctive mode of their affirmation. In what manner the object exists for them, is the characteristic mode of their *gratification*.

(2) Wherever the sensuous affirmation is the direct annulment of the object in its independent form (as in eating, drinking, working up of the object, etc.), this is the affirmation of the object.

(3) Insofar as man, and hence also his feeling, etc., are *human*, the affirmation of the object by another is likewise his own enjoyment.

(4) Only through developed industry—i.e., through the medium of private property—does the ontological essence of human passion come to be both in its totality and in its humanity; the science of man is therefore itself a product of man's establishment of himself by practical activity.

(5) The meaning of private property—liberated from its estrangement—is the *existence of essential objects* for man, both as objects of enjoyment and as objects of activity.

By possessing the *property* of buying everything, by possessing the property of appropriating all objects, *money* is thus the *object* of eminent possession. The universality of its *property* is the omnipotence of its being. It therefore functions as the almighty being. Money is the *pimp* between man's need and the object, between his life and his means of life. But *that which* mediates *my* life for me, also *mediates* the existence of other people *for me*. For me it is the *other* person.

"What, man! confound it, hands and feet
And head and backside, are all yours!
And what we take while life is sweet,
 Is that to be declared not ours?
Six stallions, say, I can afford,
Is not their strength my property?
I tear along, a sporting lord,
As if their legs belonged to me."

(Goethe: *Faust*–Mephistopheles.[2])

Shakespeare in *Timon of Athens*:

"Gold? Yellow, glittering, precious gold? No, Gods,
I am no idle votarist! . . . Thus much of this will make black white, foul fair.
Wrong, right, base noble, old young, coward valiant. . . .Why, this
Will lug your priests and servants from your sides,
Pluck stout men's pillows from below their heads:
This yellow *slave*
Will knit and break religions, bless the accursed;
Make the hoar leprosy adored, place thieves
And give them title, knee and approbation
With senators on the bench: This is it
That makes the wappen'd widow wed again;
She, whom the spital-house and ulcerous sores
Would cast the gorge at, this embalms and spices
To the April day again. . . . Damned earth,
Thou common whore of mankind, that putt'st odds
Among the rout of nations."[3]

And also later:

"O thou sweet king-killer, and dear divorce
Twixt natural son and sire! thou bright defiler
of Hymen's purest bed! thou valiant Mars!
Thou ever young, fresh, loved and delicate wooer,
Whose blush doth thaw the consecrated snow
That lies on Dian's lap! Thou *visible God!*
That solder'st close *impossibilities,*
And maest them kiss! That speak'st with every tongue,
To every purpose! O thou touch of hearts!
Think, thy slave man rebels, and by thy virtue
Set them into confounding odds, that beasts
 May have the world in empire!"[4]

Shakespeare excellently depicts the real nature of *money*. To understand him, let us begin, first of all, by expounding the passage from Goethe.
    That which is for me through the medium of *money*—that for which I can pay (i.e., which money can buy)—that am *I*, the possessor of the money. The extent

of the power of money is the extent of my power. Money's properties are my properties and essential powers—the properties and powers of its possessor.

Thus, what I *am* and *am capable* of is by no means determined by my individuality. I am ugly, but I can buy for myself the most *beautiful* of women. Therefore I am not *ugly*, for the effect of *ugliness*—its deterrent power—is nullified by money. I, in my character as an individual, am *lame*, but money furnishes me with twenty-four feet. Therefore I am not lame. I am bad, dishonest, unscrupulous, stupid; but money is honored, and therefore so is its possessor. Money is the supreme good, therefore its possessor is good. Money, besides, saves me the trouble of being dishonest: I am therefore presumed honest. I am *stupid*, but money is the *real mind* of all things and how then should its possessor be stupid? Besides, he can buy talented people for himself, and is he who has power over the talented not more talented than the talented? Do not I, who thanks to money am capable of *all* that the human heart longs for, possess all human capacities? Does not my money therefore transform all my incapacities into their contrary?

If *money* is the bond binding me to *human* life, binding society to me, binding me and nature and man, is not money the bond of all *bonds?* Can it not dissolve and bind all ties? Is it not, therefore, the universal *agent of divorce?* It is the true *agent of divorce* as well as the true *binding agent*—the [universal][5] galvano-chemical power of Society.

Shakespeare stresses especially two properties of money:

(1) It is the visible divinity—the transformation of all human and natural properties into their contraries, the universal confounding and overturning of things: it makes brothers of impossibilities. (2) It is the common whore, the common pimp of people and nations.

The overturning and confounding of all human and natural qualities, the fraternization of impossibilities—the *divine* power of money—lies in its *character* as men's estranged, alienating and self-disposing *species-nature.* Money is the alienated *ability of mankind.*

That which I am unable to do as a *man,* and of which therefore all my individual essential powers are incapable, I am able to do by means of *money.* Money thus turns each of these powers into something which in itself it is not—turns it, that is, into its *contrary.*

If I long for a particular dish or want to take the mail-coach because I am not strong enough to go by foot, money fetches me the dish and the mail-coach: that is, it converts my wishes from something in the realm of imagination, translates them from their meditated, imagined or willed existence into their *sensuous, actual* existence—from imagination to life, from imagined being into real being. In effecting this mediation, money is the *truly creative* power.

No doubt *demand* also exists for him who has no money, but his demand is a mere thing of the imagination without effect or existence for me, for a third party, for the others, and which therefore remains for me *unreal* and *objectless*. The difference between effective demand based on money and ineffective demand based on my need, my passion, my wish, etc., is the difference between *being* and *thinking*, between the imagined which *exists* merely within me and the imagined as it is for me outside me as a *real object*.

If I have no money for travel, I have no *need*—that is, no real and self-realizing need—to travel. If I have the *vocation* for study but no money for it, I have *no* vocation for study— that is, no *effective*, no *true* vocation. On the other hand, if I have really *no* vocation for study but have the will *and* the money for it, I have an *effective* vocation for it. Being the external, common *medium* and *faculty* for turning an *image* into *reality* and *reality* into a mere *image* (a faculty not springing from man as man or from human society as society), *money* transforms the *real essential powers of man and nature* into what are merely abstract conceits and therefore *imperfections*—into tormenting chimeras—just as it transforms *real imperfections and chimeras*— essential powers which are really impotent, which exist only in the imagination of the individual—into *real powers* and *faculties*.

In the light of this characteristic alone, money is thus the general overturning of *individualities* which turns them into their contrary and adds contradictory attributes to their attributes.

Money, then, appears as this *overturning* power both against the individual and against the bonds of society, etc., which claim to be *essences* in themselves. It transforms fidelity into infidelity, love into hate, hate into love, virtue into vice, vice into virtue, servant into master, master into servant, idiocy into intelligence and intelligence into idiocy.

Since money, as the existing and active concept of value, confounds and exchanges all things, it is the general *confounding* and *compounding* of all things—the world upside-down—the confounding and compounding of all natural and human qualities.

He who can buy bravery is brave, though a coward. As money is not exchanged for any one specific quality, for any one specific thing, or for any particular human essential power, but for the entire objective world of man and nature, from the standpoint of its possessor it therefore serves to exchange every property for every other, even contradictory, property and object: it is the fraternization of impossibilities. It makes contradictions embrace.

Assume *man* to be *man* and his relationship to the world to be a human one: then you can exchange love only for love, trust for trust, etc. If you want to enjoy art, you must be an artistically-cultivated person; if you want to exercise influence over other people, you must be a person with a stimulating and encouraging effect on other people. Every one of your relations to man and to nature must be a *specific expression*, corresponding to the object of your will, of your *real individual* life. If you love without evoking love in return—that is, if your loving as loving does not produce reciprocal love; if through a *living expression* of yourself as a loving person you do not make yourself a *loved person*, then your love is impotent— a misfortune.

Footnotes

[1. This word is illegible.—*Ed.*]

[2. Goethe, *Faust.* Part I —Faust's Study, III. cf. Goethe's *Faust.* Part I, translated by Philip Wayne(Penguin 1949. page 91).— *Ed.*]

[3. Shakespeare, *Timon of Athens.* Act 4, Sc. 3. (Marx quotes the Schlegel-Tieck translation.)—*Ed.*]

[4. Ibid.]

[5. An end of the page is torn out in the manuscript.—*Ed.*]

Critique of the Hegelian Dialectic and Philosophy as a Whole

(6) This is perhaps the place[1] at which, by way of explaining and justifying the ideas here presented, we might offer some considerations in regard to the Hegelian dialectic generally and especially its exposition in the *Phenomenology* and *Logic*,[2] and also, lastly, the relation to it of the modern critical movement.

So powerful was modern German criticism's preoccupation with the past—so completely was it possessed in its development by its subject-matter—that there prevailed a completely uncritical attitude to the method of criticizing, together with a complete lack of awareness about the *seemingly formal*, but really *vital* question: how do we now stand as regards the Hegelian *dialectic?* This lack of awareness about the relationship of modern criticism to the Hegelian philosophy as a whole and especially to the Hegelian dialectic has been so great that critics like *Strauss* and *Bruno Bauer* still remain wholly within the confines of the Hegelian Logic; the former completely so and the latter at least implicitly so in his *Synoptics*[3] (where, in opposition to Strauss, he replaces the substance of "abstract nature" by the "self-consciousness" of abstract man), and even in *Christianity Discovered.*[4] Thus in *Christianity Discovered*, for example, you get:

"As though in positing the world, self-consciousness posits that which is different from itself, and in what it posits it posits itself, because it in turn annuls the difference between what it has posited and itself, inasmuch as it itself has being only in the positing and the movement.—How then can it not have its purpose in this movement?" etc.; or again: "They" (the French materialists) "have not yet been able to see that it is only as the movement of self-consciousness that the movement of the universe has actually come to be for itself, and achieved unity with itself."

Such expressions do not even show any verbal divergence from the Hegelian approach, but on the contrary repeat it word for word.

How little consciousness there was in relation to the Hegelian dialectic during the act of criticism (Bauer, *The Synoptics*), and how little this consciousness came into being even after the act of material criticism is proved by Bauer when, in his *The Good of Freedom*[5] he dismisses the brash question put by Herr Gruppe—"What about logic now?"—by referring him to future critics.

But even now—now that *Feuerbach* both in his *Theses* in the *Anecdotis* and, in detail, in *The Philosophy of the Future*, has in principle overthrown the old dialectic and philosophy; now that that school of criticism, on the other hand, which was incapable of accomplishing this has all the same seen it accomplished and has proclaimed itself pure, resolute, absolute criticism—criticism that has come into the clear with itself; now that this criticism, in its spiritual pride, has reduced the whole process of history to the relation between the rest of the world and itself (the rest of the world, in contrast to itself, falling under the category of "the masses") and dissolved all dogmatic antithesis into the *single* dogmatic antithesis of its own cleverness and the stupidity of the world—the antithesis of the critical Christ and Mankind, the *rabble*; now that daily and hourly it has demonstrated its own excellence against the dullness of the masses; now, finally, that it has proclaimed the critical *Last Judgment* in the shape of an announcement that the day is approaching when the whole of expiring humanity will assemble before it and be sorted by it into groups, each particular mob receiving its *testimonium paupertatis*;[6] now that it has made known in print[7] its superiority to human feelings as well as its superiority to the world, over which it sits enthroned in sublime solitude, only letting fall from time to time from its sarcastic lips the ringing laughter of the Olympian Gods—even now, after all these delightful antics of moribund idealism in the guise of criticism (i.e., of Young-Hegelianism)—even now it has not expressed the suspicion that the time was ripe for a critical settling of accounts with the mother of Young-Hegelianism—the Hegelian dialectic—and even had [nothing] to say about its critical attitude towards the Feuerbachian dialectic. Criticism with a completely uncritical attitude to itself!

Feuerbach is the only one who has a *serious, critical* attitude to the Hegelian dialectic and who has made genuine discoveries in this field. He is in fact the true conqueror of the old philosophy. The extent of his achievement, and the unpretentious simplicity with which he, Feuerbach, gives it to the world, stand in striking contrast to the reverse.

Feuerbach's great achievement is:

(1) The proof that philosophy is nothing else but religion rendered into thoughts and thinkingly expounded, and that it has therefore likewise to be condemned as another form and manner of existence of the estrangement of the essence of man;

(2) The establishment of *true materialism* and of *real science*, since Feuerbach also makes the social relationship "of man to man" the basic principle of the theory;

(3) His opposing to the negation of the negation, which claims to be the absolute positive, the self-supporting positive, positively grounded on itself.

Feuerbach explains the Hegelian dialectic (and thereby justifies starting out from the positive, from sense-certainty) as follows:

Hegel sets out from the estrangement of Substance (in Logic, from the Infinite, the abstractly universal)—from the absolute and fixed abstraction; which means, put popularly, that he sets out from religion and theology.

Secondly, he annuls the infinite, and establishes the actual, sensuous, real, finite, particular (philosophy—annulment of religion and theology).

Thirdly, he again annuls the positive and restores the abstraction, the infinite—Restoration of religion and theology.

Feuerbach thus conceives the negation of the negation *only* as a contradiction of philosophy with itself—as the philosophy which affirms theology (the transcendent, etc.) after having denied it, and which it therefore affirms in opposition to itself.

The position or self-affirmation and self-confirmation contained in the negation of the negation is taken to be a position which is not yet sure of itself, which is therefore burdened with its opposite, which is doubtful of itself and therefore in need of proof, and which, therefore, is not a position establishing itself by its existence—not a position that justifies itself; hence it is directly and immediately confronted by the self-grounded position of sense-certainty.[8]

But because Hegel has conceived the negation of the negation from the point of view of the positive relation inherent in it as the true and only positive, and from the point of view of the negative relation inherent in it as the only true act and self-realizing act of all being, he has only found the *abstract, logical, speculative* expression for the movement of history; and this historical process is not yet the *real* history of man—of man as a given subject, but only man's *act of genesis*—the *story* of man's *origin*. We shall explain both the abstract form of this process and the difference between this process as it is in Hegel in contrast to modern criticism, that is, in contrast to the same process in Feuerbach's *Wesen des Christentums (Essence of Christianity)*, or rather the *critical* form of this in Hegel still uncritical process.

Let us take a look at the Hegelian system. One must begin with Hegel's *Phenomenology*, the true point of origin and the secret of the Hegelian philosophy.

PHENOMENOLOGY[9]

A. *Self-Consciousness*
I. *Consciousness*. (a) Certainty at the level of sense-experience; or the "This" and *Meaning*. (b) *Perception*, or the Thing with Its Properties, and *Deception*. (c) Force and Understanding, Appearance and the Supersensible World.

II. *Self-consciousness.* The Truth of Certainty of Self. (a) Independence and Dependence of Self-consciousness; Lordship and Bondage. (b) Freedom of Self-consciousness: Stoicism, Skepticism, the Unhappy Consciousness.

III. *Reason.* Reason's Certainty and Reason's Truth. (a) Observation as a Process of Reason. Observation of Nature and of Self-consciousness. (b) Realization of Rational Self-consciousness through its own Activity. Pleasure and Necessity. The Law of the Heart and the Frenzy of Self-conceit. Virtue and the Course of the World. (c) The Individuality Which is Real In and For Itself. The Spiritual Animal Kingdom and the Deception, or the Real Fact. Reason as Lawgiver. Reason Which Tests Laws.

B. *Mind*
I. *True* Mind; the Ethical Order.
II. Mind in Self-Estrangement—Culture.
III. Mind Certain of Itself, Morality.

C. *Religion*
Natural Religion; *Religion in the Form of Art; Revealed* Religion.

D. *Absolute Knowledge*
Hegel's *Encyclopaedia,*[10] beginning as it does with Logic, with *pure speculative thought,* and ending with *Absolute Knowledge*—with the self-consciousness, self-comprehending, philosophic or absolute (i.e., superhuman) abstract mind—is in its entirety nothing but the *display,* the self-objectification, of the *essence* of the philosophic mind, and the philosophic mind is nothing but the estranged mind of the world thinking within its self-estrangement—i.e., comprehending itself abstractly. *Logic* (mind's *coin of the realm,* the speculative or *thought-value* of man and nature—their essence grown totally indifferent to all real determinateness, and hence their unreal essence) is *alienated thinking,* and therefore thinking which abstracts from nature and from real man: *abstract* thinking. Then: *The externality of this abstract thinking. . . nature,* as it is for this abstract thinking. Nature is external to it—its self-loss; and it apprehends nature also in an external fashion, as abstract thinking—but as alienated abstract thinking. Finally, *Mind,* this thinking returning home to its own point of origin—the thinking which, as the anthropological, phenomenological, psychological, ethical, artistic and religious mind is not valid for itself, until ultimately it finds itself, and relates itself to itself, as *absolute* knowledge in the hence absolute, i.e., abstract mind, and so receives its conscious embodiment in a mode of being corresponding to it. For its real mode of being is *abstraction.*

There is a double error in Hegel.

The first emerges most clearly in the *Phenomenology*, the Hegelian philosophy's place of origin. When, for instance, wealth, state-power, etc., are understood by Hegel as entities estranged from the *human* being, this only happens in their form as thoughts. . . . They are thought-entities, and therefore merely an estrangement of *pure*, i.e., abstract, philosophical thinking. The whole process therefore ends with Absolute Knowledge. It is precisely abstract thought from which these objects are estranged and which they confront with their arrogation of reality. The *philosopher* sets up himself (that is, one who is himself an abstract form of estranged man) as the *measuring-rod* of the estranged world. The whole *history of the alienation-process* and the whole *process of the retraction* of the alienation is therefore nothing but the *history of the production* of abstract (i.e., absolute) thought—of logical, speculative thought. The *estrangement*, which therefore forms the real interest of this alienation and of the transcendence of this alienation, is the opposition of *in itself* and *for itself*,[11] of *consciousness* and *self-consciousness*, of *object* and *subject*—that is to say, it is the opposition, within thought itself, between abstract thinking and sensuous reality or real sensuousness. All other oppositions and movements of these oppositions are but the *semblance, the cloak, the exoteric* shape of these oppositions which alone matter, and which constitute the *meaning* of these other, profane oppositions. It is not the fact that the human being *objectifies himself inhumanly*, in opposition to himself, but the fact that he *objectifies himself* in *distinction* from and in *opposition* to abstract thinking, that is the posited essence of the estrangement and the thing to be superseded.

The appropriation of man's essential powers, which have become objects—indeed, alien objects—is thus in the *first place* only an *appropriation* occurring in *consciousness*, in *pure thought* —i.e., in *abstraction*: it is the appropriation of these objects as *thoughts* and as *movements of thought*. Consequently, despite its thoroughly negative and critical appearance and despite the criticism really contained in it, which often anticipates far later development, there is already latent in the *Phenomenology* as a germ, a potentiality, a secret, the uncritical positivism and the equally uncritical idealism of Hegel's later works—that philosophic dissolution and restoration of the existing empirical world. In the *second place*: the vindication of the objective world for man—for example, the realization that *sensuous* consciousness is not an *abstractly* sensuous consciousness but a *humanly* sensuous consciousness—that religion, wealth, etc., are but the estranged world of *human* objectification, of *man's* essential powers given over to work and that they are therefore but the *path* to the true *human* world—this appropriation or the insight into this process consequently appears in Hegel in this form, that *sense, religion, state-power, etc.*, are *spiritual* entities; for only *mind* is the *true* essence of man, and the true form of mind is thinking mind, the logical, speculative mind. The *humanness* of nature and of the nature begotten by history—the humanness of man's products—appears in the form that they are *products* of abstract mind and as such, therefore, phases of *mind—thought entities*. The *Phenomenology* is, therefore, an occult critique— still to itself obscure and mystifying criticism; but inasmuch as it keeps steadily in view man's *estrangement*, even though man appears only in the shape of mind, there lie concealed in it *all* the elements of criticism, already *prepared* and *elaborated* in a manner often rising far above the Hegelian standpoint. The "Unhappy Consciousness," the "Honest Consciousness," the struggle of the "Noble and Base Consciousness,"[12] etc., etc.,— these separate sections contain, but still in an estranged form, the *critical* elements of whole spheres such as religion, the state, civil life, etc. Just as *entities, objects,* appear as *thought-entities*, so the *subject* is always *consciousness* or *self-consciousness*; or rather the object appears only as *abstract* consciousness, man only as *self-consciousness*: the distinct forms of estrangement which make their appearance are, therefore, only various forms of consciousness and self-consciousness. Just as *in itself* abstract consciousness (the form in which the object is conceived) is merely a moment of distinction of self-consciousness, what appears as the result of the movement is the identity of self-consciousness with consciousness—absolute knowledge—the movement of abstract thought no longer directed outwards but going on now only within its own self: that is to say, the dialectic of pure thought is the result.

The outstanding thing in Hegel's *Phenomenology* and its final outcome—that is, the dialectic of negativity as the moving and generating principle—is thus first that Hegel conceives the self-genesis of man as a process, conceives objectification as loss of the object, as alienation and as transcendence of this alienation; that he thus grasps the essence of *labor* and comprehends objective man—true, because real man—as the outcome of man's *own labor*. The *real*, active orientation of man to himself as a species being, or his manifestation as a real species being (i.e., as a human being), is only possible by his really bringing out of himself all the *powers* that are his as the *species* man— something which in turn is only possible through the totality of man's actions, as the result of history—is only possible by man's treating these generic powers as objects: and this, to begin with, is again only possible in the form of estrangement.

We shall now demonstrate in detail Hegel's one-sidedness and limitations as they are displayed in the final chapter of the *Phenomenology*, "Absolute Knowledge"—a chapter which contains the concentrated spirit of the *Phenomenology*, the relationship of the *Phenomenology* to speculative dialectic, and also Hegel's *consciousness* concerning both and their relationship to one another.

Let us provisionally say just this much in advance: Hegel's standpoint is that of modern political economy. He grasps *labor* as the *essence* of man—as man's essence in the act of proving itself: he sees only the positive, not the negative side of labor. Labor is man's *coming-to-be for himself* within *alienation*, or as *alienated* man. The only labor which Hegel knows and recognizes is *abstractly mental* labor. Therefore, that which constitutes the *essence* of philosophy—the *alienation of man in his knowing of himself*, or *alienated* science *thinking itself*— Hegel grasps as its essence; and he is therefore able *vis-à-vis* preceding philosophy to gather its separate elements and phases, and to present his philosophy as *the* philosophy. What the other philosophers did—that they grasped separate phases of nature and of human life as phases of self-consciousness, and indeed of abstract self-consciousness—is *known* to Hegel as the *doings* of philosophy. Hence his science is absolute.

Let us now turn to our subject.

Absolute Knowledge. The last chapter of the "Phenomenology."

The main point is that the *object of consciousness* is nothing else but *self-consciousness*, or that the object is only *objectified self-consciousness*—self-consciousness as object.

(Positing of man = self-consciousness.)

The issue, therefore, is to surmount the *object of consciousness*. Objectivity as such is regarded as an *estranged* human relationship which does not correspond to the *essence of man*, to self-consciousness. The *re-appropriation* of the objective essence of man, begotten in the form of estrangement as something alien, has the meaning therefore not only to annul *estrangement*, but *objectivity* as well. Man, that is to say, is regarded as a *non-objective, spiritual* being.

The movement of *surmounting the object of consciousness* is now described by Hegel in the following way:

The *object* reveals itself not merely as *returning into the self*—for Hegel that is the *one-sided* way of apprehending this movement, the grasping of only one side. Man is posited as equivalent to self. The self, however, is only the *abstractly* conceived man—man begotten by abstraction. Man *is* egotistic. His eye, his ear, etc., are *egotistic*. In him every one of his essential powers has the quality of *selfhood*. But it is quite false to say on that account "*Self-consciousness* has eyes, ears, essential powers." Self-consciousness is rather a quality of human nature, of the human eye, etc.; it is not human nature that is a quality of *self-consciousness*.

The self-abstracted and fixed for itself is man as *abstract egoist*—egoism raised in its pure abstraction to the level of thought. (We shall return to this point later.)

For Hegel the *essence of man—man*—equals *self-consciousness*. All estrangement of the human essence is therefore *nothing but estrangement of self-consciousness*. The estrangement of self-consciousness is not regarded as an *expression* of the *real* estrangement of the human being—its expression reflected in the realm of knowledge and thought. Instead, the *real* estrangement—that which appears *real*—is from its *innermost*, hidden nature (a nature only brought to light by philosophy) nothing but the *manifestation* of the estrangement of the real essence of man, of *self-consciousness*. The science which comprehends this is therefore called *Phenomenology*. All re-appropriation of the estranged objective essence appears, therefore, as a process of incorporation into self-consciousness: The man who takes hold of his essential being is *merely* the self-consciousness which takes hold of objective essences. Return of the object into the self is therefore the re-appropriation of the object.

The *surmounting of the object of consciousness, comprehensively* expressed, means:13.

(1) That the object as such presents itself to consciousness as something vanishing. (2) That it is the alienation of self-consciousness which establishes thinghood. (3) That this externalization[14] of self-consciousness has not merely a *negative* but a *positive* significance. (4) That it has this meaning not merely *for us* or *intrinsically*, but *for self-consciousness itself*. (5) For *self-consciousness*, the negative of the object, its annulling of itself, has *positive* significance—self-consciousness *knows* this nullity of the object—because self-consciousness itself alienates itself; for in this alienation it establishes *itself* as object, or, for the sake of the indivisible unity of *being-for-self*, establishes the object as itself. (6) On the other hand, there is also this other moment in the process, that self-consciousness has also just as much annulled and superseded this alienation and objectivity and resumed them into itself, being thus at home with *itself* in *its* other-being *as such*. (7) This is the movement of *consciousness* and in this movement consciousness is the totality of its moments. (8) Consciousness must similarly have taken up a relation to the object in all its aspects and phases, and have comprehended it from the point of view of each of them. This totality of its determinate characteristics makes the object *intrinsically a spiritual being*; and it becomes so in truth for consciousness through the apprehending of each single one of them as *self* or through what was called above the *spiritual* attitude to them.

As to (1): That the object as such presents itself to consciousness as something vanishing—this is the above-mentioned *return of the object into the self*.

As to (2): The *alienation of self-consciousness* establishes *thinghood*. Because man equals self-consciousness, his alienated, objective essence, or *thinghood*, equals *alienated self-consciousness*, and *thinghood* is thus established through this alienation (thinghood being *that* which is an *object for man* and an object for him is really only that which is to him an essential object, therefore his *objective* essence. And since it is not *real* Man, nor therefore *Nature*—Man being *human*

Nature— who as such is made the subject, but only the abstraction of man—self-consciousness—thinghood cannot be anything but alienated self-consciousness.). It is only to be expected that a living, natural being equipped and endowed with objective (i.e., material) essential powers should have *real natural objects* of his essence; as is the fact that his self-alienation should lead to the establishing of a *real*, objective world—but a world in the form of *externality*—a world, therefore, not belonging to his own essential being, and an overpowering world. There is nothing incomprehensible or mysterious in this. It would be mysterious, rather, if it were otherwise. But it is equally clear that a *self-consciousness*—can only establish *thinghood* through its alienation—i.e., establish something which itself is only an abstract thing, a thing of abstraction and not a *real* thing. It is clear, further, that thinghood is therefore utterly without any *independence*, any *essentiality vis-à-vis* self-consciousness; that on the contrary it is a mere creature—something *posited* by self-consciousness. And what is posited, instead of confirming itself, is but a confirmation of the act of positing in which is concentrated for a moment the energy of the act as its product, *seeming* to give the de-posit—but only for a moment—the character of an independent, real substance.[15]

Whenever real, corporeal *man*, man with his feet firmly on the solid ground, man exhaling and inhaling all the forces of nature, *establishes* his real, objective *essential powers* as alien objects by his externalization, it is not the *act of positing* which is the subject in this process: it is the subjectivity of *objective* essential powers, whose action, therefore, must also be something *objective*. A being who is objective acts objectively, and he would not act objectively if the objective did not reside in the very nature of his being. He creates or establishes only *objects*, *because* he is established by objects—because at bottom he is *nature*. In the act of establishing, therefore, this objective being does not fall from his state of "pure activity" into a *creating of the object*; on the contrary, his *objective* product only confirms his *objective* activity, establishing his activity as the activity of an objective, natural being.

Here we see how consistent naturalism or humanism distinguishes itself both from idealism and materialism, constituting at the same time the unifying truth of both. We see also how only naturalism is capable of comprehending the act of world history.

Man is directly a *natural being*. As a natural being and as a living natural being he is on the one hand furnished with *natural powers of life*—he is an *active* natural being. These forces exist in him as tendencies and abilities—as *impulses*. On the other hand, as a natural, corporeal, sensuous, objective being he is a *suffering*, conditioned and limited creature, like animals and plants. That is to say, the *objects* of his impulses exist outside him, as *objects* independent of him; yet these objects are *objects* of his *need*—essential *objects*, indispensable to the manifestation and confirmation of his essential powers. To say that man is a *corporeal*, living, real, sensuous, objective being full of natural vigor is to say that he has *real*, *sensuous*, *objects* as the objects of his being or of his life, or that he can only *express* his life in real, sensuous objects. To be objective, natural and sensuous, and at the same time to have object, nature and sense outside oneself, or oneself to be object, nature and sense for a third party, is one and the same thing. *Hunger* is a natural *need*; it therefore needs a *nature* outside itself, an *object* outside itself, in order to satisfy itself, to be stilled. Hunger is an acknowledged need of my body for an *object* existing outside it, indispensable to its integration and to the expression of its essential being. The sun is the *object* of the plant—an indispensable object to it, confirming its life—just as the plant is an object of the sun, being an *expression* of the life-awakening power of the sun, of the sun's *objective* essential power.

A being which does not have its nature outside itself is not a *natural* being, and plays no part in the system of nature. A being which has no object outside itself is not an objective being. A being which is not itself an object for some third being has no being for its *object*; i.e., it is not objectively related. Its be-ing is not objective.[16]

An unobjective being is a *nullity*—an *un-being*.

Suppose a being which is neither an object itself, nor has an object. Such a being, in the first place, would be the *unique* being: there would exist no being outside it—it would exist solitary and alone. For as soon as there are objects outside me, as soon as I am not *alone*, I am *another*—*another reality* than the object outside me. For this third object I am thus an *other reality* than it; that is, I am *its* object. Thus, to suppose a being which is not the object of another being is to presuppose that *no* objective being exists. As soon as I have an object, this object has me for an object. But a *non-objective* being is an unreal, nonsensical thing—something merely thought of (merely imagined, that is)—a creature of abstraction. To be *sensuous*, that is, to be an object of sense, to be a *sensuous* object, and thus to have sensuous objects outside oneself—objects of one's sensuousness. To be sensuous is to *suffer*.[17]

Man as an objective, sensuous being is therefore a *suffering* being—and because he feels what he suffers, *a passionate* being. Passion is the essential force of man energetically bent on its object.

But man is not merely a natural being: he is a *human* natural being. That is to say, he is a being for himself. Therefore he is a *species being*, and has to confirm and manifest himself as such both in his being and in his knowing. Therefore, *human* objects are not natural objects as they immediately present themselves, and neither is *human sense* as it immediately is—as it is objectively—*human* sensibility, human objectivity. Neither nature objectively nor nature subjectively is directly given in a form adequate to the *human* being. And as everything natural has to have its *beginning, man* too has his act of coming-to-be—*history*—which, however, is for him a known history, and hence as an act of coming-to-be it is a conscious self-transcending act of coming-to-be. History is the true natural history of man (on which more later).

Thirdly, because this establishing of thinghood is itself only a sham, an act contradicting the nature of pure activity, it has to be cancelled again and thinghood denied.

Re. 3, 4, 5 and 6. (3) This externalization of consciousness has not merely a *negative* but a *positive* significance, and (4) it has this meaning not merely *for us* or intrinsically, but for consciousness itself.[18] (5) *For consciousness* the negative of the object, its annulling of itself, has *positive* significance—consciousness *knows* this nullity of the object because it alienates *itself*; for in this alienation it knows itself as object, or, for the sake of the indivisible unity of *being-for-itself* the object as itself. (6) On the other hand, there is also this other moment in the process, that consciousness has also just as much annulled and superseded this alienation and objectivity and resumed them into itself, being thus *at home with itself* in its *other-being as such.*

As we have already seen: the appropriation of what is estranged and objective, or the annulling of objectivity in the form of *estrangement* (which has to advance from indifferent foreignness to real, antagonistic estrangement) means equally or even primarily for Hegel that it is *objectivity* which is to be annulled, because it is not the *determinate* character of the object, but rather its *objective* character that is offensive and constitutes estrangement for self-consciousness. The object is therefore something negative, self-annulling—a *nullity.* This nullity of the object has not only a negative but *a positive* meaning for consciousness, for such a *nullity* of the object is precisely the *self-confirmation* of the non-objectivity, of the *abstraction* of itself. For *consciousness itself* this nullity of the object has a positive meaning because it *knows* this nullity, the objective being, as its *self-alienation;* because it knows that it exists only as a result of its own *self-alienation....*

The way in which consciousness is, and in which something is for it, is *knowing.* Knowing is its sole act. Something therefore comes to be for consciousness insofar as the latter *knows* this *something.* Knowing is its sole objective relation. Consciousness, then, knows the nullity of the object (i.e., knows the non-existence of the distinction between the object and itself, the non-existence of the object for it) because it knows the object as its *self-alienation;* that is, it knows itself—knows knowing as the object— because the object is only the *semblance* of an object, a piece of mystification, which in its essence, however, is nothing else but knowing itself, which has confronted itself with itself and in so doing has confronted itself with a *nullity*—a something which has *no* objectivity outside the knowing. Or: knowing knows that in relating itself to an object it is only *outside* itself—that it only externalizes itself; that *it itself appears* to itself only as *an object*—or that that which appears to it as an object is only it itself.

On the other hand, says Hegel, there is at the same time this other moment in this process, that consciousness has just as much annulled and superseded this externalization and objectivity and resumed them into itself, being thus *at home* in its *other-being as such*.

In this discussion are brought together all the illusions of speculation.

First of all; consciousness—self-consciousness—is *at home with itself in its other-being as such*. It is therefore—or if we here abstract from the Hegelian abstraction and put the self-consciousness of man instead of Self-consciousness—*it is at home with itself in its other-being as such*. This implies, for one thing that consciousness (knowing as knowing, thinking as thinking) pretends to be directly the *other* of itself—to be the world of sense, the real world, life—thought over-reaching itself in thought (Feuerbach).[19] This aspect is contained herein, inasmuch as consciousness as mere consciousness takes offense not at estranged objectivity, but at *objectivity as such*.

Secondly, this implies that self-conscious man, insofar as he has recognized and annulled and superseded the spiritual world (or his world's spiritual, general mode of being) as self-alienation, nevertheless again confirms this in its alienated shape and passes it off as his true mode of being—re-establishes it, and pretends to be *at home in his other-being as such*. Thus, for instance, after annulling and superseding religion, after recognizing religion to be a product of self-alienation, he yet finds confirmation of himself in *religion as religion*. Here is the root of Hegel's *false* positivism, or of his merely *apparent* criticism: this is what Feuerbach designated as the positing, negating and re-establishing of religion or theology—but it has to be grasped in more general terms. Thus reason is at home in unreason as unreason. The man who has recognized that he is leading an alienated life in politics, law, etc., is leading his true human life in this alienated life as such. Self-affirmation, *in contradiction* with itself—in contradiction both with the knowledge of and with the essential being of the object—is thus true *knowledge* and *life*.

There can therefore no longer be any question about an act of accommodation of Hegel's part *vis-à-vis* religion, the state, etc., since this lie is *the* lie of his principle.

If I *know* religion as *alienated* human self-consciousness, then what I know in it as religion is not my self-consciousness, but my alienated self-consciousness confirmed in it. I therefore know my own self, the self-consciousness that belongs to its very nature, confirmed not in *religion* but rather in *annihilated* and *superseded* religion.

In Hegel, therefore, the negation of the negation is not the confirmation of the true essence, effected precisely through negation of the pseudo-essence. With him the negation of the negation is the confirmation of the pseudo-essence, or of the self-estranged essence in its denial; or it is the denial of this pseudo-essence as an objective being dwelling outside man and independent of him, and its transformation into the subject.

A peculiar role, therefore, is played by the act of *superseding* in which denial and preservation—denial and affirmation—are bound together.

Thus, for example, in Hegel's *Philosophy of Right*, *Private Right* superseded equals *Morality*, Morality superseded equals the *Family*, the Family superseded equals *Civil Society*, Civil Society superseded equals the *State*, the State superseded equals *World History*. In the *actual world* private right, morality, the family, civil society, the state, etc., remain in existence, only they have become *moments* of man—state of his existence and being— which have no validity in isolation, but dissolve and engender one another, etc. They have become *moments of motion*.

In their actual existence this *mobile* nature of theirs is hidden. It first appears and is made manifest in thought, in philosophy. Hence my true religious existence is my existence in the *philosophy of religion*; my true political existence is my existence within the *philosophy of right*; my true natural existence, existence in the *philosophy of nature*; my true artistic existence, existence in the *philosophy of art*; my true *human* existence, my existence in *philosophy*. Likewise the true existence of religion, the state, nature, art, is the *philosophy* of religion, of nature, of the state and of art. If, however, the philosophy of religion, etc., is for me the sole true existence of religion, then, too, it is only as a *philosopher of religion* that I am truly religious, and so I deny *real* religious sentiment and the really *religious* man. But at the same time I *assert* them, in part within my own existence or within the alien existence which I oppose to them—for this *is* only their *philosophic* expression—and in part I assert them in their own original shape, for they have validity for me as merely the *apparent* other-being, as allegories, forms of their own true existence (i.e., of my *philosophical* existence) hidden under sensuous disguises.

In just the same way, *Quality* superseded equals *Quantity*, Quantity superseded equals *Measure*, Measure superseded equals *Essence*, Essence superseded equals *Appearance*, Appearance superseded equals *Actuality*, Actuality superseded equals the *Concept*, the Concept superseded equals *Objectivity*, Objectivity superseded equals the *Absolute Idea*, the Absolute Idea superseded equals *Nature*, Nature superseded equals *Subjective* Mind, Subjective Mind superseded equals *Ethical* Objective Mind, Ethical Mind superseded equals *Art*, Art superseded equals *Religion*, Religion superseded equals *Absolute Knowledge.*20

On the one hand, this act of superseding is a transcending of the thought entity; thus, Private Property as *a thought* is transcended in the *thought* of morality. And because thought imagines itself to be directly the other of itself, to be *sensuous reality*—and therefore takes its own action for *sensuous, real action*—this superseding in thought, which leaves its object standing in the real world, believes that it has really overcome it. On the other hand, because the object has now become for it a moment of thought, thought takes it in its reality too to be self-confirmation of itself—of self-consciousness, of abstraction.

From the one point of view the existent which Hegel *supersedes* in philosophy is therefore not *real* religion, the *real* state, or *real* nature, but religion itself already become an object of knowledge, i.e., *Dogmatics*; the same with *Jurisprudence*, *Political Science* and *Natural Science*. From the one point of view, therefore, he stands in opposition both to the *real* thing and to immediate, unphilosophic *science* or the unphilosophic *conceptions* of this thing. He therefore contradicts their conventional conceptions.[21]

On the other hand, the religious man, etc., can find in Hegel his final confirmation.

It is now time to lay hold of the *positive* aspects of the Hegelian dialectic within the realm of estrangement.

(a) *Annulling* as an objective movement of *retracting* the alienation *into self*. This is the insight, expressed within the estrangement, concerning the *appropriation* of the objective essence through the annulment of its estrangement; it is the estranged insight into the *real objectification* of man, into the real appropriation of his objective essence through the annihilation of the *estranged* character of the objective world, through the annulment of the objective world in its estranged mode of being—just as atheism, being the annulment of God, is the advent of theoretic humanism, and communism, as the annulment of private property, is the justification of real human life as man's possession and thus the advent of practical humanism (or just as atheism is humanism mediated with itself through the annulment of religion, while communism is humanism mediated with itself through the annulment of private property). Only through the annulment of this mediation—which is itself, however, a necessary premise—does positively self-deriving humanism, *positive humanism*, come into being.

But atheism and communism are no flight, no abstraction; they are not a losing of the objective world begotten by man— of man's essential powers given over to the realm of objectivity; they are not a returning in poverty to unnatural, primitive simplicity. On the contrary, they are but the first real coming-to-be, the realization become real for man, of man's essence— of the essence of man as something real.

Thus, by grasping the *positive* meaning of self-referred negation (if even again in estranged fashion) Hegel grasps man's self-estrangement, the alienation of man's essence, man's loss of objectivity and his loss of realness as finding of self, change of his nature, his objectification and realization. In short, within the sphere of abstraction, Hegel conceives labor as man's act of *self-genesis*—conceives man's relation to himself as an alien being and the manifesting of himself as an alien being to be the coming-to-be of *species-consciousness* and *species-life*.

(b) However, apart from, or rather in consequence of, the perverseness already described, this act appears in Hegel:

First of all as *a merely formal,* because abstract, act, because the human essence itself is taken to be only an *abstract, thinking essence,* conceived merely as self-consciousness. And,

secondly, because the conception is *formal* and *abstract,* the annulment of the alienation becomes a confirmation of the alienation; or again, for Hegel this movement of *self-genesis* and *self-objectification* in the form of *self-alienation* and *self-estrangement* is the *absolute,* and hence final, *expression of human life*—of life with itself as its aim, of life at rest in itself, of life that has attained oneness with its essence.

This movement, in its abstract form as dialectic, is therefore regarded as *truly human life,* and because it is nevertheless an abstraction—an estrangement of human life—it is regarded as a *divine process,* but as the divine process of man, a process traversed by man's abstract, pure, absolute essence that is distinct from him.

Thirdly, this process must have a bearer, a subject. But the subject first emerges as a result. This result—the subject knowing itself as absolute self-consciousness—is therefore God— *absolute Spirit—the self-knowing and self-manifesting Idea.* Real man and real nature become mere predicates—symbols of this esoteric, unreal man and of this unreal nature. Subject and predicate are therefore related to each other in absolute inversion— a *mystical subject-object* or a *subjectivity reaching beyond the object—the absolute subject* as a *process,* as subject *alienating* itself and returning from alienation into itself, but at the same time retracting this alienation into itself, and the subject as this process; a pure, *restless* revolving within itself.

First, the *formal and abstract* conception of man's act of self-genesis or self-objectification.

Hegel having posited man as equivalent to self-consciousness, the estranged object—the estranged essential reality of man— is nothing but *consciousness,* the thought of estrangement merely —estrangement's *abstract* and therefore empty and unreal expression, *negation*. The annulment of the alienation is therefore likewise nothing but an abstract, empty annulment of that empty abstraction—the *negation of the negation*. The rich, living, sensuous, concrete activity of self-objectification is therefore reduced to its mere abstraction, *absolute negativity*—an abstraction which is again fixed as such and thought of as an independent activity— as sheer activity. Because this so-called negativity is nothing but the *abstract, empty* form of that real living act, its content can in consequence be merely *a formal* content begotten by abstraction from all content. As a result there are general, abstract *forms of abstraction* pertaining to every content and on that account indifferent to, and, consequently, valid for, all content— the thought-forms or logical categories torn from *real* mind and from *real* nature. (We shall unfold the *logical* content of absolute negativity further on.)

Hegel's positive achievement here, in his speculative logic, is that the *determinate concepts*, the universal *fixed thought-forms* in their independence vis-à-vis nature and mind are a necessary result of the general estrangement of the human essence and therefore also of human thought, and that Hegel has therefore brought these together and presented them as moments of the abstraction-process. For example, superseded Being is Essence, superseded Essence is Concept, the Concept superseded is ... the Absolute Idea. But what, then, is the Absolute Idea? It supersedes its own self again, if it does not want to traverse once more from the beginning the whole act of abstraction, and to acquiesce in being a totality of abstractions or in being the self-comprehending abstraction. But abstraction comprehending itself as abstraction knows itself to be nothing: it must abandon itself— abandon abstraction—and so it arrives at an entity which is its exact contrary—at *nature*. Thus, the entire *Logic* is the demonstration that abstract thought is nothing in itself; that the Absolute Idea is nothing in itself; that only *Nature* is something.

The absolute idea, the *abstract* idea, which "*considered* with regard to its unity with itself is *intuiting*"[22] (Hegel's *Encyclopaedia*, 3rd edition, p. 222), and which "in its own absolute truth *resolves* to let the moment of its particularity or of initial characterization and other-being—the *immediate idea*, as its reflection, *go forth freely from itself as nature*" (l.c.)—this whole idea which behaves in such a strange and singular way, and which has given the Hegelians such terrible headaches, is from beginning to end nothing else but *abstraction* (i.e., the abstract thinker)— abstraction which, made wise by experience and enlightened concerning its truth, resolves under various (false and themselves still abstract) conditions to *abandon itself* and to replace its self-absorption, nothingness, generality and indeterminateness by its other-being, the particular, and the determinate; resolves to let *nature*, which it held hidden in itself only as an abstraction, as a thought-entity, *go forth freely from itself*: that is to say, abstraction resolves to forsake abstraction and to have a look at nature *free* of abstraction. The abstract idea, which without mediation becomes *intuiting,* is nothing else through-and-through but abstract thinking that gives itself up and resolves on *intuition.* This entire translation from Logic to Natural Philosophy is nothing else but the transition—so difficult to effect for the abstract thinker and therefore so queer in his description of it—from *abstracting* to *intuiting.* The *mystical* feeling which drives the philosopher forward from abstract thinking to intuiting is *boredom*—the longing for a content.

(The man estranged from himself is also the thinker estranged from his *essence*—that is, from the natural and human essence. His thoughts are therefore fixed mental shapes or ghosts dwelling outside nature and man. Hegel has locked up all these fixed mental forms together in his *Logic,* laying hold of them first as negation—that is, as an *alienation of human* thought—and then as negation of the negation—that is, as a superseding of this alienation, as a *real* expression of human thought. But as even this still takes place within the confines of the estrangement, this negation of the negation is in part the restoring of these fixed forms in their estrangement; in part a stopping-short at the last act—the act of self-reference in alienation—as the true mode of being of these fixed mental forms;[23] and in part, to the extent that this abstraction apprehends itself and experiences an infinite weariness with itself, there makes its appearance in Hegel, in the form of the resolution to recognize *nature* as the essential being and to go over to intuition, the abandonment of abstract thought—the abandonment of thought revolving solely within the orbit of thought, of thought devoid of eyes, of teeth, of ears, of everything.)

But *nature* too, taken abstractly, for itself—nature fixed in isolation from man—is *nothing* for man. It goes without saying that the abstract thinker who has committed himself to intuiting, intuits nature abstractly. Just as nature lay enclosed in the thinker in the form of the absolute idea, in the form of a thought-entity—in a shape which is his and yet is esoteric and mysterious even to him—so what he has let go forth from himself in truth is only this *abstract nature,* only nature as a *thought-entity*— but with the significance now of being the other-being of thought, of being real, intuited nature—of being nature distinguished from abstract thought. Or, to talk a human language, the abstract thinker learns in his intuition of nature that the entities which he thought to create from nothing, from pure abstraction—the entities he believed he was producing in the divine dialectic as pure products of the labor of thought forever weaving in itself and never looking outward—are nothing else but *abstractions* from *characteristics of nature.* To him, therefore, the whole of nature merely repeats the logical abstractions in a sensuous, external form. He *analyzes* it and these abstractions over again. Thus, his intuition of nature is only the act of confirming his abstraction from the intuition of nature—is only the conscious repetition by him of the process of begetting his abstraction. Thus, for example, Time equals Negativity referred to itself (l.c, p. 238): to the superseded Becoming as Being there corresponds, in natural form, superseded Movement as Matter. Light is *Reflection-in-Itself*, in *natural* form. Body as *Moon* and *Comet* is the *natural* form of the *antithesis* which according to the *Logic* is on the one side the *Positive resting on itself* and on the other side the *Negative* resting on itself. The Earth is the *natural* form of the logical *Ground*, as the negative unity of the antithesis, etc.[24]

Nature as nature—that is to say, insofar as it is still sensuously distinguished from that secret sense hidden within it—nature isolated, distinguished from these abstractions, is *nothing*—a nothing *proving itself to be nothing*—is *devoid of sense*, or has only the sense of being an externality which has to be annulled.

"In the *finite-theological* position is to be found the correct premise that nature does not contain within itself the absolute purpose" (p. 225).

Its purpose is the confirmation of abstraction.

"Nature has shown itself to be the Idea in the *form* of *other-being*. Since the *Idea* is in this form the negative of itself or *external to itself*, nature is not just relatively external *vis-à-vis* this idea, but *externality* constitutes the form in which it exists as nature" (p. 227).

Externality here is not to be understood as the *self-externalizing world of sense* open to the light, open to the man endowed with senses. It is to be taken here in the sense of alienation— a mistake, a defect, which ought not to be. For what is true is still the Idea. Nature is only the *form of the Idea's other-being.* And since abstract thought is the *essence*, that which is external to it is by its essence something merely *external.* The abstract thinker recognizes at the same time that *sensuousness—externality* in contrast to thought weaving *within itself*— is the essence of nature. But he expresses this contrast in such a way as to make this *externality of nature*, its *contrast* to thought, its *defect*, so that inasmuch as it is distinguished from abstraction, nature is something defective. Something which is defective not merely for me or in my eyes but in itself—intrinsically—has something outside itself which it lacks. That is, its being is something other than it itself. Nature has therefore to supersede itself for the abstract thinker, for it is already posited by him as a potentially *superseded* being.

"For us. Mind has *nature* for its *premise,* being nature's *truth* and for that reason its *absolute prius.* In this truth nature *has vanished,* and mind has resulted as the Idea arrived at being-for-itself, the *object* of which, as well as the *subject,* is the *concept.* This identity is *absolute negativity,* for whereas in nature the concept has its perfect external objectivity, this its alienation has been superseded, and in this alienation the concept has become identical with itself. But it is this identity, therefore, only in being a return out of nature" (p. 392).

"As the *abstract* idea, *revelation* is unmediated transition to, the *coming-to-be* of, nature; as the revelation of the mind, which is free, it is the *establishing* of nature as the *mind's* world—an establishing which at the same time, being reflection, is a *presupposing* of the world as independently-existing nature. Revelation in conception is the creation of nature as the mind's being, in which the mind procures the *affirmation* and the *truth* of its freedom."[25] *"The absolute is mind.* This is the highest definition of the absolute."

Footnotes

[1. Reference is made to the concluding portion of the part which directly precedes these words and which (because the chapter about Hegel, which Marx qualified in the "Introduction" as the "final chapter," has been put at the end of the volume) is given above under the editor's heading "Private Property and Communism. Various Stages of Development of Communist Views. Crude, Equalitarian Communism and Communism as Socialism Coinciding with Humaneness."—Ed.]

[2. *System der Wissenschaft.* von G. W. F. Hegel. Erste Teil: *Phänomenologie des Geistes.* Bamberg und Nuernberg, 1807. *Wissenschaft der Logik,* 2 Bande, 1812-16. English translations: *The Phenomenology of Mind,* by G. W. F. Hegel, Translated with an Introduction and Notes by J. B. Baillie, 2nd Edition, 1931, reprinted 1949 (London): *The Science of Logic,* by G. W. F. Hegel, Translated by Johnston and Struthers, in 2 vols., (Cambridge, 1929).—Ed.]

[3. Bruno Bauer, *Kritik der evangelischen Geschichte der Synoptiker (Critique of the Synoptic Gospels),* Band 1-2, Leipzig, 1841; Band 3, Braunschweig, 1842. In religious literature the authors of the first three Gospels are known as the Synoptics.—Ed.]

[4. *Das Entdeckte Christentum. Eine Erinnerung des Achtzehnten Jahrhundert und eine Beitrag zur Krisis des Neunzehnten. (Christianity Discovered: A Memorial of the Eighteenth Century and a Contribution to the Crisis of the Nineteenth),* von Bruno Bauer. Zürich und Winterthur, 1843.]

[5. *Die Gute Sache der Freiheit und meine Eigene Angelegenheit (The Good of Freedom and My Own Affair),* von Bruno Bauer, Zürich und Winterthur, 1842.— Ed.]

[6. Certificate of poverty.—Ed.]

[7. Reference is made to the *Allgemeine Literatur-Zeitung.*—Ed.]

[8. Feuerbach views negation of negation, the definite concept, as thinking surpassing itself in thinking and as thinking wanting to be directly awareness, nature, reality. (Reference is here made by Marx to Feuerbach's critical observations about Hegel in §§29-30 of his *Grundsätze der Philosophie der Zukunfl.)*—Ed.]

[9. What follows here are the main chapter and section-headings of Hegel's *Phenomenology of Mind.* Here and in later quotations from the *Phenomenology,* the translator has followed Baillie's translation very closely, departing from it only on the few occasions where this was necessary to keep the terminology in line with that used throughout the present volume.—Ed.]

[10. *Enzyklopädie der Philosophischen Wissenschafien.* von G. W. F. Hegel (Heidelberg, 1st edition, 1817, 3rd edition, 1830). Hegel's *Encyclopaedia of the Philosophical Sciences* is a single volume falling into three main parts: the subject of the first is Logic (cf. *The Logic of Hegel*, translated by William Wallace, 2nd edition, Oxford, 1892); the subject of the second part is the philosophy of nature (of which no English translation has been published), and that of the third the Philosophy of Mind. (Cf. Hegel's *Philosophy of Mind*, translated by William Wallace, Oxford, 1894.)—Ed.]

[11. See footnote on page 93.—Ed.]

[12. "The unhappy consciousness," etc.—Forms of mind, and phases and factors in human history, distinguished and analyzed in particular sections of Hegel's *Phenomenology.—Ed.*]

[13. The paragraph which follows is a transcript of the second and third paragraphs of the last chapter of Hegel's *Phenomenology* (Baillie's translation, 2nd edition, p. 789).— Ed.]

[14. Externalization—*Entäusserung.* See "Translator's Note on Terminology."—Ed.]

[15. Substance— *Wesen.*— Ed.]

[16. Being—*Wesen;* nature—*Nature;* system—*Wesen;* be-ing—*Sein.* See *Wesen* in "Translator's Note on Terminology."—Ed.]

[17. To be sensuous is to suffer—*Sinnlkh sein ist leidendsein.* Here "to suffer" should probably be understood in the sense of "to undergo"—to be the object of another's action. Note the transition in the next sentence from *Leiden* (suffering) to *leidenschaftlich* (passionate).—Ed.]

[18. Here Marx has taken the impersonal pronoun es (it) to represent *Bewusstsein* (consciousness); but it seems that Baillie is more correct in reading this as standing for *Selbstbewusstsein* (self-consciousness). In the first quotation of this passage (cf. p. 154) Marx simply uses es without specifying what it represents, and the translation has followed Baillie in interpreting it as "self-consciousness." In the present repetition of the passage, Marx's specification of the "it" as "consciousness," has been followed in the translation.—Ed.]

[19. Marx refers to §30 of Feuerbach's Grundsätze der Philosophie der Zukunfl, which says: "Hegel is a thinker who transcends himself in thinking."— Ed.]

[20. This sequence gives the major "categories" or "thought-forms" of Hegel's *Encyclopaedia* in the order in which they occur and are superseded. Similarly, the sequence on p. 159 from "private right" to "world history," gives the major categories of Hegel's *Philosophy of Right,* in the order in which they there appear.—Ed.]

[21. The conventional conception of theology, jurisprudence, political science, natural science, etc.—Ed.]

[22. *The Logic of Hegel,* tr. by Wallace, para. 244. "Intuiting" is here used to render *Anschauen.* In popoular usage *Anschauen* means "to contemplate," but Hegel is here using the word, like Kant, as a technical term in philosophy meaning, roughly, "to be aware through the senses." "Intuiting," likewise, should be understood here not in its popular sense but as the philosophical term which is the recognized English equivalent of *Anschauen.* —Ed.]

[23. This means that what Hegel does is to put in place of these fixed abstractions the act of abstraction which revolves in its own circle. In so doing, he has the merit, in the first place, of having indicated the source of all these inappropriate concepts which, as originally presented, belonged to disparate philosophies: of having brought them together: and of having created the entire compass of abstraction exhaustively set out as the object of criticism, instead of some specific abstraction. (Why Hegel separates thought from the *subject* we shall sec later: at this stage it is already clear, however, that when man is not. his characteristic expression also cannot he human. and so neither could thought he grasped as an expression of man as a human and natural subject endowed with eves. ears. etc.. and living in society, in the world, and in nature.)]

[24. Time, Motion, Matter, Light, etc., are forms distinguished within Hegel's *Philosophy of Nature*. Becoming, etc., are of course categories of the *Logic.—Ed.*]

[25. Cf. Hegel's *Philosophy of Mind.* tr. by Wallace, para. 381. But in rendering these passages from the *Encyclopaedia*, the present translator has not followed Wallace closely.—*Ed.*]

Outlines of a Critique of Political Economy[1]

by Frederick Engels

Political economy came into being as a natural result of the expansion of trade, and with its appearance elementary, unscientific swindling was replaced by a developed system of licensed fraud—a complete get-rich economy.

This political economy or science of enrichment born of the merchants' mutual envy and greed, bears on its brow the mark of the most loathsome selfishness. People still lived in the naive belief that gold and silver were wealth, and considered nothing more urgent than the prohibition everywhere of the export of the "precious" metals. The nations faced each other like misers, each clasping to himself with both arms his precious money-bag, eyeing his neighbors with envy and distrust. Every conceivable means was employed to lure from the nations with whom one had commerce as much ready cash as possible, and to retain snugly within the customs-boundary all which had happily been gathered in.

A rigorously consistent pursuit of this principle would have killed trade. People therefore began to go beyond this first stage. They came to appreciate that capital locked up in a chest was dead capital, while capital in circulation multiplied itself continuously. They then became more philanthropic, sent off their ducats as call-birds to bring others back with them, and recognized that there is no harm in paying A too much for his commodity so long as it can be disposed of to B at a higher price.

On this basis the *mercantile system* was built. The avaricious character of trade was to some extent already beginning to be hidden. The nations drew slightly nearer to one another, concluded trade and friendship agreements, did business with one another and, for the sake of larger profits, treated one another with all possible love and kindness. But basically there was still the old rage for money and selfishness which from time to time erupted in wars, which in that day were all based on trade jealousy. In these wars it also became evident that trade, like robbery, is based on the law of the strong hand. No scruples whatever were felt about exacting by cunning or violence such treaties as were held to be the most advantageous.

The cardinal point in the whole mercantile system is the theory of the balance of trade. Fro as they still subscribed to the dictum that gold and silver were wealth, only such transactions as would finally bring ready cash into the country were considered profitable. To ascertain this, exports were compared with imports. When more had been exported than imported, it was believed that the difference had come into the country in ready cash, and that the country was richer by that difference. The art of the economists, therefore, considered in ensuing that at the end of each year exports should show a favorable balance over imports; and for the sake of this ridiculous illusion thousands of men have been slaughtered! Trade, too, has had its crusades and inquisitions.

The eighteenth century, the century of revolution, also revolutionized economics. But just as all the revolutions of this century were one-sided and bogged down in antitheses—just as abstract materialism was set in opposition to abstract spiritualism, the republic to monarchy, the social contract to divine right—likewise the economic revolution did not get beyond antithesis. The premises remained everywhere in force: materialism did not contend with the Christian contempt for and humiliation of Man, and merely posited Nature instead of the Christian God as the Absolute facing Man. In politics no one dreamed of examining the premises of the State as such. It did not occur to economics to question *the validity of private property*. Therefore, the new economics was only half an advance. It was obliged to betray and to disavow its own premises, to have recourse to sophistry and hypocrisy so as to cover up the contradictions in which it became entangled, so as to reach the conclusions to which it was driven not by its premises but by the humane spirit of the century. Thus economics took on a philanthropic character. It withdrew its favor from the producers and bestowed it on the consumers. It affected a solemn abhorrence of the bloody terror of the mercantile system, and proclaimed trade to be a bond of friendship and union among nations as among individuals. All was pure splendor and magnificence— yet the premises reasserted themselves soon enough, and in contrast to this sham philanthropy produced the Malthusian population theory—the crudest, most barbarous theory that ever existed, a system of despair which struck down all those beautiful phrases about love of neighbor and world citizenship. The premises begot and reared the factory-system and modern slavery, which yields nothing in inhumanity and cruelty to ancient slavery. Modern economics—the system of free trade based on Adam Smith's *Wealth of Nations*—reveals itself to be that same hypocrisy, inconsistency and immorality which now confront free humanity in every sphere.

But was Smith's system, then, not an advance? Of course it was, and a necessary advance at that. It was necessary to overthrow the mercantile system with its monopolies and hindrances to trade, so that the true consequences of private property could come to light. It was necessary for all these petty, local and national considerations to recede into the background, so that the struggle of our time could become a universal human struggle. It was necessary for the theory of private property to leave the purely empirical path of merely objective enquiry and to acquire a more scientific character which would also make it responsible for the consequences, and thus transfer the matter to a universally human sphere. It was necessary to carry the immorality contained in the old economics to its highest pitch, by attempting to deny it and by veiling it in hypocrisy (a necessary result of that attempt). All this lay in the nature of the matter.

We gladly concede that it is only thanks to the establishment and development of free trade that we were placed in a position from which we can go beyond the economics of private property; but we must at the same time have the right to demonstrate the utter theoretical and practical nullity of this free trade.

The nearer to our time the economists whom we have to judge, the more severe must our judgment become. For while Smith and Malthus only had scattered fragments to go by, the modern economists had the whole system complete before them: the consequences had all been drawn; the contradictions came clearly enough to light; yet they did not come to examining the premises—and still undertook, the responsibility for the whole system. The nearer the economists come to the present time, the further they depart from honesty. With every advance of time, sophistry necessarily increases, so as to prevent economics from lagging behind the times. This is why *Ricardo*, for instance, is more guilty than *Adam Smith*, and *MacCullouch* and *Mill* more guilty than *Ricardo*.

Modern economics cannot even judge the mercantile system correctly, since it is itself one-sided and as yet fenced in by that very system's premises. Only that view which rises above the opposition of the two systems, which criticizes the premises common to both and proceeds from a purely human, universal basis, can assign to both their proper position.

It will become evident that the protagonists of free trade are more inveterate monopolists than the old mercantilists themselves. It will become evident that the sham humanity of the modern economists hides a barbarism of which their predecessors knew nothing; that the predecessors' conceptual confusion is simple and consistent compared with the double-tongued logic of their attackers, and that neither of the two can reproach the other with anything which would not recoil upon himself.

This is why modern liberal economics cannot comprehend the restoration of the mercantile system by List,[2] while for us the matter is quite simple. The inconsistency and two-sidedness of liberal economics must of necessity dissolve again into its basic components. Just as theology must either regress to blind faith or progress towards free philosophy, free trade must produce the restoration of monopolies on the one hand and the abolition of private property on the other.

The *only positive* advance which liberal economics has made is the unfolding of the laws of private property. These are contained in it, at any rate, although not yet fully unfolded and clearly expressed. It follows that on all points where it is a question of deciding which is the shortest road to wealth—i.e., in all strictly economic controversies—the protagonists of free trade have right on their side. That is, needless to say, in controversies with the monopolists—not with the opponents of private property, for the English Socialists have long since proved both practically and theoretically that the latter are in a position to settle economic questions more correctly even from an economic point of view.

In the critique of political economy, therefore, we shall examine the basic categories, uncover the contradiction introduced by the free-trade system, and bring out the consequences of both sides of the contradiction. The term "national wealth" has only arisen as a result of the liberal economists' passion for generalization. As long as private property exists, this term has no meaning. The "national wealth" of the English is very great and yet they are the poorest people under the sun. One either dismisses this term completely, or one accepts such premises as give it meaning. Similarly with the terms "national economy" and "political or public economy." In the present circumstances that science ought to be called *private* economy, for its public connections exist only for the sake of private property.

The immediate consequence of private property is *trade*— exchange of reciprocal demand—buying and selling. This trade, like every activity, must under the dominion of private property become a direct source of gain for the trader; i.e., each must seek to sell as dear as possible and buy as cheap as possible. In every purchase and sale, therefore, two men with diametrically opposed interests confront each other. The confrontation is decidedly antagonistic, for each knows the intentions of the other—knows that they are opposed to his own. Therefore, the first consequence is mutual mistrust, on the one hand, and the justification of this mistrust—the application of immoral means to attain an immoral end—on the other. Thus, the first maxim in trade is "discretion"—the concealment of everything which might reduce the value of the article in question. The result is that in trade it is permitted to take the utmost advantage of the ignorance, the trust, of the opposing party, and likewise to bestow qualities on one's commodity which it does not possess. In a word, trade is legalized fraud. Any merchant who wants to give truth its due can bear me witness that actual practice conforms with this theory.

The mercantile system still had a certain artless Catholic candor and did not in the least conceal the immoral nature of trade. We have seen how it openly paraded its mean avarice. The mutually hostile attitude of the nations in the eighteenth century, loathsome envy and trade jealousy, were the logical consequences of trade as such. Public opinion had not yet become humanized. Why, therefore, conceal things which resulted from the inhuman, hostile nature of trade itself?

But when the *economic Luther*, Adam Smith, criticized past economics things had changed considerably. The century had been humanized; reason had asserted itself; morality began to claim its eternal right. The extorted trade treaties, the commercial wars, the surly isolation of the nations, offended too greatly against advanced consciousness. Protestant hypocrisy took the place of Catholic candor. Smith proved that humanity, too, was rooted in the nature of trade; that trade, instead of being "the most fertile source of discord and animosity" must become a "bond of union and friendship among nations as among individuals" (cf. *Wealth of Nations*, Bk. 4, ch. 3, §2); that after all it lay in the nature of things for trade, taken overall, to be profitable to *all* parties concerned.

Smith was right to eulogize trade as humane. There is nothing absolutely immoral in the world. Trade, too, has an aspect wherein it pays homage to morality and humanity. But what homage! The law of the strong hand, the open highway robbery of the Middle Ages, became humanized when it passed over into trade; and trade became humanized when, in its first stage characterized by the prohibition to export money, it passed over into the mercantile system. Now the mercantile system itself was humanized. Naturally, it is in the interest of the trader to be on good terms with the one from whom he buys cheap as well as with the other to whom he sells dear. A nation therefore acts very imprudently if it fosters feelings of animosity in its suppliers and customers. The more friendly, the more profitable. Such is the humanity of trade. And this hypocritical way of misusing morality for immoral purposes is the pride of the free-trade system.

"Have we not overthrown the barbarism of the monopolies?" exclaim the hypocrites. "Have we not carried civilization to distant parts of the world? Have we not brought about the fraternization of the peoples, and reduced the number of wars?" Yes, all this you have done—but *how!* You have destroyed the small monopolies so that the *one* great basic monopoly, property, may function the more freely and unrestrictedly. You have civilized the ends of the earth to win new terrain for the deployment of your vile avarice. You have brought about the fraternization of the peoples—but the fraternity is the fraternity of thieves. You have reduced the number of wars—to earn all the bigger profits in peace, to intensify to the utmost the enmity between individuals, the ignominious war of competition! When have you done anything out of pure humanity, from consciousness of the nullity of the opposition between the general and individual interest? When have you been moral without being interested, without harboring at the back of your mind immoral, egoistical motives?

After liberal economics had done its best to universalize enmity by dissolving nationalities so as to transform mankind into a horde of ravenous beasts (for what else are competitors?) who devour one another just *because* each has identical interests with all the others—after this preparatory work there remained but one step to take before the goal was reached—the dissolution of the family.

To accomplish this, economy's own beautiful invention, the factory-system, came to its aid. The last vestige of common interests, the community of possessions constituted by the family, is being undermined by the factory-system and—at least here in England—is already in the process of dissolution. It is a common practice for children, as soon as they are capable of work (i.e., as soon as they reach the age of nine), to spend their wages themselves, to look upon their parental home as a mere boarding-house, and to make their parents an allowance of a certain sum for food and lodging. How can it be otherwise? What else can result from the separation of interests, such as forms the basis of the free-trade system? Once a principle is set in motion, it works by its own impetus through all its consequences, whether the economists like it or not.

But the economist does not know himself what cause he serves. He does not know that with all his egoistical reasoning he nevertheless forms but a link in the chain of mankind's universal progress. He does not know that by his dissolution of all sectional interests he merely paves the way for the great transformation to which the century is moving—the reconciliation of mankind with nature and with itself.

The next category established by trade is *value*. There is no quarrel between the modern economists and their predecessors over this category, just as there is none over all the others, since the monopolists in their obsessive mania for getting rich had no time left to concern themselves with categories. All controversies over such points stem from the modern economists.

The economist who lives by antitheses has also of course a *double* value—abstract or real, and exchange-value. There was a protracted quarrel over the nature of real value between the English, who defined the costs of production as the expression of real value, and the Frenchman, Say, who claimed to measure this value by the utility of an object. The quarrel hung in doubt from the beginning of the century, then became dormant without a decision having been reached. The economists cannot decide anything.

The English—MacCulloch and Ricardo in particular—thus claim that the abstract value of a thing is determined by the costs of production. The abstract value, of course, not the exchange-value, the "exchangeable value,"[3] value in trade—that, they say, is something quite different. Why are the costs of production the measure of value? Because—listen to this!— because no one in ordinary conditions and leaving aside the circumstance of competition would sell an object for less than the cost to him of its production. Would sell—? What have we to do with "selling" here, where it is not a question of *trade* value? So we find trade again, which we are specifically supposed to leave aside—and what trade! A trade in which the cardinal factor, the circumstance of competition, is not to be taken into account! First, an abstract value; now also an abstract trade— a trade without competition, i.e., a man without a body, a thought without a brain to produce thoughts. And does the economist never stop to think that as soon as competition is left out of account there is no guarantee at all that the producer will sell his commodity just at the cost of production? What confusion!

Furthermore: Let us concede for a moment that everything is as the economist says. Supposing someone were to make something utterly useless with tremendous exertion and at enormous cost—were to make something which no one desires: is that also worth its production costs? Certainly not, says the economist: Who will want to buy it? So we suddenly have not only Say's despised utility but alongside it—with "buying"—the circumstance of competition. It can't be done—the economist cannot for one moment hold on to his abstraction. Not only what he painfully seeks to remove—competition—but also what he attacks—utility—crops up at every moment. Abstract value and its determination by the costs of production are, after all, only abstractions, nonentities.

But let us suppose once more for a moment that the economist is correct—how then will he determine the costs of production without taking account of competition? When examining the costs of production we shall see that this category too is based on competition, and here once more it becomes evident how little the economist is able to substantiate his claims.

If we turn to Say, we find the same abstraction. The utility of an object is something purely subjective, something which cannot be decided absolutely, and certainly something not to be decided, anyway, so long as one still roams about in antitheses. According to this theory, the necessities of life ought to possess more value than luxury articles. The only possible way to arrive at a more or less objective, *apparently* general decision on the greater or lesser utility of an object is, under the dominion of private property, by the circumstance of competition; and yet it is precisely that circumstance which is to be left aside. But if the circumstance of competition is admitted, production costs enter it as well; for no one will sell for less than what he has himself invested in production. Thus, here, too, the one side of the opposition passes over involuntarily into the other.

Let us try to introduce clarity into this confusion. The value of an object includes both factors, which the contending parties so rudely separate—and, as we have seen, without success. Value is the relation of production costs to utility. The first application of value is the decision as to whether a thing ought to be produced at all; i.e., as to whether utility counterbalances production costs. Only then can one talk of the application of value to exchange. The production costs of two objects being equal, the deciding factor determining their comparative value will be utility.

This basis is the only just basis of exchange. But if one proceeds from this basis, who is to decide the utility of the object? The mere opinion of the parties concerned? Then in any event *one* will be cheated. Or is this decision a determination grounded in the inherent utility of the object independent of the parties concerned, and not apparent to them? If so, the exchange can only be effected *by coercion*, and each party considers itself cheated. The opposition between the real inherent utility of the thing and the determination of that utility, between the determination of utility and the freedom of those who exchange, cannot be superseded without superseding private property; and once this is superseded, there can no longer be any question of exchange as it exists at present. The practical application of the concept of value will then be increasingly confined to the decision about production, and that is its proper sphere.

But how do matters stand at present? We have seen how the concept of value is violently torn asunder, and how the detached sides are each substituted for the whole. Production costs, distorted from the outset by competition, are supposed to be value itself. So is mere subjective utility—since no other kind of utility can exist at this stage. To help these lame definitions on to their feet, we must in both cases have recourse to competition; and the best of it is that with the English competition represents utility, in contrast to the costs of production, while inversely with Say it introduces the costs of production in contrast to utility. But what kind of utility, what kind of production costs, does it introduce? Its utility depends on chance, on fashion, on the whim of the rich; its production costs fluctuate with the fortuitous relationship of demand and supply.

The difference between real value and exchange-value is based on the fact—namely, that the value of a thing differs from the so-called equivalent given for it in trade; i.e., that this equivalent is not an equivalent. This so-called equivalent is the *price* of the thing, and if the economist were honest, he would employ this term for trade value. But he has still to keep up some sort of pretense that price is somehow bound up with value, lest the immorality of trade become too obvious. It is, however, quite correct, and a fundamental law of private property, *thai price* is determined by the reciprocal action of production costs and competition. This purely empirical law was the first to be discovered by the economist; and from this law he then abstracted his "real value," i.e., the price at the time when competition is in a state of equilibrium, when demand and supply cover each other. Then, of course, what remains over are the costs of production and it is these which the economist proceeds to call "real value," while they are merely the determinateness of price. Thus everything in economics stands on its head. Value, the origin or source of price, is made dependent on that which is its own product. As is well known, this inversion is the essence of abstraction; on which see Feuerbach.

According to the economists, the production costs of a commodity consist of three elements: the rent for the piece of land required to produce the raw material; the capital with its profit; and the wages for the labor required for production and manufacture. But it becomes immediately evident that capital and labor are identical, since the economists themselves confess that capital is "stored-up labor." We are therefore left with only two sides—the natural objective side, land; and the human, subjective side, labor, which includes capital and, besides capital, a third factor which the economist does not think about—I mean the spiritual element of invention, of thought, alongside the physical element of sheer labor. What has the economist to do with the spirit of invention? Have not all inventions come flying to him without any effort on his part? Has *one* of them cost him anything? Why then should he bother about them in the calculation of production costs? Land, capital and labor are for him the conditions of wealth, and he requires no more. Science is no concern of his. What does it matter to him that he has received its gifts through Berthollet, Davy, Liebig, Watt, Cart-wright, etc.—gifts which have benefited him and his production immeasurably? He does not know how to calculate such things; the advances of science go beyond his figures. But in a rational order which has gone beyond the division of interests as it is found with the economist, the spiritual element certainly belongs among the elements of production and will find its place, too, in economics among the costs of production. And here it is certainly gratifying to know that the promotion of science also brings its material reward; to know that a single achievement of science like James Watt's steam-engine has brought in more for the world in the first fifty years of its existence than the world has spent on the promotion of science since the beginning of time.

We have, then, two elements of production in operation— nature and man, with man again active physically and spiritually, and can go back to the economist and his production costs.

What cannot be monopolized has no value, says the economist— a proposition which we shall examine more closely later on. If we say "has no *price*," then the proposition is valid for the order which rests on private property. If land could be had as easily as air, no one would pay rent. Since this is not the case, but since, rather, the extent of a piece of land to be acquired is limited in any particular case, one pays rent for the acquired, i.e., the monopolized land, or one pays down a purchase price for it. After this enlightenment about the origin of ground-rent it is, however, very strange to have to hear from the economist that the rent of land is the difference between the yield from the rented land and from the worst land worth cultivating at all. As is well known, this is the definition of rent fully developed for the first time by Ricardo. This definition is no doubt correct in practice if one presupposes that a fall in demand reacts *instantaneously* on rent, and at once puts a corresponding amount of the worst cultivated land out of cultivation. This, however, is not the case, and the definition is therefore inadequate. Moreover, it does not cover the causation of rent, and must therefore be dismissed for that reason alone. In opposition to this definition, Col. T. P. Thompson, the champion of the Anti-Corn Law League, revived Adam Smith's definition, and consolidated it. According to him, rent is the relation between the competition of those striving for the use of the land and the limited quantity of available land. Here at least is a return to the origin of rent; but this explanation does not take into account the varying fertility of the soil, just as the previous explanation leaves out competition.

Once more, therefore, we have two one-sided and hence only imperfect definitions of a single object. As in the case of the concept of value, we shall again have to bring together these two definitions so as to find the correct definition which will follow from the development of the thing itself and thus embrace all practice. Rent is the relation between the productivity of the land—between the natural side (which in turn consists of *natural* fertility and *human* cultivation—labor applied to effect improvement), and the human side, competition. The economists may shake their heads over this "definition"; they will discover to their horror that it embraces everything relevant to this matter.

The *landowner* has nothing with which to reproach the merchant.

He practices robbery in monopolizing the land. He practices robbery in exploiting for his own benefit the increase in population which increases competition and thus the value of his estate; in turning into a source of personal advantage that which has not been his own doing—that which is his by sheer accident. He practices robbery in *leasing his land*, when he eventually seizes for himself the improvements effected by his tenant. This is the secret of the ever-increasing wealth of the great landowners.

The axioms which qualify as robbery the landowner's method of deriving an income—namely, that each has a right to the product of his labor, or that no one shall reap where he has not sown—are not something we have set forth. The first excludes the duty of feeding children; the second deprives each generation of the right to live, since each generation starts with what it inherits from the preceding generation. These axioms are, rather, implications of private property. Either one implements its implications or one abandons private property as a premise.

Indeed, the original act of appropriation itself is justified by the assertion of the still earlier *common* property-right. Thus, wherever we turn, private property leads us into contradictions.

To make earth an object of huckstering—the earth which is our one and all, the first condition of our existence—was the last step towards making oneself an object of huckstering. It was and is to this very day an immorality surpassed only by the immorality of self-alienation. And the original appropriation—the monopolization of the earth by a few, the exclusion of the rest from that which is the condition of their life—yields nothing in immorality to the subsequent huckstering of the earth.

If here again we abandon private property, rent is reduced to its truth, to the rational notion which essentially lies at its root. The value of the land divorced from it as rent then reverts to the land itself. This value, to be measured by the productivity of equal areas of land subjected to equal applications of labor, should, however, be taken into account as part of the production costs when determining the value of products; and like rent, it is the relation of productivity to competition—but to *true* competition, such as will be developed when its time comes.

We have seen how capital and labor are initially identical; we see further from the explanations of the economist himself, how, in the process of production, capital, the result of labor, is immediately transformed again into the substratum, into the material of labor; and how therefore the momentarily established separation of capital from labor immediately gives way to the unity of both. And yet the economist separates capital from labor, and yet insists on the division without giving any other recognition to their unity than by his defining capital as "stored-up labor." The split between capital and labor resulting from private property is nothing but the inner dichotomy of labor corresponding to this divided condition and arising out of it. And after this separation is accomplished, capital divides itself once more into the original capital and profit—the increment of capital, which it receives in the process of production; although in practice profit is immediately lumped together with capital and set into motion with it. Indeed, even profit is in its turn split into interest and profit proper. In the case of interest, the absurdity of these splits is carried to the extreme. The immorality of interest-loans, of receiving without working, for merely lending, though already inherent in private property, is only too obvious, and has long ago been recognized for what it is by unsophisticated popular consciousness, which in such matters is usually right. All these minute splits and divisions stem from the original separation of capital from labor and from the culmination of this separation—the division of mankind into capitalists and workers—a division which daily becomes ever more acute, and which, as we shall see, is *bound* to deepen. This separation, however, like the separation already considered of land from capital and labor, is in the final analysis an impossible separation. What share land, capital and labor each have in any particular product cannot be determined. The three magnitudes are incommensurable. The soil creates the raw material, but not without capital and labor. Capital presupposes land and labor. And labor presupposes *at least* land, and usually also capital. The functions of these three elements are completely different, and are not to be measured by a fourth common standard. Therefore, when it comes to dividing the proceeds among the three elements under existing conditions, there is no inherent standard; it is an entirely alien and to them fortuitous standard that decides—competition, the slick right of the stronger. Rent implies competition; profit on capital is solely determined by competition; and the position with regard to wages we shall see presently.

If we abandon private property, then all these unnatural divisions disappear. The difference between interest and profit disappears; capital is nothing without labor, without movement. The significance of profit is reduced to the weight which capital carries in the determination of the costs of production; and profit thus remains inherent in capital, in the same way as capital itself reverts to its original unity with labor.

Labor—the main factor in production, the "source of wealth," free human activity—comes off badly with the economist. Just as capital was previously separated from labor, likewise labor is now in turn split for a second time: the product of labor confronts labor as wages, is separated from it, and is as usual once more determined by competition—there being, as we have seen, no firm standard determining labor's share in production. If we do away with private property, this unnatural separation also disappears. Labor becomes its own reward, and the true significance of the wages of labor, hitherto alienated, comes to light—namely, the significance of labor for the determination of the production costs of a thing.

We have seen that in the end everything comes down to competition, so long as private property exists. It is the economist's principal category—his most beloved daughter, whom he ceaselessly caresses—and look out for the medusa's head which she will show you!

The immediate consequence of private property was the split of production into two opposing sides—the natural and the human sides, the soil which without fertilization by man is dead and sterile, and human activity, whose first condition is that very soil. Furthermore we have seen how human activity in its turn was dissolved into labor and capital, and how these two sides antagonistically confronted each other. Thus already we had the struggle of the three elements against one another, instead of their mutual support; and to make matters worse, private property brings in its wake the splintering of each of these elements. One estate stands confronted by another, one piece of capital by another, one unit of labor-power by another. In other words, because private property isolates everyone in his own crude solitariness, and because, nevertheless, everyone has the same interest as his neighbor, one landowner stands antagonistically confronted by another, one capitalist by another, one worker by another. In this discord of identical interests resulting precisely from this identity is consummated the immorality of mankind's condition hitherto; and this consummation is competition.

The opposite of *competition* is *monopoly*. Monopoly was the war-cry of the mercantilists; competition the battle-cry of the liberal economists. It is easy to see that this antithesis is again a quite hollow antithesis. Every competitor *cannot but* desire to have the monopoly, be he worker, capitalist or landowner. Each smaller group of competitors cannot but desire to have the monopoly for itself against all others. Competition is based on self-interest, and self-interest in turn breeds monopoly. In short, competition passes over into monopoly. On the other hand, monopoly cannot stem the tide of competition—indeed, it itself breeds competition; just as high tariffs, for instance, or a prohibition of imports positively breed the competition of smuggling. The contradiction of competition is exactly the same as that of private property. It is in the interest of each to possess everything, but in the interest of the whole that each possess an equal amount. Thus, the general and the individual interest are diametrically opposed to each other. The contradiction of competition is that each cannot but desire the monopoly, while the whole as such is bound to lose by monopoly and must therefore remove it. Moreover, competition already presupposes monopoly—namely, the monopoly of property (and here the hypocrisy of the liberals comes once more to light); and so long as the monopoly of property exists, for just so long the possession of monopoly is equally justified—for monopoly, once it exists, is also property. What a pitiful half-measure, therefore, to attack the small monopolies, and to leave untouched the basic monopoly! And if we here bring in the economist's proposition mentioned above, that nothing has value which cannot be monopolized—that nothing, therefore, which does not permit of such monopolization can enter this arena of competition—then our assertion that competition presupposes monopoly is completely justified.

The law of competition is that demand and supply always strive to complement each other, and therefore never do so. The two sides are torn apart again and transformed into flat opposition. Supply always follows close on demand without ever quite covering it. It is either too big or too small, never corresponding to demand; because in this unconscious condition of mankind no one knows how big supply or demand is. If demand is greater than supply the price rises and, as a result, supply is to a certain degree stimulated. As soon as it comes on to the market, prices fall; and if it becomes greater than demand, then the fall in prices is so significant that demand is once again stimulated. So it goes on unendingly—a permanently unhealthy state of affairs—a constant alternation of over-stimulation and collapse which precludes all advance—a state of perpetual fluctuation perpetually unresolved. This law with its constant balancing, in which whatever is lost here is gained there, seems to the economist marvelous. It is his chief glory—he cannot see enough of it, and considers it in all its possible and impossible applications. Yet it is obvious that this law is a purely natural law, and not a law of the mind. It is a law which produces revolution. The economist comes along with his lovely theory of demand and supply, proves to you that "one can never produce too much," and practice replies with trade crises, which re-appear as regularly as the comets, and of which we have now on the average one every five to seven years. For the last eighty years these trade crises have come just as regularly as the great plagues did in the past—and they have brought in their train more misery and more immorality than the latter. (Compare Wade: *History of the Middle and Working Classes*, London, 1835, p. 211.) Of course, these trade crises confirm the law, confirm it exhaustively—but in a manner different from that which the economist would have us believe to be the case. What are we to think of a law which can only assert itself through periodic crises? It is just a natural law based on the unconsciousness of the participants. If the producers as such knew how much the consumers required, if they were to organize production, if they were to share it out among themselves, then the fluctuations of competition and its tendency to crisis would be impossible. Produce with consciousness as human beings—not as dispersed atoms without consciousness of your species—and you are beyond all these artificial and untenable antitheses. But as long as you continue to produce in the present unconscious, thoughtless manner, at the mercy of chance—for just so long trade crises will remain; and each successive crisis is bound to become more universal and therefore worse than the preceding one; is bound to impoverish a larger body of small capitalists, and to augment in increasing proportion the numbers of that class who live by labor alone, thus visibly enlarging the mass of labor to be employed (the major problem of our economists) and finally causing a social revolution such as has never been dreamed of by the school-wisdom of the economists.

The perpetual fluctuation of prices such as is created by the condition of competition completely deprives trade of its last vestige of morality. *Value* is no longer even mentioned; the same system which appears to attach such importance to value, which confers on the abstraction of value in money form the honor of having an existence of its own—this very system destroys by means of competition the inherent value of all things, and daily and hourly changes the value-relationship of all things to one another. Where does there remain any possibility of an exchange based on a moral foundation in this whirlpool? In this continuous up-and-down, every one *must* seek to hit upon the most favorable moment for purchase and sale; every one must become a speculator—that is to say, must reap where he has not sown; must enrich himself at the expense of others, must calculate on the misfortune of others, or let chance win for him. The speculator always counts on disasters, particularly on bad harvests. He utilizes everything—for instance, the New York fire in its time—and immorality's culminating point is the speculation on the Stock Exchange, where history, and with it mankind, is demoted to a means of gratifying the avarice of the calculating and gambling speculator. And let not the honest "respectable" merchant rise above the gambling on the Stock Exchange with a Pharisaic "I thank thee, O Lord ..." etc. He is as bad as the speculators in stocks and shares. He speculates just as much as they do. He has to: competition compels him to. And his trading activity therefore implies the same immorality as theirs. The truth of the relationship of competition is the relationship of the power of consumption to the power of production. In a world worthy of mankind there will be no other competition than this. The community will have to calculate what it can produce with the means at its disposal; and in the light of the relationship of this productive power to the mass of consumers it will determine how far it has to raise or lower production, how far it has to give way to, or curtail, luxury. But so that they may be able to pass a correct judgment on this relationship and on the increase in productive power to be expected from a rational state of affairs within the community, I invite my readers to consult the writings of the English Socialists, and partly also those of Fourier.

Subjective competition—the contest of capital against capital, or labor against labor, etc.—will under these conditions be reduced to the spirit of emulation grounded in human nature (a concept tolerably developed so far only by Fourier), which after the transcendence of opposing interests will be confined to its proper and rational sphere.

The struggle of capital against capital, of labor against labor, of land against land, drives production to a fever-pitch at which production turns all natural and rational relations upside-down. No capital can stand the competition of another if it is not brought to the highest pitch of activity. No estate can be profitably cultivated if it does not continuously increase its productive power. No worker can hold his own against his competitors if he does not devote all his powers to labor. No one at all who becomes involved in the struggle of competition can stand the strain without the utmost exertion of his powers, without renouncing every truly human purpose. The consequence of this over-exertion on the one side is, inevitably, collapse on the other. When the fluctuation of competition is small, when demand and supply, consumption and production, are almost equal, a stage must be reached in the development of production where there is so much superfluous productive power that the great mass of the nation has nothing to live on, that the people starve from sheer abundance. For some considerable time England has found herself in this crazy position, in this living absurdity. When, as a necessary consequence of such a situation, production is subject to greater fluctuations, then the alternation of boom and crisis, over-production and slump, sets in. The economist has never been able to explain to himself this mad situation. In order to explain it, he invented the Population Theory, which is just as senseless—indeed even more senseless—than the contradiction of co-existing wealth and poverty. The economist *could not afford* to see the truth; he could not afford to admit that this contradiction is a simple consequence of competition; for otherwise his entire system would have fallen to bits.

For us the matter is easy to explain. The productive power at mankind's disposal is immeasurable. The productivity of the soil can be increased *ad infinitum* by the application of capital, labor and science. According to the most able economists and statisticians (cf. Alison's *Principles of Population*, Vol. I, chs. 1 and 2),[4] "over-populated" Great Britain can be brought within ten years to produce a corn yield sufficient for a population of six times its present size. Capital increases daily; the power of labor grows with population; and day by day science increasingly makes the power of nature subject to man. This immeasurable productive capacity, handled with consciousness and in the interest of all, would soon reduce to a minimum the labor falling to the share of mankind. Left to competition, it does the same, but within a context of antitheses. One part of the land is cultivated in the best possible manner, while another part—in Great Britain and Ireland thirty million acres of good land—lies barren. One part of capital circulates with amazing speed; another lies dead in the chest. One part of the workers works fourteen to sixteen hours a day, while another part stands idle and inactive, and starves. Or the division leaves this realm of simultaneousness: today trade is good; demand is very considerable; everyone works; capital is turned over with miraculous speed; farming flourishes; the workers work themselves sick. Tomorrow, a slump sets in. The cultivation of the land is not worth the effort; entire stretches of land remain untilled; the flow of capital freezes; the workers have no employment, and the whole country labors under surplus wealth and surplus population.

The economist cannot afford to accept this exposition of the subject as correct; otherwise, as has been said, he would have to give up his whole system of competition. He would have to recognize the hollowness of his antithesis of production and consumption, of surplus population and surplus wealth. To bring fact and theory into conformity with each other—since this fact just could not be denied—the Population Theory was invented.

Malthus, the originator of this doctrine, maintains that population is always pressing on the means of subsistence; that as soon as production increases, population increases in the same proportion; and that the inherent tendency of the population to multiply in excess of the available means of subsistence is the root of all misery and all vice. For, when there are too many people, they have to be disposed of in one way or another: either they must be killed by violence or they must starve. But when this has happened, there is once more a gap which other multipliers of the population immediately start to fill up once more: and so the old misery begins all over again. What is more, this is the case in all circumstances—not only in civilized, but also in primitive, conditions. In New Holland,[5] with a population density of one per square mile, the savages suffer just as much from over-population as England. In short, if we want to be consistent, we must admit that *the earth was already over-populated when only one man existed*. The implications of this line of thought are that since it is just the poor who are the surplus, nothing should be done for them except to make their starvation as easy as possible, to convince them that it cannot be helped and that there is no other salvation for their whole class than keeping propagation down to the absolute minimum. Or if this does not work, then it is always better to establish a state institution for the painless killing of the children of the poor, such as "Marcus"[6] has suggested, whereby each working-class family would be allowed to have two and a half children, any excess being painlessly killed. Charity would be a crime, since it supports the augmentation of the surplus population. Indeed, it will be very advantageous to declare poverty a crime and to turn poor-houses into prisons, as has already happened in England as a result of the new "liberal" Poor Law. Admittedly it is true that this theory ill conforms with the Bible's doctrine of the perfection of God and of His creation; but "it is a poor refutation to enlist the Bible against facts."

Am I to go on any longer elaborating this vile, infamous theory, this revolting blasphemy against nature and mankind? Am I to pursue its consequences any further? Here at last we have the immorality of the economist brought to its highest pitch. What are all the wars and horrors of the monopoly system compared with this theory! And it is just this theory which is the keystone of the liberal system of free trade, whose fall entails the downfall of the entire edifice. For if here competition is proved to be the root cause of misery, poverty and crime, who then will still dare to speak up for it?

In his above-mentioned work, Alison has shaken the Malthusian theory by involving the productive power of the earth, and by opposing to the Malthusian principle the fact that each adult can produce more than he himself needs—a fact without which mankind could not multiply, indeed could not even exist; for what else could those still growing up live on? But Alison does not go to the root of the matter, and therefore in the end reaches the same conclusion as Malthus. True enough, he proves that Malthus's principle is incorrect, but cannot gainsay the facts which have impelled Malthus to his principle.

If Malthus had not considered the matter so one-sidedly, he could not have failed to see that surplus population or labor-power is invariably tied up with surplus wealth, surplus capital and surplus landed property. The population is only too large where the productive power as a whole is too large. The condition of every over-populated country, particularly England, since the time when Malthus wrote, makes this abundantly clear. These were the facts which Malthus ought to have considered in their totality, and whose consideration was bound to have led to the correct conclusion. Instead, he selected one fact, gave no consideration to the others, and therefore arrived at his crazy conclusion. The second error he committed was to confuse means of subsistence with means of employment. That population is always pressing on the means of employment—that the number of people produced varies with the number of people who can be employed—in short, that the production of labor-power has been regulated so far by the law of competition and is therefore also exposed to periodic crises and fluctuations—this is a fact whose establishment constitutes Malthus's merit. But the means of employment are not the means of subsistence. Only in their end-result are the means of employment increased by the increase in machine-power and capital. The means of subsistence increase as soon as productive power increases even slightly. Here a new contradiction in economics comes to light. The economist's "demand" is not the real demand; his "consumption" is an artificial consumption. For the economist, only that person really demands, only that person is a real consumer, who has an equivalent to offer for what he receives. But if it is a fact that every adult produces more than he himself can consume, that children are like trees which give superabundant returns on the outlays invested in them—and these certainly are facts, are they not?—then one ought to believe that each worker should be able to produce far more than he needs and that the community, therefore, should be very glad to provide him with everything he needs; one ought to believe that a large family should be looked upon by the community as a very welcome gift. But the economist, with his crude outlook, knows no other equivalent than that which is paid to him in tangible ready cash. He is so firmly set in his antitheses that the most striking facts are of as little concern to him as the most scientific principles.

We destroy the contradiction simply by transcending it. With the fusion of the interests now opposed to each other there disappears the opposition between excess population here and excess wealth there; there disappears the miraculous fact (more miraculous than all the miracles of all the religions put together) that a nation has to starve from sheer wealth and plenty; and there disappears the crazy assertion that the earth lacks the power to feed men. This assertion is the pinnacle of Christian economics—and that our economics is essentially Christian I could have proved from every proposition, from every category, and shall in fact do so when the time comes. The Malthusian theory is but the economic expression of the religious dogma concerning the contradiction of spirit and nature and the resulting corruption of both. So far as religion is concerned, this contradiction has been resolved long ago. I hope that in the sphere of economics I have equally demonstrated the utter emptiness of this contradiction. Moreover, I shall not accept as competent any defense of the Malthusian theory which does not from the outset explain to me on the basis of its own principles how a people can starve from sheer plenty and bring this into harmony with reason and fact.

At the same time, the Malthusian theory has been an absolutely necessary point of transition which has taken us infinitely further. Thanks to this theory, as to economics as a whole, our attention has been drawn to the productive power of the earth and of mankind; and after overcoming this economic despair we have been made forever secure against the fear of overpopulation. We derive from it the most powerful economic arguments for a social transformation. For even if Malthus were completely right, this transformation would have to be undertaken on the spot; for only this transformation, and the education of the masses which it alone provides, makes possible that moral restraint of the propagative instinct which Malthus himself presents as the most effective and easiest remedy for overpopulation. Through this theory we have come to know the deepest degradation of man, his dependence on the realm of competition. It has shown us how in the last instance private property has turned man into a commodity whose production and destruction also depend solely on demand;

how the system of competition has thus slaughtered, and daily continues to slaughter, millions of men. All this we have seen, and all this drives us to the abolition of this degradation of mankind through the abolition of private property, competition and the opposing interests.

Yet, so as to deprive the universal fear of over-population of any possible basis, let us once more return to the relationship of productive power to population. Malthus establishes a formula on which he bases his entire system: population is said to increase in a geometrical progression—1 = 2 = 4 = 8 = 16 = 32, etc.; the productive power of the land in an arithmetical progression— 1 = 2 = 3 = 4 = 5 = 6. The difference is obvious, is terrifying; but is it correct? Where has it been proved that the productivity of the land increases in an arithmetical progression? The extent of land is limited. All right! The labor-power to be employed on this land-surface increases with population. Let us even assume that the increase in yield due to increase in labor does not always rise in proportion to the labor: there still remains a third element which, of course, never means anything to the economist—science —whose progress is as unceasing and at least as rapid as that of population. What progress does the agriculture of this century owe to chemistry alone—indeed, to two men alone, Sir Humphrey Davy and Justus Liebig! But science increases at least as much as population. The latter increases in proportion to the size of the previous generation, science advances in proportion to the knowledge bequeathed to it by the previous generation, and thus under the most ordinary conditions also in geometrical progression. And what is impossible to science? But it is absurd to talk of over-population so long as "there is enough waste land in the valley of the Mississippi for the whole population of Europe to be transplanted there";[7] so long as no more than one-third of the earth can be considered cultivated, and so long as the production of this third itself can be raised sixfold and more by the application of improvements already known.

Thus, competition sets capital against capital, labor against labor, landed property against landed property; and likewise each of these elements against the other two. In the struggle the stronger wins; and in order to predict the outcome of the struggle, we shall have to investigate the strength of the contestants. At first, land and capital are stronger than labor, for the worker must work to live, while the landowner can live on his rents, and the capitalist on his interest, or if the need arises, on his capital or on capitalized property in land. The result is that only the very barest necessities, the mere means of subsistence, fall to the lot of labor; while the largest part of the products is shared between capital and landed property. Moreover, the stronger worker drives the weaker out of the market, just as larger capital drives out smaller capital, and larger landed property drives out smaller landed property. Practice confirms this conclusion.

The advantages which the larger manufacturer and merchant enjoy over the smaller, and the big landowner over the owner of a single acre, are well known. The result is that already under ordinary conditions, in accordance with the law of the stronger, large capital and large landed property swallow small capital and small landed property—i.e., centralization of property. In crises of trade and agriculture, this centralization proceeds much more rapidly. Large property as such increases much more rapidly than small property, since a much smaller portion is deducted from its proceeds as property-expenses. This law of the centralization of private property is as immanent in private property as all the others. The middle classes must increasingly disappear until the world is divided into millionaires and paupers, into large landowners and poor farm laborers. All the laws, all the dividing of landed property, all the possible splitting-up of capital, are of no avail: this result must and will come, unless it is anticipated by a total transformation of social conditions, a fusion of opposed interests, a transcendence of private property.

Free competition, the key-word of our present-day economists, is an impossibility. Monopoly at least intended to protect the consumer against counterfeit, even if it could not in fact do so. The abolition of monopoly, however, opens the door wide to counterfeit. You say that competition carries with it the remedy for counterfeit, since no one will buy bad articles. But that means that everyone has to be an expert in every article, which is impossible. Hence the necessity for monopoly, which many articles in fact reveal. Apothecaries, etc., *must* have a monopoly. And the most important article—money—requires a monopoly most of all. Whenever the circulating medium has ceased to be a state monopoly it has invariably produced a trade crisis; and the English economists, Dr. Wade among them, do concede in this case the necessity for monopoly. But even monopoly is no protection against counterfeit money. One can take one's stand on either side of the question: the one is as difficult as the other. Monopoly produces free competition, and the latter, in turn, produces monopoly. Therefore, both must fall, and these difficulties must be resolved through the transcendence of the principle which gives rise to them.

Competition has penetrated all the relationships of our life and completed the reciprocal bondage in which men now hold themselves. Competition is the great mainspring which again and again jerks into activity our ageing and withering social order, or rather disorder; but with each new exertion it also saps a part of this order's waning strength. Competition governs the numerical advance of mankind; it likewise governs its moral advance. Anyone who has any knowledge of the statistics of crime must have been struck by the peculiar regularity with which crime advances year by year, and with which certain causes produce certain crimes. The extension of the factory-system is followed everywhere by an increase in crime. The number of arrests, of criminal cases—indeed, the number of murders, robberies, petty thefts, etc., for a large town or for a district— can be predicted year by year with unfailing precision, as has been done often enough in England. This regularity proves that crime, too, is governed by competition; that society creates a *demand* for crime which is met by a corresponding *supply*; that the gap created by the arrest, transportation or execution of a certain number is at once filled by others, just as every gap in population is at once filled by new arrivals; in other words, this regularity proves that crime presses on the means of punishment just as the people press on the means of employment. How just it is to punish criminals under these circumstances, quite part from any other considerations, I leave to the judgment of my readers. Here I am merely concerned in demonstrating the extension of competition into the moral sphere, and to show to what deep degradation private property has brought man.

In the struggle of capital and land against labor, the first two elements enjoy yet another special advantage over labor—the assistance of science; for in present conditions science, too, is directed against labor. Almost all mechanical inventions, for instance, have been occasioned by the lack of labor-power; especially so, Hargreaves's, Crompton's and Arkwright's cotton-spinning machines. There has never been an intense demand for labor which did not result in an invention that increased labor productivity considerably, thus diverting demand away from human labor. The history of England from 1770 until now is one long proof of this. The last great invention in cotton-spinning, the self-acting mule, was occasioned simply and solely by the demand for labor, and rising wages. It doubled machine-labor, and thereby cut down hand-labor by half; it threw half the workers out of employment, and thereby depressed the wages of the other half; it crushed a joint scheme of the workers against the factory-owners, and destroyed the last vestige of strength with which labor had still held out in the unequal struggle against capital. (Cf. Dr. Ure, *Philosophy of Manufactures*, Vol. 2.) The economist now says, however, that in its final result machinery is favorable to the workers, since it makes production cheaper and thus creates a new and larger market for its products, and since in so doing it ultimately re-employs the workers put out of work. Quite right. But is the economist forgetting, then, that the production of labor-power is regulated by competition; that labor-power is always pressing on the means of employment, and that, therefore, when these advantages are due to become operative, a surplus of competitors for work is already waiting for them, and will thus render these advantages illusory; while the disadvantages—the sudden withdrawal of the means of subsistence from one half of the workers and the fall in wages for the other half—are not illusory? Is the economist forgetting that the progress of invention never stands still, and that these disadvantages, therefore, perpetuate themselves? Is he forgetting that with the division of labor, developed to such a degree by our civilization, a worker can only live if he can be used at this particular machine for this particular detailed operation; that the change-over from one type of employment to another newer type is almost invariably an absolute impossibility for the adult worker?

In turning my attention to the effects of machinery, I am brought to another subject less directly relevant,—the factory-system; and I have neither the inclination nor the time to treat this here. Besides, I hope to have an early opportunity to expound in detail the despicable immorality of this system, and to expose mercilessly the economist's hypocrisy which here appears in all its glitter.[8]

Footnotes

[1. *Outlines of a Critique of Political Economy* is the first economic work of Frederick Engels in which he examines the bourgeois economic system and the basic categories of bourgeois political economy from the standpoint of socialism. Marx rated this work of Engels's highly even later, calling it "a brilliant outline of a critique of economic categories" (See "Introduction" to *Zur Kritik der Politischen Ekonomie* [*A Contribution to the Critique of Political Economy*], 1859). Evidencing Engels's final departure from idealism to materialism and from revolutionary democracy to communism, the work is not, however, free from the influence of ethical "philosophical" communism. In a number of passages Engels still criticizes bourgeois society from the standpoint of abstract principles of universal morals and humaneness.—Ed.]

[2. *Friedrich List* (1789-1846), a well-known German economist, advocated the abolition of customs barriers within Germany but at the same time the protection by tariffs, etc., of German industry from foreign competition.—Ed.]

[3. "Exchangeable value"—English term quoted by Engels.—Ed.]

[4. A. Alison, *The Principles of Population, and Their Connection with Human Happiness.* Vols. I, II. London, 1840.—Ed.]

[5. The old name for Australia.—Ed.]

[6. Three pamphlets appeared under the pseudonym of "Marcus," namely: *On the Possibility of Limiting Populousness,* by Marcus, Printed by John Hill, Black Horse Court, Fleet Street, 1838, 46 pp.; *The Book of Murder! A Vade Mecum for the Commissioners and Guardians of the New Poor Law . . . Being an Exact Reprint of the Infamous Essay on the Possibility of Limiting Populousness,* by Marcus, one of the three. . . now Reprinted for the Instruction of the Labourer,* by William Dugdale, 37 Holywell Street, Strand.; *The Theory of Painless Extinction,* by Marcus. Cf. N.M.W.: *Advertisements* 29. VIII. 1840.

An anonymous pamphlet, *An Essay on Populousness, printed for private circulation; printed for the author.* 1838. 27 pp.—contains the basic ideas of the "Marcus" pamphlets. Cf. also Thomas Carlyle, *Chartism,* London, 1840, p. 110 sqq.—Ed.]

[7. A. Alison, l.c, p. 548.—Ed.]

[8. Engels refers to a work on England's social history which he intended to write and for which he was collecting material during his stay in that country (November 1842-August

1844). In this work Engels meant to devote a special chapter to the condition of the English workers. Later he changed his mind and decided to write a special book about the English proletariat. He did so on returning to Germany. The book, *Condition of the Working Class in England*, was published in Leipzig in 1845.—Ed.]

Manifesto of the Communist Party

From the English Edition of 1888
Edited by Friedrich Engels

Contents

Introduction. 148

Bourgeois and Proletarians. 149

Proletarians and Communists. 160

Socialist and Communist Literature. 169

Position of the Communists in Relation to the Various Existing Opposition Parties. 178

Introdution

A spectre is haunting Europe—the spectre of Communism. All the Powers of old Europe have entered into a holy alliance to exorcise this spectre: Pope and Czar, Metternich and Guizot, French Radicals and German police-spies.

Where is the party in opposition that has not been decried as Communistic by its opponents in power? Where is the Opposition that has not hurled back the branding reproach of Communism, against the more advanced opposition parties, as well as against its reactionary adversaries?

Two things result from this fact.

I. Communism is already acknowledged by all European Powers to be itself a Power.

II. It is high time that Communists should openly, in the face of the whole world, publish their views, their aims, their tendencies, and meet this nursery tale of the Spectre of Communism with a Manifesto of the party itself.

To this end, Communists of various nationalities have assembled in London, and sketched the following Manifesto, to be published in the English, French, German, Italian, Flemish and Danish languages.

Bourgeois and Proletarians

The history of all hitherto existing societies is the history of class struggles.

Freeman and slave, patrician and plebeian, lord and serf, guild-master and journeyman, in a word, oppressor and oppressed, stood in constant opposition to one another, carried on an uninterrupted, now hidden, now open fight, a fight that each time ended, either in a revolutionary re-constitution of society at large, or in the common ruin of the contending classes.

In the earlier epochs of history, we find almost everywhere a complicated arrangement of society into various orders, a manifold gradation of social rank. In ancient Rome we have patricians, knights, plebeians, slaves; in the Middle Ages, feudal lords, vassals, guild-masters, journeymen, apprentices, serfs; in almost all of these classes, again, subordinate gradations.

The modern bourgeois society that has sprouted from the ruins of feudal society has not done away with class antagonisms. It has but established new classes, new conditions of oppression, new forms of struggle in place of the old ones. Our epoch, the epoch of the bourgeoisie, possesses, however, this distinctive feature: it has simplified the class antagonisms. Society as a whole is more and more splitting up into two great hostile camps, into two great classes, directly facing each other: Bourgeoisie and Proletariat.

From the serfs of the Middle Ages sprang the chartered burghers of the earliest towns. From these burgesses the first elements of the bourgeoisie were developed.

The discovery of America, the rounding of the Cape, opened up fresh ground for the rising bourgeoisie. The East-Indian and Chinese markets, the colonisation of America, trade with the colonies, the increase in the means of exchange and in commodities generally, gave to commerce, to navigation, to industry, an impulse never before known, and thereby, to the revolutionary element in the tottering feudal society, a rapid development.

The feudal system of industry, under which industrial production was monopolised by closed guilds, now no longer sufficed for the growing wants of the new markets. The manufacturing system took its place. The guild-masters were pushed on one side by the manufacturing middle class; division of labour between the different corporate guilds vanished in the face of division of labour in each single workshop.

Meantime the markets kept ever growing, the demand ever rising. Even manufacture no longer sufficed. Thereupon, steam and machinery revolutionised industrial production. The place of manufacture was taken by the giant, Modern Industry, the place of the industrial middle class, by industrial millionaires, the leaders of whole industrial armies, the modern bourgeois.

Modern industry has established the world-market, for which the discovery of America paved the way. This market has given an immense development to commerce, to navigation, to communication by land. This development has, in its time, reacted on the extension of industry; and in proportion as industry, commerce, navigation, railways extended, in the same proportion the bourgeoisie developed, increased its capital, and pushed into the background every class handed down from the Middle Ages.

We see, therefore, how the modern bourgeoisie is itself the product of a long course of development, of a series of revolutions in the modes of production and of exchange.

Each step in the development of the bourgeoisie was accompanied by a corresponding political advance of that class. An oppressed class under the sway of the feudal nobility, an armed and self-governing association in the mediaeval commune; here independent urban republic (as in Italy and Germany), there taxable "third estate" of the monarchy (as in France), afterwards, in the period of manufacture proper, serving either the semi-feudal or the absolute monarchy as a counterpoise against the nobility, and, in fact, corner-stone of the great monarchies in general, the bourgeoisie has at last, since the establishment of Modern Industry and of the world-market, conquered for itself, in the modern representative State, exclusive political sway. The executive of the modern State is but a committee for managing the common affairs of the whole bourgeoisie.

The bourgeoisie, historically, has played a most revolutionary part.

The bourgeoisie, wherever it has got the upper hand, has put an end to all feudal, patriarchal, idyllic relations. It has pitilessly torn asunder the motley feudal ties that bound man to his "natural superiors," and has left remaining no other nexus between man and man than naked self-interest, than callous "cash payment." It has drowned the most heavenly ecstasies of religious fervour, of chivalrous enthusiasm, of philistine sentimentalism, in the icy water of egotistical calculation. It has resolved personal worth into exchange value, and in place of the numberless and feasible chartered freedoms, has set up that single, unconscionable freedom—Free Trade. In one word, for exploitation, veiled by religious and political illusions, naked, shameless, direct, brutal exploitation.

The bourgeoisie has stripped of its halo every occupation hitherto honoured and looked up to with reverent awe. It has converted the physician, the lawyer, the priest, the poet, the man of science, into its paid wage labourers.

The bourgeoisie has torn away from the family its sentimental veil, and has reduced the family relation to a mere money relation.

The bourgeoisie has disclosed how it came to pass that the brutal display of vigour in the Middle Ages, which Reactionists so much admire, found its fitting complement in the most slothful indolence. It has been the first to show what man's activity can bring about. It has accomplished wonders far surpassing Egyptian pyramids, Roman aqueducts, and Gothic cathedrals; it has conducted expeditions that put in the shade all former Exoduses of nations and crusades.

The bourgeoisie cannot exist without constantly revolutionising the instruments of production, and thereby the relations of production, and with them the whole relations of society. Conservation of the old modes of production in unaltered form, was, on the contrary, the first condition of existence for all earlier industrial classes. Constant revolutionising of production, uninterrupted disturbance of all social conditions, everlasting uncertainty and agitation distinguish the bourgeois epoch from all earlier ones. All fixed, fast-frozen relations, with their train of ancient and venerable prejudices and opinions, are swept away, all new-formed ones become antiquated before they can ossify. All that is solid melts into air, all that is holy is profaned, and man is at last compelled to face with sober senses, his real conditions of life, and his relations with his kind.

The need of a constantly expanding market for its products chases the bourgeoisie over the whole surface of the globe. It must nestle everywhere, settle everywhere, establish connexions everywhere.

The bourgeoisie has through its exploitation of the world-market given a cosmopolitan character to production and consumption in every country. To the great chagrin of Reactionists, it has drawn from under the feet of industry the national ground on which it stood. All old-established national industries have been destroyed or are daily being destroyed. They are dislodged by new industries, whose introduction becomes a life and death question for all civilised nations, by industries that no longer work up indigenous raw material, but raw material drawn from the remotest zones; industries whose products are consumed, not only at home, but in every quarter of the globe. In place of the old wants, satisfied by the productions of the country, we find new wants, requiring for their satisfaction the products of distant lands and climes. In place of the old local and national seclusion and self-sufficiency, we have intercourse in every direction, universal inter-dependence of nations. And as in material, so also in intellectual production. The intellectual creations of individual nations become common property. National one-sidedness and narrow-mindedness become more and more impossible, and from the numerous national and local literatures, there arises a world literature.

The bourgeoisie, by the rapid improvement of all instruments of production, by the immensely facilitated means of communication, draws all, even the most barbarian, nations into civilisation. The cheap prices of its commodities are the heavy artillery with which it batters down all Chinese walls, with which it forces the barbarians' intensely obstinate hatred of foreigners to capitulate. It compels all nations, on pain of extinction, to adopt the bourgeois mode of production; it compels them to introduce what it calls civilisation into their midst, i.e., to become bourgeois themselves. In one word, it creates a world after its own image.

The bourgeoisie has subjected the country to the rule of the towns. It has created enormous cities, has greatly increased the urban population as compared with the rural, and has thus rescued a considerable part of the population from the idiocy of rural life. Just as it has made the country dependent on the towns, so it has made barbarian and semi-barbarian countries dependent on the civilised ones, nations of peasants on nations of bourgeois, the East on the West.

The bourgeoisie keeps more and more doing away with the scattered state of the population, of the means of production, and of property. It has agglomerated production, and has concentrated property in a few hands. The necessary consequence of this was political centralisation. Independent, or but loosely connected provinces, with separate interests, laws, governments and systems of taxation, became lumped together into one nation, with one government, one code of laws, one national class-interest, one frontier and one customs-tariff. The bourgeoisie, during its rule of scarce one hundred years, has created more massive and more colossal productive forces than have all preceding generations together. Subjection of Nature's forces to man, machinery, application of chemistry to industry and agriculture, steam-navigation, railways, electric telegraphs, clearing of whole continents for cultivation, canalisation of rivers, whole populations conjured out of the ground—what earlier century had even a presentiment that such productive forces slumbered in the lap of social labour?

We see then: the means of production and of exchange, on whose foundation the bourgeoisie built itself up, were generated in feudal society. At a certain stage in the development of these means of production and of exchange, the conditions under which feudal society produced and exchanged, the feudal organisation of agriculture and manufacturing industry, in one word, the feudal relations of property became no longer compatible with the already developed productive forces; they became so many fetters. They had to be burst asunder; *Feudalism* they were burst asunder.

Into their place stepped free competition, accompanied by a social and political constitution adapted to it, and by the economical and political sway of the bourgeois class.

A similar movement is going on before our own eyes. Modern bourgeois society with its relations of production, of exchange and of property, a society that has conjured up such gigantic means of production and of exchange, is like the sorcerer, who is no longer able to control the powers of the nether world whom he has called up by his spells. For many a decade past the history of industry and commerce is but the history of the revolt of modern productive forces against modern conditions of production, against the property relations that are the conditions for the existence of the bourgeoisie and of its rule. It is enough to mention the commercial crises that by their periodical return put on its trial, each time more threateningly, the existence of the entire bourgeois society. In these crises a great part not only of the existing products, but also of the previously created productive forces, are periodically destroyed. In these crises there breaks out an epidemic that, in all earlier epochs, would have seemed an absurdity—the epidemic of over-production. Society suddenly finds itself put back into a state of momentary barbarism; it appears as if a famine, a universal war of devastation had cut off the supply of every means of subsistence; industry and commerce seem to be destroyed; and why? Because there is too much civilisation, too much means of subsistence, too much industry, too much commerce. The productive forces at the disposal of society no longer tend to further the development of the conditions of bourgeois property; on the contrary, they have become too powerful for these conditions, by which they are fettered, and so soon as they overcome these fetters, they bring disorder into the whole of bourgeois society, endanger the existence of bourgeois property. The conditions of bourgeois society are too narrow to comprise the wealth created by them. And how does the bourgeoisie get over these crises? On the one hand inforced destruction of a mass of productive forces; on the other, by the conquest of new markets, and by the more thorough exploitation of the old ones. That is to say, by paving the way for more extensive and more destructive crises, and by diminishing the means whereby crises are prevented.

The weapons with which the bourgeoisie felled feudalism to the ground are now turned against the bourgeoisie itself.

But not only has the bourgeoisie forged the weapons that bring death to itself; it has also called into existence the men who are to wield those weapons—the modern working class—the proletarians.

In proportion as the bourgeoisie, *i.e.*, capital, is developed, in the same proportion is the proletariat, the modern working class, developed—a class of labourers, who live only so long as they find work, and who find work only so long as their labour increases capital. These labourers, who must sell themselves piece-meal, are a commodity, like every other article of commerce, and are consequently exposed to all the vicissitudes of competition, to all the fluctuations of the market.

Owing to the extensive use of machinery and to division of labour, the work of the proletarians has lost all individual character, and consequently, all charm for the workman. He becomes an appendage of the machine, and it is only the most simple, most monotonous, and most easily acquired knack, that is required of him. Hence, the cost of production of a workman is restricted, almost entirely, to the means of subsistence that he requires for his maintenance, and for the propagation of his race. But the price of a commodity, and therefore also of labour, is equal to its cost of production. In proportion therefore, as the repulsiveness of the work increases, the wage decreases. Nay more, in proportion as the use of machinery and division of labour increases, in the same proportion the burden of toil also increases, whether by prolongation of the working hours, by increase of the work exacted in a given time or by increased speed of the machinery, etc.

Modern industry has converted the little workshop of the patriarchal master into the great factory of the industrial capitalist. Masses of labourers, crowded into the factory, are organised like soldiers. As privates of the industrial army they are placed under the command of a perfect hierarchy of officers and sergeants. Not only are they slaves of the bourgeois class, and of the bourgeois State; they are daily and hourly enslaved by the machine, by the over-looker, and, above all, by the individual bourgeois manufacturer himself. The more openly this despotism proclaims gain to be its end and aim, the more petty, the more hateful and the more embittering it is.

The less the skill and exertion of strength implied in manual labour, in other words, the more modern industry becomes developed, the more is the labour of men superseded by that of women. Differences of age and sex have no longer any distinctive social validity for the working class. All are instruments of labour, more or less expensive to use, according to their age and sex.

No sooner is the exploitation of the labourer by the manufacturer, so far at an end, that he receives his wages in cash, than he is set upon by the other portions of the bourgeoisie, the landlord, the shopkeeper, the pawnbroker, etc.

The lower strata of the middle class—the small tradespeople, shopkeepers, retired tradesmen generally, the handicraftsmen and peasants—all these sink gradually into the proletariat, partly because their diminutive capital does not suffice for the scale on which Modern Industry is carried on, and is swamped in the competition with the large capitalists, partly because their specialized skill is rendered worthless by the new methods of production. Thus the proletariat is recruited from all classes of the population.

The proletariat goes through various stages of development. With its birth begins its struggle with the bourgeoisie. At first the contest is carried on by individual labourers, then by the workpeople of a factory, then by the operatives of one trade, in one locality, against the individual bourgeois who directly exploits them. They direct their attacks not against the bourgeois conditions of production, but against the instruments of production themselves; they destroy imported wares that compete with their labour, they smash to pieces machinery, they set factories ablaze, they seek to restore by force the vanished status of the workman of the Middle Ages.

At this stage the labourers still form an incoherent mass scattered over the whole country, and broken up by their mutual competition. If anywhere they unite to form more compact bodies, this is not yet the consequence of their own active union, but of the union of the bourgeoisie, which class, in order to attain its own political ends, is compelled to set the whole proletariat in motion, and is moreover yet, for a time, able to do so. At this stage, therefore, the proletarians do not fight their enemies, but the enemies of their enemies, the remnants of absolute monarchy, the landowners, the non-industrial bourgeois, the petty bourgeoisie. Thus the whole historical movement is concentrated in the hands of the bourgeoisie; every victory so obtained is a victory for the bourgeoisie.

But with the development of industry the proletariat not only increases in number; it becomes concentrated in greater masses, its strength grows, and it feels that strength more. The various interests and conditions of life within the ranks of the proletariat are more and more equalised, in proportion as machinery obliterates all distinctions of labour, and nearly everywhere reduces wages to the same low level. The growing competition among the bourgeois, and the resulting commercial crises, make the wages of the workers ever more fluctuating. The unceasing improvement of machinery, ever more rapidly developing, makes their livelihood more and more precarious; the collisions between individual workmen and individual bourgeois take more and more the character of collisions between two classes. Thereupon the workers begin to form combinations (Trades Unions) against the bourgeois; they club together in order to keep up the rate of wages; they found permanent associations in order to make provision beforehand for these occasional revolts. Here and there the contest breaks out into riots.

Now and then the workers are victorious, but only for a time. The real fruit of their battles lies, not in the immediate result, but in the ever-expanding union of the workers. This union is helped on by the improved means of communication that are created by modern industry and that place the workers of different localities in contact with one another. It was just this contact that was needed to centralise the numerous local struggles, all of the same character, into one national struggle between classes. But every class struggle is a political struggle. And that union, to attain which the burghers of the Middle Ages, with their miserable highways, required centuries, the modern proletarians, thanks to railways, achieve in a few years.

This organisation of the proletarians into a class, and consequently into a political party, is continually being upset again by the competition between the workers themselves. But it ever rises up again, stronger, firmer, mightier. It compels legislative recognition of particular interests of the workers, by taking advantage of the divisions among the bourgeoisie itself. Thus the ten-hours' bill in England was carried.

Altogether collisions between the classes of the old society further, in many ways, the course of development of the proletariat. The bourgeoisie finds itself involved in a constant battle. At first with the aristocracy; later on, with those portions of the bourgeoisie itself, whose interests have become antagonistic to the progress of industry; at all times, with the bourgeoisie of foreign countries. In all these battles it sees itself compelled to appeal to the proletariat, to ask for its help, and thus, to drag it into the political arena. The bourgeoisie itself, therefore, supplies the proletariat with its own instruments of political and general education, in other words, it furnishes the proletariat with weapons for fighting the bourgeoisie.

Further, as we have already seen, entire sections of the ruling classes are, by the advance of industry, precipitated into the proletariat, or are at least threatened in their conditions of existence. These also supply the proletariat with fresh elements of enlightenment and progress.

Finally, in times when the class struggle nears the decisive hour, the process of dissolution going on within the ruling class, in fact within the whole range of society, assumes such a violent, glaring character, that a small section of the ruling class cuts itself adrift, and joins the revolutionary class, the class that holds the future in its hands. Just as, therefore, at an earlier period, a section of the nobility went over to the bourgeoisie, so now a portion of the bourgeoisie goes over to the proletariat, and in particular, a portion of the bourgeois ideologists, who have raised themselves to the level of comprehending theoretically the historical movement as a whole.

Of all the classes that stand face to face with the bourgeoisie today, the proletariat alone is a really revolutionary class. The other classes decay and finally disappear in the face of Modern Industry; the proletariat is its special and essential product. The lower middle class, the small manufacturer, the shopkeeper, the artisan, the peasant, all these fight against the bourgeoisie, to save from extinction their existence as fractions of the middle class. They are therefore not revolutionary, but conservative. Nay more, they are reactionary, for they try to roll back the wheel of history. If by chance they are revolutionary, they are so only in view of their impending transfer into the proletariat, they thus defend not their present, but their future interests, they desert their own standpoint to place themselves at that of the proletariat.

The "dangerous class," the social scum, that passively rotting mass thrown off by the lowest layers of old society, may, here and there, be swept into the movement by a proletarian revolution; its conditions of life, however, prepare it far more for the part of a bribed tool of reactionary intrigue.

In the conditions of the proletariat, those of old society at large are already virtually swamped. The proletarian is without property; his relation to his wife and children has no longer anything in common with the bourgeois family-relations; modern industrial labour, modern subjection to capital, the same in England as in France, in America as in Germany, has stripped him of every trace of national character. Law, morality, religion, are to him so many bourgeois prejudices, behind which lurk in ambush just as many bourgeois interests.

All the preceding classes that got the upper hand, sought to fortify their already acquired status by subjecting society at large to their conditions of appropriation. The proletarians cannot become masters of the productive forces of society, except by abolishing their own previous mode of appropriation, and thereby also every other previous mode of appropriation. They have nothing of their own to secure and to fortify; their mission is to destroy all previous securities for, and insurances of, individual property.

All previous historical movements were movements of minorities, or in the interests of minorities. The proletarian movement is the self-conscious, independent movement of the immense majority, in the interests of the immense majority. The proletariat, the lowest stratum of our present society, cannot stir, cannot raise itself up, without the whole superincumbent strata of official society being sprung into the air.

Though not in substance, yet in form, the struggle of the proletariat with the bourgeoisie is at first a national struggle. The proletariat of each country must, of course, first of all settle matters with its own bourgeoisie.

In depicting the most general phases of the development of the proletariat, we traced the more or less veiled civil war, raging within existing society, up to the point where that war breaks out into open revolution, and where the violent overthrow of the bourgeoisie lays the foundation for the sway of the proletariat.

Hitherto, every form of society has been based, as we have already seen, on the antagonism of oppressing and oppressed classes. But in order to oppress a class, certain conditions must be assured to it under which it can, at least, continue its slavish existence. The serf, in the period of serfdom, raised himself to membership in the commune, just as the petty bourgeois, under the yoke of feudal absolutism, managed to develop into a bourgeois. The modern laborer, on the contrary, instead of rising with the progress of industry, sinks deeper and deeper below the conditions of existence of his own class. He becomes a pauper, and pauperism develops more rapidly than population and wealth. And here it becomes evident, that the bourgeoisie is unfit any longer to be the ruling class in society, and to impose its conditions of existence upon society as an over-riding law. It is unfit to rule because it is incompetent to assure an existence to its slave within his slavery, because it cannot help letting him sink into such a state, that it has to feed him, instead of being fed by him. Society can no longer live under this bourgeoisie, in other words, its existence is no longer compatible with society.

The essential condition for the existence, and for the sway of the bourgeois class, is the formation and augmentation of capital; the condition for capital is wage-labour. Wage-labour rests exclusively on competition between the laborers. The advance of industry, whose involuntary promoter is the bourgeoisie, replaces the isolation of the labourers, due to competition, by their revolutionary combination, due to association. The development of Modern Industry, therefore, cuts from under its feet the very foundation on which the bourgeoisie produces and appropriates products. What the bourgeoisie, therefore, produces, above all, is its own grave-diggers. Its fall and the victory of the proletariat are equally inevitable.

Proletarians and Communists

In what relation do the Communists stand to the proletarians as a whole?

The Communists do not form a separate party opposed to other working-class parties.

They have no interests separate and apart from those of the proletariat as a whole.

They do not set up any sectarian principles of their own, by which to shape and mould the proletarian movement.

The Communists are distinguished from the other working-class parties by this only: (1) In the national struggles of the proletarians of the different countries, they point out and bring to the front the common interests of the entire proletariat, independently of all nationality. (2) In the various stages of development which the struggle of the working class against the bourgeoisie has to pass through, they always and everywhere represent the interests of the movement as a whole.

The Communists, therefore, are on the one hand, practically, the most advanced and resolute section of the working-class parties of every country, that section which pushes forward all others; on the other hand, theoretically, they have over the great mass of the proletariat the advantage of clearly understanding the line of march, the conditions, and the ultimate general results of the proletarian movement.

The immediate aim of the Communist is the same as that of all the other proletarian parties: formation of the proletariat into a class, overthrow of the bourgeois supremacy, conquest of political power by the proletariat.

The theoretical conclusions of the Communists are in no way based on ideas or principles that have been invented, or discovered, by this or that would-be universal reformer. They merely express, in general terms, actual relations springing from an existing class struggle, from a historical movement going on under our very eyes. The abolition of existing property relations is not at all a distinctive feature of Communism.

All property relations in the past have continually been subject to historical change consequent upon the change in historical conditions.

The French Revolution, for example, abolished feudal property in favour of bourgeois property.

The distinguishing feature of Communism is not the abolition of property generally, but the abolition of bourgeois property. But modern bourgeois private property is the final and most complete expression of the system of producing and appropriating products, that is based on class antagonisms, on the exploitation of the many by the few.

In this sense, the theory of the Communists may be summed up in the single sentence: Abolition of private property.

We Communists have been reproached with the desire of abolishing the right of personally acquiring property as the fruit of a man's own labour, which property is alleged to be the groundwork of all personal freedom, activity and independence.

Hard-won, self-acquired, self-earned property! Do you mean the property of the petty artisan and of the small peasant, a form of property that preceded the bourgeois form? There is no need to abolish that; the development of industry has to a great extent already destroyed it, and is still destroying it daily.

Or do you mean modern bourgeois private property?

But does wage-labour create any property for the labourer? Not a bit. It creates capital, i.e., that kind of property which exploits wage-labour, and which cannot increase except upon condition of begetting a new supply of wage-labour for fresh exploitation. Property, in its present form, is based on the antagonism of capital and wage-labour. Let us examine both sides of this antagonism.

To be a capitalist, is to have not only a purely personal, but a social status in production. Capital is a collective product, and only by the united action of many members, nay, in the last resort, only by the united action of all members of society, can it be set in motion.

Capital is, therefore, not a personal, it is a social power.

When, therefore, capital is converted into common property, into the property of all members of society, personal property is not thereby transformed into social property. It is only the social character of the property that is changed. It loses its class-character.

Let us now take wage-labour.

The average price of wage-labour is the minimum wage, i.e., that quantum of the means of subsistence, which is absolutely requisite in bare existence as a labourer. What, therefore, the wage-labourer appropriates by means of his labour, merely suffices to prolong and reproduce a bare existence. We by no means intend to abolish this personal appropriation of the products of labour, an appropriation that is made for the maintenance and reproduction of human life, and that leaves no surplus wherewith to command the labour of others. All that we want to do away with, is the miserable character of this appropriation, under which the labourer lives merely to increase capital, and is allowed to live only in so far as the interest of the ruling class requires it.

In bourgeois society, living labour is but a means to increase accumulated labour. In Communist society, accumulated labour is but a means to widen, to enrich, to promote the existence of the labourer.

In bourgeois society, therefore, the past dominates the present; in Communist society, the present dominates the past. In bourgeois society capital is independent and has individuality, while the living person is dependent and has no individuality.

And the abolition of this state of things is called by the bourgeois, abolition of individuality and freedom! And rightly so. The abolition of bourgeois individuality, bourgeois independence, and bourgeois freedom is undoubtedly aimed at.

By freedom is meant, under the present bourgeois conditions of production, free trade, free selling and buying.

But if selling and buying disappears, free selling and buying disappears also. This talk about free selling and buying, and all the other "brave words" of our bourgeoisie about freedom in general, have a meaning, if any, only in contrast with restricted selling and buying, with the fettered traders of the Middle Ages, but have no meaning when opposed to the Communistic abolition of buying and selling, of the bourgeois conditions of production, and of the bourgeoisie itself.

You are horrified at our intending to do away with private property. But in your existing society, private property is already done away with for nine-tenths of the population; its existence for the few is solely due to its non-existence in the hands of those nine-tenths. You reproach us, therefore, with intending to do away with a form of property, the necessary condition for whose existence is the non-existence of any property for the immense majority of society.

In one word, you reproach us with intending to do away with your property. Precisely so; that is just what we intend.

From the moment when labour can no longer be converted into capital, money, or rent, into a social power capable of being monopolised, *i.e.*, from the moment when individual property can no longer be transformed into bourgeois property, into capital, from that moment, you say individuality vanishes.

You must, therefore, confess that by "individual" you mean no other person than the bourgeois, than the middle-class owner of property. This person must, indeed, be swept out of the way, and made impossible.

Communism deprives no man of the power to appropriate the products of society; all that it does is to deprive him of the power to subjugate the labour of others by means of such appropriation.

It has been objected that upon the abolition of private property all work will cease, and universal laziness will overtake us.

According to this, bourgeois society ought long ago to have gone to the dogs through sheer idleness; for those of its members who work, acquire nothing, and those who acquire anything, do not work. The whole of this objection is but another expression of the tautology: that there can no longer be any wage-labour when there is no longer any capital.

All objections urged against the Communistic mode of producing and appropriating material products, have, in the same way, been urged against the Communistic modes of producing and appropriating intellectual products. Just as, to the bourgeois, the disappearance of class property is the disappearance of production itself, so the disappearance of class culture is to him identical with the disappearance of all culture.

That culture, the loss of which he laments, is, for the enormous majority, a mere training to act as a machine.

But don't wrangle with us so long as you apply, to our intended abolition of bourgeois property, the standard of your bourgeois notions of freedom, culture, law, etc. Your very ideas are but the outgrowth of the conditions of your bourgeois production and bourgeois property, just as your jurisprudence is but the will of your class made into a law for all, a will, whose essential character and direction are determined by the economical conditions of existence of your class.

The selfish misconception that induces you to transform into eternal laws of nature and of reason, the social forms springing from your present mode of production and form of property—historical relations that rise and disappear in the progress of production—this misconception you share with every ruling class that has preceded you. What you see clearly in the case of ancient property, what you admit in the case of feudal property, you are of course forbidden to admit in the case of your own bourgeois form of property.

Abolition of the family! Even the most radical flare up at this infamous proposal of the Communists.

On what foundation is the present family, the bourgeois family, based? On capital, on private gain. In its completely developed form this family exists only among the bourgeoisie. But this state of things finds its complement in the practical absence of the family among the proletarians, and in public prostitution.

The bourgeois family will vanish as a matter of course when its complement vanishes, and both will vanish with the vanishing of capital.

Do you charge us with wanting to stop the exploitation of children by their parents? To this crime we plead guilty.

But, you will say, we destroy the most hallowed of relations, when we replace home education by social.

And your education! Is not that also social, and determined by the social conditions under which you educate, by the intervention, direct or indirect, of society, by means of schools, etc.? The Communists have not invented the intervention of society in education; they do but seek to alter the character of that intervention, and to rescue education from the influence of the ruling class.

The bourgeois clap-trap about the family and education, about the hallowed co-relation of parent and child, becomes all the more disgusting, the more, by the action of Modern Industry, all family ties among the proletarians are torn asunder, and their children transformed into simple articles of commerce and instruments of labour.

But you Communists would introduce community of women, screams the whole bourgeoisie in chorus.

The bourgeois sees in his wife a mere instrument of production. He hears that the instruments of production are to be exploited in common, and, naturally, can come to no other conclusion than that the lot of being common to all will likewise fall to the women.

He has not even a suspicion that the real point is to do away with the status of women as mere instruments of production.

For the rest, nothing is more ridiculous than the virtuous indignation of our bourgeois at the community of women which, they pretend, is to be openly and officially established by the Communists. The Communists have no need to introduce community of women; it has existed almost from time immemorial.

Our bourgeois, not content with having the wives and daughters of their proletarians at their disposal, not to speak of common prostitutes, take the greatest pleasure in seducing each other's wives.

Bourgeois marriage is in reality a system of wives in common and thus, at the most, what the Communists might possibly be reproached with, is that they desire to introduce, in substitution for a hypocritically concealed, an openly legalised community of women. For the rest, it is self-evident that the abolition of the present system of production must bring with it the abolition of the community of women springing from that system, i.e., of prostitution both public and private.

The Communists are further reproached with desiring to abolish countries and nationality.

The working men have no country. We cannot take from them what they have not got. Since the proletariat must first of all acquire political supremacy, must rise to be the leading class of the nation, must constitute itself the nation, it is, so far, itself national, though not in the bourgeois sense of the word.

National differences and antagonisms between peoples are daily more and more vanishing, owing to the development of the bourgeoisie, to freedom of commerce, to the world-market, to uniformity in the mode of production and in the conditions of life corresponding thereto.

The supremacy of the proletariat will cause them to vanish still faster. United action, of the leading civilised countries at least, is one of the first conditions for the emancipation of the proletariat.

In proportion as the exploitation of one individual by another is put an end to, the exploitation of one nation by another will also be put an end to. In proportion as the antagonism between classes within the nation vanishes, the hostility of one nation to another will come to an end.

The charges against Communism made from a religious, a philosophical, and, generally, from an ideological standpoint, are not deserving of serious examination.

Does it require deep intuition to comprehend that man's ideas, views and conceptions, in one word, man's consciousness, changes with every change in the conditions of his material existence, in his social relations and in his social life?

What else does the history of ideas prove, than that intellectual production changes its character in proportion as material production is changed? The ruling ideas of each age have ever been the ideas of its ruling class.

When people speak of ideas that revolutionise society, they do but express the fact, that within the old society, the elements of a new one have been created, and that the dissolution of the old ideas keeps even pace with the dissolution of the old conditions of existence.

When the ancient world was in its last throes, the ancient religions were overcome by Christianity. When Christian ideas succumbed in the 18th century to rationalist ideas, feudal society fought its death battle with the then revolutionary bourgeoisie. The ideas of religious liberty and freedom of conscience merely gave expression to the sway of free competition within the domain of knowledge.

"Undoubtedly," it will be said, "religious, moral, philosophical and juridical ideas have been modified in the course of historical development. But religion, morality philosophy, political science, and law, constantly survived this change."

"There are, besides, eternal truths, such as Freedom, Justice, etc. that are common to all states of society. But Communism abolishes eternal truths, it abolishes all religion, and all morality, instead of constituting them on a new basis; it therefore acts in contradiction to all past historical experience."

What does this accusation reduce itself to? The history of all past society has consisted in the development of class antagonisms, antagonisms that assumed different forms at different epochs.

But whatever form they may have taken, one fact is common to all past ages, viz., the exploitation of one part of society by the other. No wonder, then, that the social consciousness of past ages, despite all the multiplicity and variety it displays, moves within certain common forms, or general ideas, which cannot completely vanish except with the total disappearance of class antagonisms.

The Communist revolution is the most radical rupture with traditional property relations; no wonder that its development involves the most radical rupture with traditional ideas.

But let us have done with the bourgeois objections to Communism.

We have seen above, that the first step in the revolution by the working class, is to raise the proletariat to the position of ruling as to win the battle of democracy.

The proletariat will use its political supremacy to wrest, by degrees, all capital from the bourgeoisie, to centralise all instruments of production in the hands of the State, *i.e.*, of the proletariat organised as the ruling class; and to increase the total of productive forces as rapidly as possible.

Of course, in the beginning, this cannot be effected except by means of despotic inroads on the rights of property, and on the conditions of bourgeois production; by means of measures, therefore, which appear economically insufficient and untenable, but which, in the course of the movement, outstrip themselves, necessitate further inroads upon the old social order, and are unavoidable as a means of entirely revolutionising the mode of production.

These measures will of course be different in different countries.

Nevertheless in the most advanced countries, the following will be pretty generally applicable.

1. Abolition of property in land and application of all rents of land to public purposes.

2. A heavy progressive or graduated income tax.

3. Abolition of all right of inheritance.

4. Confiscation of the property of all emigrants and rebels.

5. Centralisation of credit in the hands of the State, by means of a national bank with State capital and an exclusive monopoly.

6. Centralisation of the means of communication and transport in the hands of the State.

7. Extension of factories and instruments of production owned by the State; the bringing into cultivation of waste-lands, and the improvement of the soil generally in accordance with a common plan.

8. Equal liability of all to labour. Establishment of industrial armies, especially for agriculture.

9. Combination of agriculture with manufacturing industries; gradual abolition of the distinction between town and country, by a more equable distribution of the population over the country.

10. Free education for all children in public schools. Abolition of children's factory labour in its present form. Combination of education with industrial production, &c., &c.

When, in the course of development, class distinctions have disappeared, and all production has been concentrated in the hands of a vast association of the whole nation, the public power will lose its political character. Political power, properly so called, is merely the organised power of one class for oppressing another. If the proletariat during its contest with the bourgeoisie is compelled, by the force of circumstances, to organise itself as a class, if, by means of a revolution, it makes itself the ruling class, and, as such, sweeps away by force the old conditions of production, then it will, along with these conditions, have swept away the conditions for the existence of class antagonisms and of classes generally, and will thereby have abolished its own supremacy as a class.

In place of the old bourgeois society, with its classes and class antagonisms, we shall have an association, in which the free development of each is the condition for the free development of all.

Socialist and Communist Literature

1. Reactionary Socialism
A. Feudal Socialism

Owing to their historical position, it became the vocation of the aristocracies of France and England to write pamphlets against modern bourgeois society. In the French revolution of July 1830, and in the English reform agitation, these aristocracies again succumbed to the hateful upstart. Thenceforth, a serious political contest was altogether out of the question. A literary battle alone remained possible. But even in the domain of literature the old cries of the restoration period had become impossible.

In order to arouse sympathy, the aristocracy were obliged to lose sight, apparently, of their own interests, and to formulate their indictment against the bourgeoisie in the interest of the exploited working class alone. Thus the aristocracy took their revenge by singing lampoons on their new master, and whispering in his ears sinister prophecies of coming catastrophe.

In this way arose Feudal Socialism: half lamentation, half lampoon; half echo of the past, half menace of the future; at times, by its bitter, witty and incisive criticism, striking the bourgeoisie to the very heart's core; but always ludicrous in its effect, through total incapacity to comprehend the march of modern history.

The aristocracy, in order to rally the people to them, waved the proletarian alms-bag in front for a banner. But the people, so often as it joined them, saw on their hindquarters the old feudal coats of arms, and deserted with loud and irreverent laughter.

One section of the French Legitimists and "Young England" exhibited this spectacle.

In pointing out that their mode of exploitation was different to that of the bourgeoisie, the feudalists forget that they exploited under circumstances and conditions that were quite different, and that are now antiquated. In showing that, under their rule, the modern proletariat never existed, they forget that the modern bourgeoisie is the necessary offspring of their own form of society.

For the rest, so little do they conceal the reactionary character of their criticism that their chief accusation against the bourgeoisie amounts to this, that under the bourgeois regime a class is being developed, which is destined to cut up root and branch the old order of society.

What they upbraid the bourgeoisie with is not so much that it creates a proletariat, as that it creates a revolutionary proletariat.

In political practice, therefore, they join in all coercive measures against the working class; and in ordinary life, despite their high falutin phrases, they stoop to pick up the golden apples dropped from the tree of industry, and to barter truth, love, and honour for traffic in wool, beetroot-sugar, and potato spirits.

As the parson has ever gone hand in hand with the landlord, so has Clerical Socialism with Feudal Socialism.

Nothing is easier than to give Christian asceticism a Socialist tinge. Has not Christianity declaimed against private property, against marriage, against the State? Has it not preached in the place of these, charity and poverty, celibacy and mortification of the flesh, monastic life and Mother Church? Christian Socialism is but the holy, water with which the priest consecrates the heart-burnings of the aristocrat.

B. Petty-Bourgeois Socialism

The feudal aristocracy was not the only class that was ruined by the bourgeoisie, not the only class whose conditions of existence pined and perished in the atmosphere of modern bourgeois society. The mediaeval burgesses and the small peasant proprietors were the precursors of the modern bourgeoisie. In those countries which are but little developed, industrially and commercially, these two classes still vegetate side by side with the rising bourgeoisie.

In countries where modern civilisation has become fully developed, a new class of petty bourgeois has been formed, fluctuating between proletariat and bourgeoisie and ever renewing itself as a supplementary part of bourgeois society. The individual members of this class, however, are being constantly hurled down into the proletariat by the action of competition, and, as modern industry develops, they even see the moment approaching when they will completely disappear as an independent section of modern society, to be replaced, in manufactures, agriculture and commerce, by overlookers, bailiffs and shopmen.

In countries like France, where the peasants constitute far more than half of the population, it was natural that writers who sided with the proletariat against the bourgeoisie, should use, in their criticism of the bourgeois regime, the standard of the peasant and petty bourgeois, and from the standpoint of these intermediate classes should take up the cudgels for the working class. Thus arose petty-bourgeois Socialism. Sismondi was the head of this school, not only in France but also in England.

This school of Socialism dissected with great acuteness the contradictions in the conditions of modern production. It laid bare the hypocritical apologies of economists. It proved, incontrovertibly, the disastrous effects of machinery and division of labour; the concentration of capital and land in a few hands; overproduction and crises; it pointed out the inevitable ruin of the petty bourgeois and peasant, the misery of the proletariat, the anarchy in production, the crying inequalities in the distribution of wealth, the industrial war of extermination between nations, the dissolution of old moral bonds, of the old family relations, of the old nationalities.

In its positive aims, however, this form of Socialism aspires either to restoring the old means of production and of exchange, and with them the old property relations, and the old society, or to cramping the modern means of production and of exchange, within the framework of the old property relations that have been, and were bound to be, exploded by those means. In either case, it is both reactionary and Utopian.

Its last words are: corporate guilds for manufacture, patriarchal relations in agriculture.

Ultimately, when stubborn historical facts had dispersed all intoxicating effects of self-deception, this form of Socialism ended in a miserable fit of the blues.

C. German, or "True," Socialism

The Socialist and Communist literature of France, a literature that originated under the pressure of a bourgeoisie in power, and that was the expression of the struggle against this power, was introduced into Germany at a time when the bourgeoisie, in that country, had just begun its contest with feudal absolutism.

German philosophers, would-be philosophers, and beaux esprits, eagerly seized on this literature, only forgetting, that when these writings immigrated from France into Germany, French social conditions had not immigrated along with them. In contact with German social conditions, this French literature lost all its immediate practical significance, and assumed a purely literary aspect. Thus, to the German philosophers of the eighteenth century, the demands of the first French Revolution were nothing more than the demands of "Practical Reason" in general, and the utterance of the will of the revolutionary French bourgeoisie signified in their eyes the law of pure Will, of Will as it was bound to be, of true human Will generally.

The world of the German literate consisted solely in bringing the new French ideas into harmony with their ancient philosophical conscience, or rather, in annexing the French ideas without deserting their own philosophic point of view.

This annexation took place in the same way in which a foreign language is appropriated, namely, by translation.

It is well known how the monks wrote silly lives of Catholic Saints over the manuscripts on which the classical works of ancient heathendom had been written. The German literate reversed this process with the profane French literature. They wrote their philosophical nonsense beneath the French original. For instance, beneath the French criticism of the economic functions of money, they wrote "Alienation of Humanity," and beneath the French criticism of the bourgeois State they wrote "dethronement of the Category of the General," and so forth.

The introduction of these philosophical phrases at the back of the French historical criticisms they dubbed "Philosophy of Action," "True Socialism," "German Science of Socialism," "Philosophical Foundation of Socialism," and so on.

The French Socialist and Communist literature was thus completely emasculated. And, since it ceased in the hands of the German to express the struggle of one class with the other, he felt conscious of having overcome "French one-sidedness" and of representing, not true requirements, but the requirements of truth; not the interests of the proletariat, but the interests of Human Nature, of Man in general, who belongs to no class, has no reality, who exists only in the misty realm of philosophical fantasy.

This German Socialism, which took its schoolboy task so seriously and solemnly, and extolled its poor stock-in-trade in such mountebank fashion, meanwhile gradually lost its pedantic innocence.

The fight of the German, and especially, of the Prussian bourgeoisie, against feudal aristocracy and absolute monarchy, in other words, the liberal movement, became more earnest.

By this, the long wished-for opportunity was offered to "True" Socialism of confronting the political movement with the Socialist demands, of hurling the traditional anathemas against liberalism, against representative government, against bourgeois competition, bourgeois freedom of the press, bourgeois legislation, bourgeois liberty and equality, and of preaching to the masses that they had nothing to gain, and everything to lose, by this bourgeois movement.

German Socialism forgot, in the nick of time, that the French criticism, whose silly echo it was, presupposed the existence of modern bourgeois society, with its corresponding economic conditions of existence, and the political constitution adapted thereto, the very things whose attainment was the object of the pending struggle in Germany.

To the absolute governments, with their following of parsons, professors, country squires and officials, it served as a welcome scarecrow against the threatening bourgeoisie.

It was a sweet finish after the bitter pills of floggings and bullets with which these same governments, just at that time, dosed the German working-class risings.

While this "True" Socialism thus served the governments as a weapon for fighting the German bourgeoisie, it, at the same time, directly represented a reactionary interest, the interest of the German Philistines. In Germany the petty-bourgeois class, a relic of the sixteenth century, and since then constantly cropping up again under various forms, is the real social basis of the existing state of things.

To preserve this class is to preserve the existing state of things in Germany. The industrial and political supremacy of the bourgeoisie threatens it with certain destruction; on the one hand, from the concentration of capital; on the other, from the rise of a revolutionary proletariat. "True" Socialism appeared to kill these two birds with one stone. It spread like an epidemic.

The robe of speculative cobwebs, embroidered with flowers of rhetoric, steeped in the dew of sickly sentiment, this transcendental robe in which the German Socialists wrapped their sorry "eternal truths," all skin and bone, served to wonderfully increase the sale of their goods amongst such a public. And on its part, German Socialism recognised, more and more, its own calling as the bombastic representative of the petty-bourgeois Philistine.

It proclaimed the German nation to be the model nation, and the German petty Philistine to be the typical man. To every villainous meanness of this model man it gave a hidden, higher, Socialistic interpretation, the exact contrary of its real character. It went to the extreme length of directly opposing the "brutally destructive" tendency of Communism, and of proclaiming its supreme and impartial contempt of all class struggles. With very few exceptions, all the so-called Socialist and Communist publications that now (1847) circulate in Germany belong to the domain of this foul and enervating literature.

2. Conservative, or Bourgeois, Socialism

A part of the bourgeoisie is desirous of redressing social grievances, in order to secure the continued existence of bourgeois society.

To this section belong economists, philanthropists, humanitarians, improvers of the condition of the working class, organisers of charity, members of societies for the prevention of cruelty to animals, temperance fanatics, hole-and-corner reformers of every imaginable kind. This form of Socialism has, moreover, been worked out into complete systems.

We may cite Proudhon's Philosophie de la Misere as an example of this form.

The Socialistic bourgeois want all the advantages of modern social conditions without the struggles and dangers necessarily resulting therefrom. They desire the existing state of society minus its revolutionary and disintegrating elements. They wish for a bourgeoisie without a proletariat. The bourgeoisie naturally conceives the world in which it is supreme to be the best; and bourgeois Socialism develops this comfortable conception into various more or less complete systems. In requiring the proletariat to carry out such a system, and thereby to march straightway into the social New Jerusalem, it but requires in reality, that the proletariat should remain within the bounds of existing society, but should cast away all its hateful ideas concerning the bourgeoisie.

A second and more practical, but less systematic, form of this Socialism sought to depreciate every revolutionary movement in the eyes of the working class, by showing that no mere political reform, but only a change in the material conditions of existence, in economic relations, could be of any advantage to them. By changes in the material conditions of existence, this form of Socialism, however, by no means understands abolition of the bourgeois relations of production, an abolition that can be effected only by a revolution, but administrative reforms, based on the continued existence of these relations; reforms, therefore, that in no respect affect the relations between capital and labour, but, at the best, lessen the cost, and simplify the administrative work, of bourgeois government.

Bourgeois Socialism attains adequate expression, when, and only when, it becomes a mere figure of speech.

Free trade: for the benefit of the working class. Protective duties: for the benefit of the working class. Prison Reform: for the benefit of the working class. This is the last word and the only seriously meant word of bourgeois Socialism.

It is summed up in the phrase: the bourgeois is a bourgeois—for the benefit of the working class.

3. *Critical-utopian Socialism and Communism*

We do not here refer to that literature which, in every great modern revolution, has always given voice to the demands of the proletariat, such as the writings of Babeuf and others.

The first direct attempts of the proletariat to attain its own ends, made in times of universal excitement, when feudal society was being overthrown, these attempts necessarily failed, owing to the then undeveloped state of the proletariat, as well as to the absence of the economic conditions for its emancipation, conditions that had yet to be produced, and could be produced by the impending bourgeois epoch alone. The revolutionary literature that accompanied these first movements of the proletariat had necessarily a reactionary character. It inculcated universal asceticism and social levelling in its crudest form.

The Socialist and Communist systems properly so called, those of Saint-Simon, Fourier, Owen and others, spring into existence in the early undeveloped period, described above, of the struggle between proletariat and bourgeoisie (see Section 1. Bourgeois and Proletarians).

The founders of these systems see, indeed, the class antagonisms, as well as the action of the decomposing elements, in the prevailing form of society. But the proletariat, as yet in its infancy, offers to them the spectacle of a class without any historical initiative or any independent political movement.

Since the development of class antagonism keeps even pace with the development of industry, the economic situation, as they find it, does not as yet offer to them the material conditions for the emancipation of the proletariat. They therefore search after a new social science, after new social laws, that are to create these conditions.

Historical action is to yield to their personal inventive action, historically created conditions of emancipation to fantastic ones, and the gradual, spontaneous class-organisation of the proletariat to the organisation of society specially contrived by these inventors. Future history resolves itself, in their eyes, into the propaganda and the practical carrying out of their social plans.

In the formation of their plans they are conscious of caring chiefly for the interests of the working class, as being the most suffering class. Only from the point of view of being the most suffering class does the proletariat exist for them.

The undeveloped state of the class struggle, as well as their own surroundings, causes Socialists of this kind to consider themselves far superior to all class antagonisms. They want to improve the condition of every member of society, even that of the most favoured. Hence, they habitually appeal to society at large, without distinction of class; nay, by preference, to the ruling class. For how can people, when once they understand their system, fail to see in it the best possible plan of the best possible state of society?

Hence, they reject all political, and especially all revolutionary, action; they wish to attain their ends by peaceful means, and endeavour, by small experiments, necessarily doomed to failure, and by the force of example, to pave the way for the new social Gospel.

Such fantastic pictures of future society, painted at a time when the proletariat is still in a very undeveloped state and has but a fantastic conception of its own position correspond with the first instinctive yearnings of that class for a general reconstruction of society.

But these Socialist and Communist publications contain also a critical element. They attack every principle of existing society. Hence they are full of the most valuable materials for the enlightenment of the working class. The practical measures proposed in them—such as the abolition of the distinction between town and country, of the family, of the carrying on of industries for the account of private individuals, and of the wage system, the proclamation of social harmony, the conversion of the functions of the State into a mere superintendence of production, all these proposals, point solely to the disappearance of class antagonisms which were, at that time, only just cropping up, and which, in these publications, are recognised in their earliest, indistinct and undefined forms only. These proposals, therefore, are of a purely Utopian character.

The significance of Critical-Utopian Socialism and Communism bears an inverse relation to historical development. In proportion as the modern class struggle develops and takes definite shape, this fantastic standing apart from the contest, these fantastic attacks on it, lose all practical value and all theoretical justification. Therefore, although the originators of these systems were, in many respects, revolutionary, their disciples have, in every case, formed mere reactionary sects. They hold fast by the original views of their masters, in opposition to the progressive historical development of the proletariat. They, therefore, endeavour, and that consistently, to deaden the class struggle and to reconcile the class antagonisms. They still dream of experimental realisation of their social Utopias, of founding isolated "phalansteres," of establishing "Home Colonies," of setting up a "Little Icaria"—duodecimo editions of the New Jerusalem—and to realise all these castles in the air, they are compelled to appeal to the feelings and purses of the bourgeois. By degrees they sink into the category of the reactionary conservative Socialists depicted above, differing from these only by more systematic pedantry, and by their fanatical and superstitious belief in the miraculous effects of their social science.

They, therefore, violently oppose all political action on the part of the working class; such action, according to them, can only result from blind unbelief in the new Gospel.

The Owenites in England, and the Fourierists in France, respectively, oppose the Chartists and the Reformistes.

Position of the Communists in Relation to the Various Existing Opposition Parties

Section II has made clear the relations of the Communists to the existing working-class parties, such as the Chartists in England and the Agrarian Reformers in America.

The Communists fight for the attainment of the immediate aims, for the enforcement of the momentary interests of the working class; but in the movement of the present, they also represent and take care of the future of that movement. In France the Communists ally themselves with the Social-Democrats, against the conservative and radical bourgeoisie, reserving, however, the right to take up a critical position in regard to phrases and illusions traditionally handed down from the great Revolution.

In Switzerland they support the Radicals, without losing sight of the fact that this party consists of antagonistic elements, partly of Democratic Socialists, in the French sense, partly of radical bourgeois.

In Poland they support the party that insists on an agrarian revolution as the prime condition for national emancipation, that party which fomented the insurrection of Cracow in 1846.

In Germany they fight with the bourgeoisie whenever it acts in a revolutionary way, against the absolute monarchy, the feudal squirearchy, and the petty bourgeoisie.

But they never cease, for a single instant, to instil into the working class the clearest possible recognition of the hostile antagonism between bourgeoisie and proletariat, in order that the German workers may straightaway use, as so many weapons against the bourgeoisie, the social and political conditions that the bourgeoisie must necessarily introduce along with its supremacy, and in order that, after the fall of the reactionary classes in Germany, the fight against the bourgeoisie itself may immediately begin.

The Communists turn their attention chiefly to Germany, because that country is on the eve of a bourgeois revolution that is bound to be carried out under more advanced conditions of European civilisation, and with a much more developed proletariat, than that of England was in the seventeenth, and of France in the eighteenth century, and because the bourgeois revolution in

Germany will be but the prelude to an immediately following proletarian revolution.

In short, the Communists everywhere support every revolutionary movement against the existing social and political order of things.

In all these movements they bring to the front, as the leading question in each, the property question, no matter what its degree of development at the time.

Finally, they labour everywhere for the union and agreement of the democratic parties of all countries.

The Communists disdain to conceal their views and aims. They openly declare that their ends can be attained only by the forcible overthrow of all existing social conditions. Let the ruling classes tremble at a Communistic revolution. The proletarians have nothing to lose but their chains. They have a world to win.

Working Men of All Countries, Unite!

CPSIA information can be obtained
at www.ICGtesting.com
Printed in the USA
LVOW10s1512200518

577857LV00002B/350/P

9 781617 202933